ARGUING WITH ANGELS

SUNY series in Western Esoteric Traditions

David Appelbaum, editor

ARGUING WITH ANGELS

Enochian Magic & Modern Occulture

Egil Asprem

Published by State University of New York Press, Albany

Printed in the United States of America

For information, contact State University of New York Press, Albany, NY
www.sunypress.edu

Production by Ryan Morris
Marketing by Kate McDonnell

Library of Congress Cataloging-in-Publication Data

Asprem, Egil.
Arguing with angels : Enochian magic and modern occulture / Egil Asprem.
p. cm. — (SUNY series in Western esoteric traditions)
Includes bibliographical references and index.
ISBN 978-1-4384-4191-7 (hardcover : alk. paper) — ISBN 978-1-4384-4190-0 (pbk : alk. paper)
1. Enochian magic—History. 2. Occultism—History. I. Title.
BF1623.E55A87 2012
133.4'309—dc23

2011021278

10 9 8 7 6 5 4 3 2 1

CONTENTS

LIST OF TABLES

ACKNOWLEDGMENTS

The present book has been in the making approximately since the autumn of 2006. After several years of research and writing, thanks are due to a number of people who have helped out, inspired, and contributed in so many different ways along the way. First of all, my supervisor during the research for my MA degree at the University of Amsterdam between 2006 and 2008, Dr. Marco Pasi, now a colleague at the same institution, deserves a great deal of honor for guiding me through the early process of what evolved into this project. His critical comments on parts of my research have been very valuable, as have his suggestions leading to sources and new discoveries that would otherwise likely have been overlooked. Thanks are also due to other colleagues at the Centre for History of Hermetic Philosophy and Related Currents in Amsterdam, especially Prof. Dr. Wouter J. Hanegraaff, Prof. Dr. Kocku von Stuckrad (now at the University of Groningen), and Dr. Ulrike Popp-Baier, whose conversations and input in earlier stages have shaped my visions for this project. In addition I wish to thank Dr. Asbjørn Dyrendal in Trondheim, who has been a profound influence and motivation for many years, and my friends and colleagues Dr. Kennet Granholm, Jesper Aagaard Petersen, Joyce Pijnenburg, John L. Crow, for many enlightening conversations. Thanks also to Dr. Peter Forshaw, Tessel M. Bauduin, Eduard ten Houten, Joshua Levi Ian Gentzke, and Jason Rose, and to Martin Palmer and Forum Nidarosiae for giving the opportunity to try out my ideas in the summer of 2009.

Parts of the research for this book would have been impossible without contact with knowledgeable people in the world of the occult. I am especially indebted to those well-placed gentlemen who kindly responded to my various inquiries, including Dr. Michael Aquino, Steven Ashe, Al Billings, Clive Harper, Dean Hildebrandt. Runar Karlsen is especially acknowledged for giving his permission to publish parts of his magical work as an appendix to this book, and providing it with an introduction. I wish to thank friends and acquaintances who have shared their rare knowledge with me, and taken time to answer my questions, especially Kjetil Fjell and

John Færseth. Ian Rons of *The Magickal Review* has been of great assistance, and I particularly thank him for supplying the Enochian characters used in Table 1.1 of this book.

Acknowledgment is also due to the helpful and efficient staffs of the following institutions: the British Library, Bibliotheca Philosophica Hermetica, the UvA university library, and the Amsterdam Theosophical Library. Finally, chapter 2 has been developed from an article originally published in the journal *Magic, Ritual, and Witchcraft*, while other parts of arguments presented in the book have been tried out in the journals *Aries*, *The Pomegranate*, and *Chaos*. Acknowledgment is due to the editors and anonymous peer reviewers who have helped refine my arguments at various stages.

Finally, the support and constant encouragement of friends and family has been deeply appreciated. My final thanks go out to my parents, Frank and Wenche Asprem, my sister Nina and brother Isak, to Eva and Einar Asprem, and to my many good friends, both old and new. Finally, a special regard goes out to Hanne Kristin Berg, who was a source of much joy and inspiration during the period when this book started to take shape.

Egil Asprem
AMSTERDAM, FEBRUARY 2011

INTRODUCTION

"Never shall be razed out the Memorie of these Actions."
—The angel Me to John Dee, March 28, 1583

On a Friday afternoon late in January 1991 an art student in his late twenties was performing a magical ritual in a little rural house on the outskirts of Oslo. In the middle of the ritual, and quite contrary to the young magician's intentions with it, his visions were wiped out and replaced by what he experienced as a "void of purity." In a loud, thundering voice, an unknown spirit started dictating in a strange, unfamiliar language: *"Ma pratisi kolia navadigi, selig quanisi gon . . . "* The dictation continued for some time, all scribbled down by the aspiring artist and magician until it comprised a whole book of mysterious words, later to become known under the title *Dor OS zol ma thil*. Soon he was to discover that the voices he had heard and transcribed were speaking in an arcane language known as "Enochian," a language which some believed to be the tongue of the angels.[1]

At the same time, in well-assorted occult bookshops in Oslo, as in any other Western capital, one would find shelves sporting titles such as *Enochian Physics, Enochian Tarot,* and *Enochian Sex Magic*. There would be books telling that Enochian had been the language of Atlantis, rediscovered by the Rosicrucians; others that its existence constitutes the clearest proof of the supernatural, and especially the existence of angels. One would read that there existed a whole system of "Enochian magic," maybe part of a secret angelic conspiracy to set off the Apocalypse as described in the *Book of Revelation*; and one would find the Enochian tongue murmured in the liturgy of satanic rituals. If one cared to take a closer look one would even learn that Enochiana had played a role in the prophetic inception of at least two new religious movements. The truth is that Enochiana had been on the lips of occultists and ritual magicians for a hundred years.

All of these claims and theories, speculations and observations belong to the extraordinarily multifaceted reception history of John

Dee's sixteenth-century conversations with angels. During the last three decades of his life, the English renaissance scholar had sought divine help to solve puzzles in natural philosophy, and employed several so-called scryers, or crystal gazers, in attempts to uncover secrets from the angels. The best known of these scryers was no doubt Edward Kelley—in part because he was the only one which thoroughly convinced Dee of his skills, and in part because the records of their actions have survived, while those of the others were destroyed or have otherwise been lost over the tumultuous centuries since the late 1500s. In 1659, the magical workings of Dee and Kelley were canonized by the publication of Meric Casaubon's *A True and Faithful Relation*—an account brought to the public with the intention of showing how a good but gullible man was lured into damnation by a cunning nigromancer. The book at first caused a stir, tempting others to try what Dee had done rather than keeping them away from magic. Dee's actions were even discussed by the members of the early Royal Society, sometimes with open scorn for the credulousness of a past generation, sometimes with partial admiration and fascination over the complexity of his work. With the passing of a few generations, however, and the advent of the Enlightenment in the eighteenth century, the curious conversations were largely forgotten.

* * *

After centuries of relative obscurity, Dee's magical papers have been rediscovered, reconstructed, and disseminated in modern occultism, from the late-nineteenth-century Golden Dawn to today's magical discussion forums on the Internet. But reception and interpretation always involve selection and exclusion: some things will be emphasized to the neglect of other things, depending on the understanding that is unique to the context of the receiving part. As would be expected, the diffusion of the magical material found in Dee's diaries into nineteenth and especially twentieth-century occultism led to a wide array of diverging interpretations of it.

In the context of this book, the term *Enochiana* will refer to all occult speculations and practices related to one or more aspects of John Dee's angel conversations. There are several reasons why this definition is prudent. First off, having been claimed as a part of esoteric bodies of doctrine and practices by a number of different organizations, orders, and occultists over the past century, Enochiana has become an increasingly contested field of discourse. As a scholarly construct for analyzing a phenomenon within modern esotericism, our concept of Enochiana should be able to cover all these divergent and opposing positions. The common denominator is that they all claim for themselves some (or several) part(s) of Dee and Kelley's revelations.

But one cannot define Enochiana simply as "John Dee's magical system," either. That would be anachronistic, since very few contenders on the arena of modern occultism actually follow any of those magical systems, as set forth in the original sources. As a matter of fact, this is exactly where one of the major internal disputes lies: Who is the final authority when it comes to the interpretation of Enochiana? Is it Dee himself, and what the sources seem to tell us about his views and agenda? A few modern occultists would say yes. Others, probably the majority, would tend to disagree for various reasons. Among other strategies, they could claim that Enochiana is part of a perennial system, which stems from much higher authorities, whether these be the angels themselves, a selection of Atlantean or Rosicrucian secret chiefs, or other esoteric sources of knowledge. Perhaps Dee and Kelley failed to understand the significance of their revelations, or perhaps they were even deliberately misled by "the angels," whoever they were? These are core conflicts in the modern discourse on Enochiana, conflicts that are perpetuated throughout its history. Hence, making the original sources, plain and simple, the final word of what Enochiana is all about begs the very questions that we are interested in exploring. In short, it fixes authenticity, whereas we are really interested in looking at how authenticity is constructed.

* * *

A voluminous scholarly literature on John Dee and his various intellectual pursuits, including their contexts and agendas, has accumulated over the last few decades.[2] Meanwhile, close to nothing has been said about the reception history of Dee's magic. Scholars of occultism and magic in the modern period commonly appreciate the centrality and importance of Enochian magic to the figures and currents they are studying, but seldom is the topic problematized or explored in any detail. Christopher Partridge, for instance, is baffled by the complexity of "the many tables, diagrams and symbols, including the Enochian script" appearing in manuals on Golden Dawn magic, and sees Enochian magic as one among other *exempli gratia* of the enchanted worldview of modern "occulture."[3] Alex Owen's recent study of modern ritual magic includes a whole chapter on Aleister Crowley's adventurous Enochian experiments in the Algerian desert in 1909 together with his male lover, the poet Victor Neuburg.[4] Owen offers a fascinating, although somewhat psychologizing, interpretation of the events in the desert, but regarding the nature and provenance of the techniques used we learn little. It is simply referred to as "a complex magical system developed by John Dee . . . and his clairvoyant, Edward Kelley." Enochian magic is furthermore described in anachronistic terms which resonate well with Crowley's and the Golden Dawn's occultist theories, but less so with those found in the Elizabethan Renaissance.[5]

This lack of comparative diachronic perspectives must be seen as a consequence of a quite necessary division of intellectual labor. Experts on modern esoteric religion may step lightly over the often deep and complicated historical issues, focusing instead on their specific field of expertise. Experts on Renaissance intellectual life, on the other hand, generally take little interest in modern receptions of the currents they are specializing in, sometimes, perhaps, even viewing them as vulgar, inauthentic corruptions. This was certainly how Gershom Scholem felt about modern adaptations of Kabbalah.[6] While it is understandable that such a division of labor has taken place, it entails the unfortunate consequence that there now exist parallel scholarships, entire literatures that would be mutually enlightening, but which, in fact, seldom interact. In the process we lose opportunities to make diachronic comparisons that could be helpful in singling out the forms of creativity involved in processes of reception and reinterpretation, and the strategies at play in modern constructions of tradition and emic historiographies.

To my knowledge, the only presently available study dedicated to exploring Enochiana as a kind of esoteric *longue durée,* diffused through a variety of modern systems, is an article published by Marco Pasi and Philippe Rabaté in 1999.[7] The article presents a good overview, and is an excellent roadmap to anyone who wants to explore these rather unspoiled territories of Western esoteric discourse. But considering the long time span and complexity of the development of Enochiana, an article-length study must necessarily be somewhat limited in scope. For example, Pasi and Rabaté's article dealt specifically with the history of the Enochian *language*, and can only convey a somewhat fragmented picture when the whole field of Enochian magic is to be scrutinized. Additionally, modern occulture is a rapidly changing entity, and significant developments have already taken place after the article was written. Most notably the advent of the Internet made a tremendous impact, a development that will be assessed in some detail toward the end of this book.

* * *

We may conclude, then, that a detailed and careful study of Dee's place in modern and contemporary occultism is overdue. The ambition of this book is to begin filling the gap. Although the main focus is on modern Enochiana, from the nineteenth to twenty-first centuries, and the wider occulture that it is situated in, I also seek to mend some of the holes stemming from the division of labor discussed above. For this reason, the book is divided into two parts. Part One attempts to cover and contextualize what may be characterized as the Renaissance "roots" of Enochiana, and the routes of transmission that the material has traveled up to the so-called Victorian "occult revival." Part Two, on the other hand, is dedicated to analyzing the modern reconstructions, the many exchanges over legitimacy, and the accompanying discursive strategies employed by main spokespersons. While the first part lays a historical fundament, driven by the methods of historical-critical scholarship, the second uses this knowledge as a background for a more discursively driven analysis of constructions of tradition and legitimacy in a contested field of modern esoteric religiosity.

Chapter 1 revisits Elizabethan England, the main point being to present the original sources that the modern discourse on Enochian reconstructs. This is necessary primarily for the sake of comparison and the extirpation of common anachronisms, as explained already, but also since an appeal to "authenticity" based on proximity to the sources has been frequently employed by occultists in later years. It is therefore desirable to know the original sources well enough to be able to distinguish mythmaking from scholarship, emic from etic historiography, historical research from manifestations of mnemohistorical projections. Chapter 2 addresses the little-known and sometimes confusedly understood routes of transmission, and early reception history, of Dee's magic. It takes special concern with the hypothesis that has sometimes been put forth regarding a "secret tradition" through a circle of unknown ritual magicians.[8] According to this interpretation, Dee's angel conversations, and the magical systems conveyed from the heavenly messengers would have been carried on and practiced after Dee's death. Two seventeenth-century manuscripts have been mentioned in support of this thesis. As I will demonstrate in some detail in this chapter, critical scrutiny of the sources and their context does not corroborate or support such an interpretation.[9]

In chapter 3 we move on to the Victorian period, and consider the blooming interest in magic in the midst of the wider occult revival. Crystallomancy was once again on the rise, and figures such as Frederick Hockley and Kenneth Mackenzie visited the manuscript collections in the British Library in search of arcane knowledge. A little later, parts of Dee's material resurfaced in the sketchy notes of the mysterious "Cipher MS," which would become a foundation document for the seminal Hermetic Order of the Golden Dawn. It is the magical theories of this esoteric order, embedded in a startling system of initiations, which will concern us the most in this chapter. I argue that it is in context of the creative innovations of the Golden Dawn that the formation of modern Enochiana should be located. Occultists of the twentieth century largely came to see Enochian magic, and perhaps even medieval and Renaissance ritual magic at large, through the filtered perception of the Golden Dawn. Understanding the Golden Dawn's theories and their mode of formation is therefore paramount to the project of this book.

Chapter 4 concludes the historical section of the book by introducing the theoretical issues that will be at the basis for Part Two. In this chapter, I will largely be preoccupied with two theoretical points. These may be summed up, with the chapter's heading, as "the Authenticity Problem" and the problem of the "Legitimacy of Magic." Briefly speaking, these concern two interrelated questions, regarding the struggle to gain legitimacy for esoteric belief systems in modern culture. The problem of legitimacy applies to modern magic generally, and is directed toward the ideals of the dominant culture surrounding it. The authenticity problem, as I conceive of it here, regards Enochiana specifically, and is directed toward fellow occultists. The first aspect is furthermore connected with the debates concerning religion and secularization: how do modern magicians legitimize magical practice in the face of secular modernity, and how do they interpret the nature of their practices? Has modern ritual magic become a "disenchanted," secularized, or diluted ghost of its premodern counterparts, or do the magicians stand as champions for a new and genuine "re-enchantment" at the heart of secular culture? What I propose to call the authenticity problem is somewhat more myopic in focus: given the wide number of differing interpretations of Enochiana by various spokespersons, how are specific standpoints legitimized vis-à-vis competitors? What are the discursive strategies implied in the arguments, which appeals are being made by groups and individual authors or magicians to show that their interpretation is "authentic"? Furthermore, does authenticity only exist in the singular, or are a plurality of ways viable; in the terminology of Moshe Idel, does the assumed perennial wisdom follow a unilinear or a multilinear course of transmission?[10] I will show that the modern and contemporary discourse on these matters is heavily formed by the Golden Dawn and its demise. Much of what has been argued by occultists the last fifty years is a direct consequence of the nineteenth-century religious creativity and innovation that went into the construction of the Golden Dawn system.

As will become clear throughout Part Two of this book, this is not only, or even primarily, because of the continued influence of the Golden Dawn's teachings, but because of efforts to *overcome* it. Chapters 5 and 6 both portray negotiations occurring at a period close to the disintegration of the Golden Dawn, both historically and socially. Aleister Crowley's engagement with the Enochian material is considered in chapter 5, closely linked up to his mission of erecting the new "magical religion" of Thelema. Chapter 6 starts out by looking at polemical exchanges between factions of the Golden Dawn, where the very question of the legitimacy of magic as such is fought over. It continues however to look in more detail at what may be treated as the symbolical end of the Golden Dawn era, namely, the emergence of modern Satanism from the occultural counterculture of 1960s California. Despite the creation of a new satanic identity, contesting the "holy esoterica" of earlier occultists, the "angelic" system of Enochiana was interestingly incorporated into Anton LaVey's *Satanic Bible*. Furthermore, it became an arena for the struggle between two ideational positions within modern Satanism, to wit, the largely "rationalistic" and secularizing position of LaVey, and the more esoteric, reenchanted variety of Michael Aquino and the Temple of Set.

The 1960s counterculture and the popular occult explosion gave rise to the major features of contemporary occulture. The term *occulture* has recently been introduced by Christopher Partridge as a sociological category denoting an emerging cultural milieu, consisting of a "reservoir of ideas, beliefs, practices, and symbols," which relate to the esoteric, paranormal, conspiratorial, and spiritual.[11] Developed from Colin Campbell's influential concept of the "cultic milieu," occulture is also meant to include the institutions, fora, and networks through which such ideas are created, distributed, and disseminated among the population. A crucial point for Partridge is that occulture in this sense is becoming increasingly ordinary and mainstream, especially by functioning as a cultural pool of resources for popular culture; another important feature, particularly since the 1990s, is the introduction of the Internet as a new tool that has significantly altered the complexity of networking and distribution of occultural ideas.[12]

The last two chapters of this book chart out the implications that the growth of occulture has had for the discourse on Enochiana, and the major responses that have emerged from it. By its strongly individualistic, diffuse, and network-oriented structure, the development of occulture has increased the level of polyfocality in the Enochian discourse, taking questions of authority and authenticity further. Chapter 7 discusses what I call a "purist turn" in the modern Enochian discourse, which, largely in a reaction against the eclecticism of occulture, advocated a return to the source materials and a radical break with the Golden Dawn occultist heritage. From the 1970s toward the end of the 1980s the purist position was popularized, signaling important ramifications for the legitimacy of other interpretations of Enochiana. Some of these are discussed in chapter 8, where we see a variety of innovative positions flourishing amid the growing appeal of Enochiana in the occulture. As the millennium crept closer the Enochian discourse went online. The finale of this book, then, consists of a reconstruction of issues that have been vociferously discussed in the emerging global network of magicians on the Internet.

A last note on method is in order. As has been suggested implicitly already, the research questions raised in this book require a methodological focus on occult *discourse*, on polyfocality, and variety of strategies for gaining and retaining legitimacy within that discourse. The approach that I develop is therefore informed by a discursive study of religion focusing on pluralism. I aim to frame Enochiana by presenting "a polyfocal picture of a contested arena, a field of discourse on which discursive strategies are intertwined, communicated, and negotiated . . ."[13] An emphasis on polemical discourse in connection to esotericism has gained much scholarly attention in recent years.[14] The focus has however mostly been on "esotericism and its Others", that is, the polemical friction between "esoteric discourse," on the one hand, and other branches of society on the other. More often than not, this emphasis has stemmed from efforts to disentangle esoteric movements and thinkers from the discursive processes that have constructed them as "rejected," whether it was as the demonic Other of Christian theology or the irrational Other of Enlightenment historiography.[15] Meanwhile, little attention has been devoted to polemics between various positions *within* esoteric discourse. Nevertheless, I submit that such internal polemical friction has remained an important element in the dynamics of innovation and religious creativity in esoteric and occult discourse, at least in the modern and late modern contexts. In the second part of this book the emphasis is therefore on claims and counterclaims, on rhetorical and discursive strategies for attaining and defending legitimacy in the contested arena of modern occultism after the split of the Golden Dawn at the inception of the twentieth century. In doing this, my focus is much indebted to Olav Hammer's work on knowledge claims, emic epistemologies, and discursive strategies in modern esoteric literature.[16]

One practical implication of this methodological focus is that I largely attempt to present the data in a dialogical fashion. Whenever it is possible, I try to reconstruct the polemical and dialogical context of, and the frictions and interest conflicts behind, the production of occult knowledge. After the fragmentation of the Golden Dawn polemics have played a crucial part in the development of the genre of occult literature that is Enochian magic. Its contested nature has only grown with the explosion in occult publishing since the 1960s, and into the new contested arenas of cyberspace in the mid-1990s. The migration of the Enochian discourse to online forums, discussed at length in chapter 8, can aptly be considered the peak of the present investigation.

PART ONE

HISTORICAL PERSPECTIVES

1

The Magus and the Seer

A Colloquium of Angels

For almost thirty years, a good one-third of a long and productive life, the Elizabethan mathematician, astrologer, alchemist, and natural philosopher John Dee (1527–1608/9) experimented with magic. The goal of these experiments was to make contact with the angels. From around 1580 until his death in the winter of 1608/9 Dee employed at least five different "scryers," or crystal gazers, to aid him in this pursuit.[1] Of these ongoing experiments with various seers, it is the series of sessions with Edward Kelley (1555–1597) that stands out. The relationship between Dee and Kelley, a trained apothecary who had probably been convicted of coining, took place over seven intense years, from 1582 to 1589, variously against the cultural settings of London, Krakow, Prague, and various other Bohemian cities. It was a Europe marked by political intrigue, growing religious conflict, and strong apocalyptic fervors. Against this background, Kelley introduced Dee to a gallery of angelic beings and heavenly landscapes, ostensibly appearing to him in the crystal, pouring out drops of divine and esoteric secrets to the eager philosopher. Among the wonders were the lost language of Adam, knowledge of the angelic hierarchies, and secrets regarding the imminent apocalypse.

In itself, there was nothing new about scrying. Catoptromantic and crystallomantic practices, that is, the use of reflective surfaces, such as mirrors or crystals to contact spiritual entities, were folk traditions that could easily be traced back to the Middle Ages.[2] In Elizabethan England, crystal gazing had become something of an institution, with wandering scryers taking up residence with patrons for shorter periods, to provide their sought-after supernatural services. What seems new and surprising with Dee's experiments is rather the contents and setting.

What was the motivation for one of Renaissance England's brightest minds to immerse himself in angel magic? This question has caused much trouble for historians. For a long time, Dee appeared as a somewhat two-faced figure: at the one hand stood his ultimately intelligible work in Renaissance mathematics and natural philosophy; on the other stood the magician. One response, taken by such an influential scholar as Frances Yates, has been to neglect Dee's "sensational angel-summonings" altogether, focusing instead on more "respectable" parts of his work.[3] This tendency led Nicholas Clulee to lament that the angel conversations had provided "rich resources for romantic biography and writers of occult sympathies but something of an embarrassment to any attempt to consider Dee as a significant figure in the history of philosophy and science."[4] That shortcoming he sat out to mend, showing how Dee's interests in natural philosophy were reproduced and continued in the course of the angel conversations.[5]

John Dee and Renaissance Natural Philosophy

Seeing the crystal-gazing "colloquium of angels" on a continuum with the more readily explicable natural philosophy has proved a fruitful strategy. Clulee's approach was notably taken up and expanded by Deborah Harkness, who produced what is currently the best full-length monograph study of Dee's angel conversations.[6] When we take this view, it seems plausible that Dee initially found the rationale for his attempt to make contact with the divine messengers in his quest for understanding nature.[7] As a natural philosopher, Dee had produced three major works which, with hindsight, all help to put the angel magic in context of Renaissance intellectual life.

On the whole, Dee's intellectual project is situated in distinctive Renaissance habits of thought, what we might call the Renaissance *episteme*, primarily associated with the rise of the humanists and their intellectual struggles with the "scholastic" tradition.[8] A foundation for Dee's work is the view that God revealed his mysteries through three "books": the human soul, revealed Scripture, and "the Book of Nature."[9] The intellectual task of the natural philosopher largely consisted in deciphering, reading, and interpreting the Book of Nature. Setting out on this course more than half a century before Galileo famously asserted that the Book of Nature is written in the language of mathematics, Dee belonged to a generation that searched passionately for the right key to reading nature's language. Variously, he found cues in optics, kabbalistic hermeneutics, emblematics,[10] mathematics, astrology, and magic.

In his first major work, *Propaedeumata aphoristica* (1558), Dee contemplated the metaphysics of light and the prospects for an optical science to properly understand the cosmos. According to scripture, light had been God's first creation, and authorities such as Roger Bacon, whom Dee defended, held that understanding the properties and behavior of light would be the first step to a "universal science."[11] More than that, Dee advanced an argument that astrological magic, of the type one would find outlined in Agrippa's *De occulta philosophia* (1533), ought to be reformed by this emerging science. Building on the light metaphysics of the Muslim natural philosopher Al-Kindi, mediated through Grosseteste and Bacon, the idea was that the stellar and planetary influences which astrology based itself on were transported in the straight rays of light. Hence, they could also be trapped and manipulated through the careful use of mirrors or crystals. Dee had come to recommend that the wise natural philosopher would not coerce nature, but rather work with it, "forcing nature artfully" by means of the processes that God had already established; the replacement of coercive magical ritual by optical mechanics would be consistent with that principle.[12]

In the cryptic *Monas hieroglyphica* (1564) Dee applied a combination of Kabbalistic hermeneutics, astrological and alchemical theory, and symbolism to the study of the Book of Nature.[13] Whereas the *Propaedeumata aphoristica* had been largely concerned with the act of *observing* nature, the *Monas* was devoted to deciphering and interpreting its text. The tract it self consisted of a central "hieroglyph," the *monas* symbol, accompanied by twenty-four theorems explaining its various permutations and hidden layers of meaning. It was thought as a grand "symbol of symbols," comprising the domains of astrology, alchemy, mathematics, geometry, and Kabbalistic hermeneutics. In addition to covering all these early modern modes of knowledge, the Hieroglyphic Monad was to be simultaneously "mathematically, magically, cabbalistically, and anagogically explained." Between the lines, circles, dots, and semicircles that make up the structure of the *monas* symbol, the student will find mathematical proportions and relations that, ostensibly, reveal something about the universe; furthermore, by approaching the hieroglyph in ways analogous to the kabbalistic readings of texts, the glyph can be morphed into a great number of other symbols and combinations of such. By finally reading the whole "anagogically," that is, assuming that apparently mundane relations speak of higher realities, the *monas* should reveal esoteric truths about the relations of man, nature, and God. From the geometrical shapes at its foundation (the point, line, and circle) spring all the principal numbers, and from this base the planetary, elemental, metallic, and alchemical symbols can also be generated.

The track of mathematics was taken up and expanded in Dee's influential "Mathematical Preface" to Euclid (1570).[14] Anticipating to some extent the developments of the seventeenth century, Dee now argued that mathematics was at the foundation of several branches of natural philosophy, from optics and astrology to navigation and other applied arts. Following the Neoplatonism of Ficino, referencing the *Timaeus* and the *Republic* as well as the mathematical philosophy of Proclus, Dee marveled in the divine and perfect nature of mathematics, presenting a platonizing metaphysics of numbers. Numbers were intermediaries between the perfect heavenly realms and the terrestrial world; they participated in things both divine and mundane. Indeed, the numbers themselves existed in three different states: there were the "numbers numbering," reserved only for God, and implicated in the creation process, and there were the "numbers numbered," present in every creature of the corruptible and changing natural world. Thirdly, there was an intermediary state of the numbers, existing in the minds of angels and men. Thus, the human intellect was linked to a chain of understanding, the possibility of truth and certainty being guaranteed by the connection to the divine numbers. Perhaps more important, it was also in these pages that Dee prophesized about a future "Archemastrie," a perfect, unified science, wielded by the complete natural philosopher, the "Archemaster."[15] Dee considered this complete discipline to be the unification of all the branches of natural philosophy, from the propagation of rays of light, the use of mathematics, the manipulation of astral radiation through the combination of optics and astrology, as well as the practice of alchemy.[16] This new science was not merely content with speculation, but required active operation, a kind of mediating engagement with the natural world and the heavenly hierarchies.

Deborah Harkness speculates that Dee's description of the Archemastrie may indicate he was already at this point experimenting with capturing angels in crystals.[17] At the very least, it would seem that he had erected a natural philosophical and esoteric framework that inherently allowed such experiments as a possibility. Around the time that Dee had written and published the "Mathematical Preface" he had also been on the verge of an intellectual breakdown. His diary entries reveal that the persistent attempts to attain perfect understanding and mastery of the Book of Nature had only met with frustration and despair. In 1569 he had made "special supplications" to Michael the Archangel, praying for help but receiving only silence. Obscure comments about a decision to "leave this world presently" in order to "enioye the bottomless fowntayne of all wisdome" suggest that Dee may even have contemplated suicide due to his melancholy situation.[18]

The angel conversations may have provided a less violent way out. When the corrupted text of the Book of Nature refused to reveal its meaning, Dee would turn to the source of all wisdom and understanding, by enrolling in a "celestial school" run by angelic tutors. Just as God had sent his good angels to illuminate the patriarchs and prophets of old, including Enoch, Moses, Jacob, Esdras, Daniel, and Tobit, Dee was hoping to partake in the uncorrupted, perfect knowledge that could only come from a divine source.

Understanding the Spirit Diaries

Until quite recently, scholarship on Dee's magical interest has tended to focus on its novelty and break with the "dirty magic" of the Middle Ages. This was notably the point of view of the Warburg school of research into Renaissance intellectual culture. In the vision of scholars such as Frances Yates and Peter French,[19] it became important to show how John Dee, framed as Renaissance "Hermetic Magus," was anticipating the more reputable disciplines of modern science and technological innovation with his *magia,* rather than hailing backward to the superstitious practices of medieval warlocks and necromancers. Crucial to this understanding was presenting Dee as a link between the Renaissance philosophers dedicated to the rediscovered *Hermetica,* Marsilio Ficino and Giovanni Pico della Mirandola in particular, and the "Scientific Revolution" yet to emerge in the coming centuries.[20] To a considerable extent, this led to the *neglect* of studying the angel diaries in any real extent, as they remained to the Warburg scholars an embarrassing facet of the otherwise progressive character.

The many studies of John Dee that have emerged since the 1980s, by Christopher Whitby, Nicholas Clulee, Deborah Harkness, Stephen Clucas, György Szőnyi, Håkan Håkansson, and others, have considerably remedied this shortcoming.[21] That the angel diaries now occupy a more significant part of Dee scholarship is readily apparent from reviewing the various articles in Clucas's fairly recent, representative and interdisciplinary anthology on John Dee.[22] As was suggested above, the main strategy of these newer studies has been to point out the consistencies and overlaps between Dee's natural philosophy and the contents and main aspirations and goals of the extant angel diaries. Dee may have found the final solution to his insatiable thirst for natural philosophical knowledge in crystals and conjurations, perhaps viewed primarily as a new optical science.[23] One should keep in mind that Dee operated with a clear division in the state of knowledge, connected to the biblical idea of the Fall. Adam had enjoyed a perfect, nondiscursive knowledge in Paradise, but after the Fall the sciences became imperfect, and prone to error and inaccuracy. Verily, the world itself, the Book of Nature, became a corrupted and unstable text after the Fall. Against this context, crystallomantic evocations of angels were seen as the *via regia* to a reconstitution of a lost, prelapsarian science.

Harkness has suggested that the three main aims of the angelic conferences were all connected to this project: recovering the original and perfect *lingua adamica*; restoring the prelapsarian Kabbalah, as it had originally been revealed to Adam by the angel Raziel; and use these in combination to reconstruct, mend, and read the fallen and corrupted text of the Book of Nature.[24] The centrality of the Fall and the imminent apocalyptic restoration places the diaries thematically at the heart of late-sixteenth-century intellectual culture. So does the all-important search for the Adamic language, one of the more famous features of the angel conversations.[25]

Enthusiasm about finding the primordial or universal language was a trend of the times. This endeavor had, as we have seen, a unique significance in the episteme of the Renaissance. The linguistic theories of the times held that the primordial language would possess a unique quality to refer directly to the things in the world, by naming their essences. This special quality had been gradually lost with the Fall, and the confusion of tongues, accounting in part for the inaccuracy both in language and in our knowledge of the world. Discovering or reconstructing the perfect tongue would have radical consequences for natural philosophy.

It is not unlikely that Dee himself found much inspiration for this pursue in abbot Johannes Trithemius of Sponheim, one of his favorite scholars.[26] Other notable scholars of the era who speculated on the issue of the primordial language, and whom Dee certainly knew well, include the humanist and Christian Kabbalist Johannes Reuchlin (1455–1522), who considered the three biblical languages as being closest to the Adamic language, and Guillaume Postel (1510–1581), who tended to side with Hebrew exclusively. A more colorful opinion was given somewhat later by the Swedish natural philosopher Andreas Kempe (1622–1689), arguing that God had spoken Swedish, that Adam named the animals in Danish, and that the Serpent had tempted Eve in French.[27] This was no doubt a convenient position in the context of the Swedish imperial ambitions at the time; however comical, it nicely illustrates the diffusion of the discourse on the primordial language and its correlations with contemporary natural languages.

While these considerations frame the angel conversations motivationally and thematically in light of Renaissance intellectual culture, another great asset of recent research has been that the *novelty* typically reserved for Dee's magical practices has been challenged. Among the more obvious observations is the fact that catoptromantic practices, including crystallomancy, had been a common folk tradition for generations. Indeed, Dee's manner of calling forth angels seems more influenced by "low" folk magic than intellectual "Hermetic" magic.[28] Additionally, Clucas has pointed out that much of the magical paraphernalia used by Dee and Kelley in the angel workings seems to be taken almost directly from medieval sources, such as the pseudo-Solomonic tradition of the *Ars Notoria*.[29] We will look closer at some of these connections later, as we proceed to analyze and classify some of the "results" of the angelic scrying sessions.

The Magus and the Seer

These latter points bring us to another issue with the angel diaries that has, perhaps surprisingly, evaded attention in the scholarly literature. We usually talk about "Dee's conversations with angels," effectively downplaying the importance of his scryers. The primary reason is clearly that Dee has been the protagonist in the historical narratives that comment on the angel conversations, while very few studies have focused on the conversations in themselves, separated from the broader biography of Dee, mundane, magical, scientific, or otherwise. As we saw already, these narratives did for a long time find the conversations somewhat embarrassing, and when they were finally incorporated the main strategy was to place them in a continuum with Dee's lofty natural philosophy. What, then, of the scryers? What was the role of Edward Kelley, the person who was actually doing the talking on behalf of such entities as "Gabriel," "Ave," "Nalvage," or "Madimi"?[30] The tough question is, then: What really went on in the angel sessions?

It is not correct to say that this question has been completely left out of the literature. In fact, two models have frequently been assumed, although not developed in any systematic fashion: either Kelley was a charlatan, who duped his old master to gain influence over him, or else he was simply deranged. Both these models stand in opposition, of course, to the more esoteric claim that there was, in fact, supernatural agency involved in creating the angel sessions. As later chapters of this book will show, the supernaturalistic interpretation has been common among occultists, and continues in various forms to be so today. The "charlatan theory," by far the dominating paradigm in the scholarly discourse, goes all the way back to the seventeenth century, where it was posited in the polemical "Preface" to Meric Casaubon's *True and Faithful Relations* (*T&FR*), the first publication of (some of) Dee's magical diaries. Casaubon held that Dee, an otherwise pious Christian, had been deceived by a diabolical nigromancer, and offered his volume as a warning against dabbling with magic. Without the theological accusations, the suspicion of fraud has been taken up in modern scholarship, especially in the Warburg tradition. Yates, for one, wrote explicitly that "Kelly was a fraud who deluded his pious master," while French added the possibility that he "had some form of mental illness" as well.[31] It is also noteworthy that those scholars who have taken it upon themselves to analyse the contents of the angel conversations in later years, including Harkness, Clulee, Szőnyi, and Håkansson, largely sidestep the difficult issue of "what went on," steering by a kind of "methodologically agnostic" principle instead. This may have been a wise decision in light of the specific research questions that have been asked and answered, but it has also left a hole in our current understanding of this episode.

There is something unsatisfying about a situation where the question of what went on is left a battle between claims of fraud and madness on the one side, and supernaturalism on the other. Recently, James Justin Sledge attempted to remedy this gap in a close analysis of the angel diaries, with the ambitious goal of creating a satisfying "etiology" of the conversations.[32] While recognizing that the charlatan theory has a few merits (Kelley was a known forger, had been in and out of prison, and had a financial motive for staying with Dee, who paid a high salary), Sledge rightly finds it wanting because of the serious inconsistencies it creates. From the sources it seems clear that Dee was the persistent, steadfast director and enthusiast of the actions, while Kelley was volatile, and at several occasions tried to opt out of the experiments, claiming the spirits to be wicked, or otherwise suggesting that there are better things to do than summoning angels (alchemy, for instance). The problem is that the charlatan theory requires casting Dee as deceived and exploited.[33] This does not make perfect sense, especially given Dee's now quite clear rationale for engaging in these actions. One is reminded of the somewhat unorthodox but still intriguing remark made by Geoffrey James, that it was *Kelley* who was the exploited part in the duo, doing as he was told to earn his wages: "It was Dee, not Kelley, who was gaining the benefit from the magical ceremonies, for it sated his lust for 'radical truths.'"[34]

Sledge proposes that a combination of four considerations make the spirit actions fully explicable. First, a material contextualization, placing the angel conversations in the middle of the cultural, religious, and political environment of the late sixteenth century makes much of the content and the undertaking itself understandable. This is hardly controversial, and an understanding on these grounds may be said to have emerged already with the recent wave of Dee scholarship discussed above. Sledge's second consideration consists in probing the extant material for signs of consistent behavioral traits that may indicate a preexisting psychotic condition in Kelley. This is a partial acknowledgment of the "madness thesis," but one which urges a more systematic approach, informed by our best psychiatric models. Thirdly, it is suggested that the records could also be analyzed looking for signs of "altered states of consciousness," arising either due to specific conditions that obtain during the séances, by the very procedures observed in the rituals, or also in combination with the possible preexisting mental condition. Here too, the analysis should, according to Sledge, rest on what can be salvaged from contemporary research, particularly research looking for correlations between brain states identifiable and verifiable by neurobiology, and claims to special mental states associated with religious and "mystical" observance. Finally, Sledge argues that the abovementioned factors can be tied together in an analysis of the "formative epistemological processes" that allowed Kelley to operate somewhere between "wilful deception" and sincerity in his role and capabilities as seer.

Sledge's analysis is a welcome contribution, refreshingly pointing at questions that everyone have found intriguing, but few have dared to answer. Nevertheless, one is left with the impression that some of the pathologizing is overstated, and perhaps even redundant. Indeed, one possible shortcoming with a theory that rests in part on the psychopathology of Edward Kelley is that what we need to account for goes beyond his mere person. Although Kelley was clearly the most famous and apparently most successful scryer that Dee employed, he was only working in about one-third of the total angel scrying sessions. What we need to explain, then, is not the particular case of Kelley (although it is a good and exceptionally well-documented case), but rather the entire cultural practice, the *institution* of scrying. We know that Dee had worked with the scryer Barnabas Saul prior to meeting Kelley in 1582, and suspect that he had at least one more scyer before this. But also after his collaboration with Kelley was terminated Dee continued with other scryers. He attempted to use his seven-year-old son, Arthur, but was not content with his performance. Finally he ended up with one Bartholomew Hickman, who must have done a pretty good job, since he continued to work with Dee for a total of sixteen years. Unfortunately, we know very little about the nature of these sessions since so little of the material survives. No doubt this is partly because Dee's endeavor with Hickman had been built on an angelic prophecy stating that September 1600 would mark some tremendous breakthrough in his project. When nothing happened, Dee demonstrated his frustration by burning the records from nine years of angel conversations.[35] However, it is worth noting that the problem was not Hickman's scrying abilities as such—they must surely have been convincing enough, since Dee continued to work with him on and off for seven more years even after this incident.

In order to assess the whole cultural practice of scrying, then, I will suggest that contextual factors, coupled perhaps with analyses of the actual practices (i.e., the techniques, procedures, use of paraphernalia, etc.) should, in the main, suffice. Additionally, restating and expanding Sledge's fourth consideration may be particularly fruitful: the "formative epistemological processes" he is concerned with, involving active imagination, mythmaking, and role play is conceived of as something akin to Tanya Luhrmann's concept of "interpretive drift" observed in her fieldwork of contemporary witchcraft and magical groups in England.[36] Erecting an updated theoretical framework, which could help explain such processes more generally, I submit, would do well to consider the vast literature and research in cognitive and social psychology on the centrality of role play and social expectations on memory, identity, and reports of "anomalous experiences" and behavior. The sociocognitive framework has proved successful for making sense of such things as hypnosis, "multiple personalities," false memories (about past lives, alien abductions, satanic ritual abuse, etc.), "trance," and, indeed, spirit possession and exorcism.[37] All of these are sociocultural phenomena which, I think most would agree, share some vague family resemblance to claims we associate with the practice of scrying. Such an approach would focus on the institutional role of scrying in the given period, its cultural significance and recognition, and the social *expectations* embedded in the practice, especially the tensions between expert and client. Some of the mystique of the angel conversations is unveiled when we consider the relation between Kelley and Dee as taking part in a culturally sanctioned practice, probably not the most common one, but one which was certainly not exceptional or unheard of.

A further demystification of Kelley may arise from looking at him through different sources, and hence different eyes. As Susan Bassnett has pointed out, the perception of Kelley changes somewhat when we see him described from the perspective of the Bohemians whom he spent the height of his career with, instead of through Dee's eyes, which perspective obviously dominates in the diaries.[38] First of all, we should note with some interest that when Kelley and Dee parted company on the occasion of Dee's return to England in 1588, Kelley's days as a scryer were numbered. This reminds us again of Geoffrey James's claim that Kelley had only stayed in the scrying business because of Dee's will and lust for "radical truths." It would at the very least seem as if Kelley was better off after he parted with Dee, working as a successful and sought-after alchemist. His acquisition of land and property, including a gold mine, his involvement in political intrigue, and his being knighted by the emperor Rudolph II in or about 1589, all testify to this.[39] Indeed, Bassnett has suggested that Kelley's success and upward social mobility in Bohemia may have produced feelings of envy and resentment in Dee, who finally decided to turn homeward.[40] At any rate, a quite different picture of Kelley emerges from these perspectives.

The Magic of the Angelic Conferences: Toward a Typology

With these background considerations we may proceed to the content of the magical diaries, looking for a way to localize, classify, and analyze the components that in modern times have become "Enochian magic." Dee and Kelley's cooperation started in 1582, and lasted for about five years, until 1587. Over these years hundreds of pages of transcripts of angel conversations were produced, along with several *libri* detailing specific magical instructions, prepared separately on the angels' command. Apart from the diary transcripts published by Casaubon in 1659, the remains of these actions are preserved in the manuscript collections of the British Library.[41]

There are several ways one could approach this material in order to make a typology. One effort of classifying the themes of the extant material has been submitted by György E. Szőnyi. Szőnyi divides the totality of material received from the angels into four thematic categories:[42]

1. Descriptions of visions of the divine cosmic order and the world of angels sustaining it;
2. Descriptions of rituals and magical invocations (i.e., more or less explicitly magical material);
3. Apocalyptic/prophetic prognostications, predictions foretelling the fall of various empires and the rise of new, spiritually pious regimes;
4. Instructions on the *lingua adamica*.

This may seem a pertinent classification if only to get a clear overview of the themes covered: we certainly find major portions of the angel diaries dealing with mystical cosmology, various kinds of apocalypticism, magical instructions, and the Adamic language. However, these are *not* separate concerns. They all mix together and relate to one another, in such a way that, for instance, the magical instructions, which mainly concern us here, heavily incorporate the Adamic language as a component, and are embedded in both the metaphysical/theological visions of the universe and in apocalyptic speculations. The magical system (or systems) appearing in the context of the angelic revelations cannot be separated from these other concerns. Thus, the typology is not helping us much further if we want to get a clearer overview of the *magical* component itself.

I will propose a slightly different approach, which better fits the agenda of this book and, I believe, does more justice to the magical component of Dee and Kelley's workings. First of all, a line should be drawn between the angel conversations themselves, that is, the way Dee and Kelley actually *worked,* and the arcane magical material "received" *through* these conversations. In other words, level one of "Dee's magic" is a catoptromantic, Ars Notoria inspired crystal gazing, aimed at communion with the angels and revelations of higher knowledge concerning natural philosophy, the apocalypse, and God's salvific project; level two, on the other hand, comprises a number of magical systems, grimoire-like in form, which appear in the course of the angel diaries.

I should take haste to mention that this distinction does not work in an absolute sense, since in the earliest sessions instructions were given to make certain ritual tools, which seem to have been put to general use later, when contacting the angels. In other words, at least some of the practices observed by Dee and Kelley when contacting the angels already came from Kelley, "through revelation," in the same way as I argue for the second category. Already in Dee and Kelley's very first session together, on March 10, 1582, there were given designs for a "Holy Table" or altar, and a waxen Sigillum Dei.[43] These were built, and apparently used in consequent scrying sessions, together with more such instruments described by the angels. But in addition to these instructions large quantities of other arcane information was imparted: letter squares, invocations in the Adamic language, names of spiritual entities (angels, Princes, "Seniors," and even cacodaemons), and ways of calling them forth. It is this kind of material which I believe must be distinguished from the procedure of the workings through which it was "received."

Furthermore, this magical material can be subdivided in various ways. I find it most prudent to divide the magical system received in the angel conversations first into five components, based on a distinction made by Dee himself, and which also seems to signify important differences in content and intended function. This classification relates to the way the outcome of the angelic conversations was recorded. To begin with, Dee recorded every session diligently and chronologically, containing the dialogues with the angels, including all their commands, answers, and revelations. These diary entries are preserved in MS Sloane 3188 and Cotton Appendix XLVI, the latter of which forms the basis for Casaubon's 1659 publication, *A True & Faithful Relation*. But in addition to these "proceedings" Dee was also on a few occasions commanded to prepare special books, where more or less independent parts of the magical revelations were concentrated and systematized. The result was a total of five separate texts, which I will refer to as "revealed books," none of which were published by Casaubon. The contents of these books show, in concentrated and systematized form, the magical system(s) revealed through the conversations. For this reason they present themselves as a pertinent basis for a classification of the magical material.

A brief summary of the five received books is in order. The first book is the one commonly referred to as *Liber Logaeth/Loagaeth,* or "the Book of the Speech of God."[44] The book is the condensation of the angel conversations that started March 23 to 29, 1583, and went on for about a month, and saw the first transmission of the alleged Angelic or Adamic language.[45] It takes the form of ninety-five gridded tables, mostly of forty-nine by forty-nine squares each, filled up with letters, and forty-nine "calls" or prayers prefacing the tables.[46] Interestingly, John Reeds made the discovery that eight of the tables in *Liber Loagaeth* are actually copied from Dee's *Book of Soyga* in Sloane 8, meaning that not all of them were created by Kelley/the angels.[47] The prefacing prayers are in the Angelic tongue and were not translated, with the exception of a few individual words. Also included toward the end of the manuscript is the twenty-one-letter Angelic alphabet, revealed by Kelley on March 26. Although the intended use of these letter tables is somewhat unclear, the angels did tell Dee that "when the time is right" the book should be used together with the Holy Table to initiate the apocalyptic "redefinition of the natural world."[48] No other instructions of its function or use are extant, except obscure hints that the mysteries of the tables will only be revealed by God at his chosen moment.[49] With reference to Szőnyi's classification discussed above, this already demonstrates clearly the way in which apocalypticism, speculations on *lingua adamica,* and magic are all interconnected in Dee's angel diaries.

Angelic letter							
Name	Pa	Veh	Ged	Gal	Or	Un	Graph
Latin equivalent	B	C	G	D	F	A	E

Angelic letter							
Name	Tal	Gon	Na	Ur	Mals	Ger	Drux
Latin equivalent	M	I	H	L	P	Q	N

Angelic letter							
Name	Pal	Med	Don	Ceph	Van	Fan	Gisg
Latin equivalent	X	O	R	Z	U	S	T

TABLE 1.1. The 21 letters of the Angelic alphabet, in the order they appear at the bottom of the last leaf of Sloane 3189 (Liber Loagaeth). The table shows the names of the letters, and their Latin equivalents, as explained in Dee and Kelley's angel diaries.

The second revealed book bears the title *De heptarchia mystica,* and is a rather compendious collection of the essential information received by Dee and Kelley before they left England for the continent in 1583.[50] The content of this book forms a magical system wherewith the magician can call upon the "heptarchical Kings and Princes," purportedly ruling the seven days of the week.[51] The book includes names of these "good Heptarchical Angels," their various seals and sigils, the nature of their offices (e.g., imparting arcane knowledge, or teaching alchemy), and supplications to call them forth. The system of angels set over the seven days of the week reminds one of earlier magical manuals of similar intent, such as the *Heptameron* attributed to the medieval Italian physician and astrologer Pietro d'Abano.[52] One should add, however, that Dee's spirit names and conjurations were, as always, idiosyncratic, and it is the structure and intent rather than concrete names and sigils that bear resemblance.

The third revealed book is the *48 Claves angelicae,* the forty-eight angelic keys.[53] These are really nineteen short verses, written in the Angelic language, with English translations given at the angels' discretion. While the first eighteen are freestanding invocations of unclear function, the nineteenth is dedicated to the so-called thirty "Aires," a set of obscure entities that are explained more systematically in the *fourth* revealed book, *Liber scientiae, auxilii, et victoriae terrestris* ("Book of terrestrial science, support, and victory").[54] The thirty Aires seem to be certain spirits, spiritual realms, or principles located in various parts of the air surrounding the earth. Each of these thirty Aires control a small number of spirits (an average of three each, or ninety-one in total), which further control legions of lesser spirits, extending in a vast hierarchy of angelic creatures—comprising a total of 491,577 angels.

What is particularly interesting is that each of the ninety-one spirits corresponds to a country or geographical region in the world, as it looked through European Renaissance eyes (or more precisely, as it had looked in late antiquity: the geographical names are all derived from Ptolemy), and a mystic name is given to each of the regions. For instance we learn that Egypt is Occodon, Syria Pascomb, and Mesopotamia Valgars, that these are ruled by the angels Zarzilg, Zinggen, and Alpudus, sat under the Aire called LIL.[55] Furthermore, the twelve tribes of ancient Israel are also listed, with directions apparently pointing out where, in their dispersion, each has gone. The intention of this system seems to be that by "calling" the right Aires with the nineteenth "key" of the *Claves angelicae* the magician can gain the authority over the geographical entities and presumably the power to control great geopolitical events (thus indicated by the title of the book, "terrestrial victory"). In other words, this was a form of magic most desirable for Dee, being the occasional counselor to the Imperial Elizabethan throne. As Harkness has commented, it also seems that another intention was to localize and order the twelve lost tribes.[56] According to the prophecies, the tribes should return to Israel with the onset of the apocalypse; Dee may have envisioned a role for himself in this apocalyptic project. It should be noted that politics and the rearrangement of empires and nations feature frequently in the apocalyptic discourse of the angel conversations generally as well.

The fifth and last revealed book is known as *Tabula bonorum angelorum*, "the table of good angels."[57] Again, this is a collection of prayers or invocations, but this time related to a specific fourfold magical square or table, referred to by Dee as the "Great Table" or "table of good angels." comprising four lesser "Watchtowers." These letter squares were transmitted by Kelley on two consecutive days, June 25–26, 1584, while Dee and Kelley were in Krakow.[58] From the four "watchtower" squares, connected to form the "Great Table" by inserting what is referred to as "the black cross" between them (a cross scribbled black by Dee, containing more mysterious names), are extracted numerous angels, "Seniors" (purportedly the six that stand before the throne of God in *Revelations*), Kings, secret names of God, and even demons; all ordered in an elaborate hierarchy.

The methods of extracting the names, as well as the function of each entity, were described on June 26, when the angel Ave declared the tables to contain:

1. All human knowledge.
2. Out of it springeth Physick
3. *The knowledge of the elemental Creatures, amongst you. How many* kinds there are, and for what use they were created. *Those that live in the air, by themselves. The* property *of the fire*—which is the secret life of all things.
4. *The knowledge, finding and use of Metals.*
   The vertues of *them.*
   The congelations, and vertues of *Stones.*
5. *The Conjoining and knitting together of Natures. The destruction of Nature, and of things that may perish.*
6. *Moving from place to place [as into this Country, or that Country at pleasure]*
7. *The knowledge of all crafts Mechanical.*
8. Transmutatio formalis, sed non essentialis.[59]

No small set of feats, to be sure. The *Tabula angelorum bonorum* is Dee's systematic ordering of the material relating to this Great Table. In addition to the table itself, it includes lists of angels and divine names,

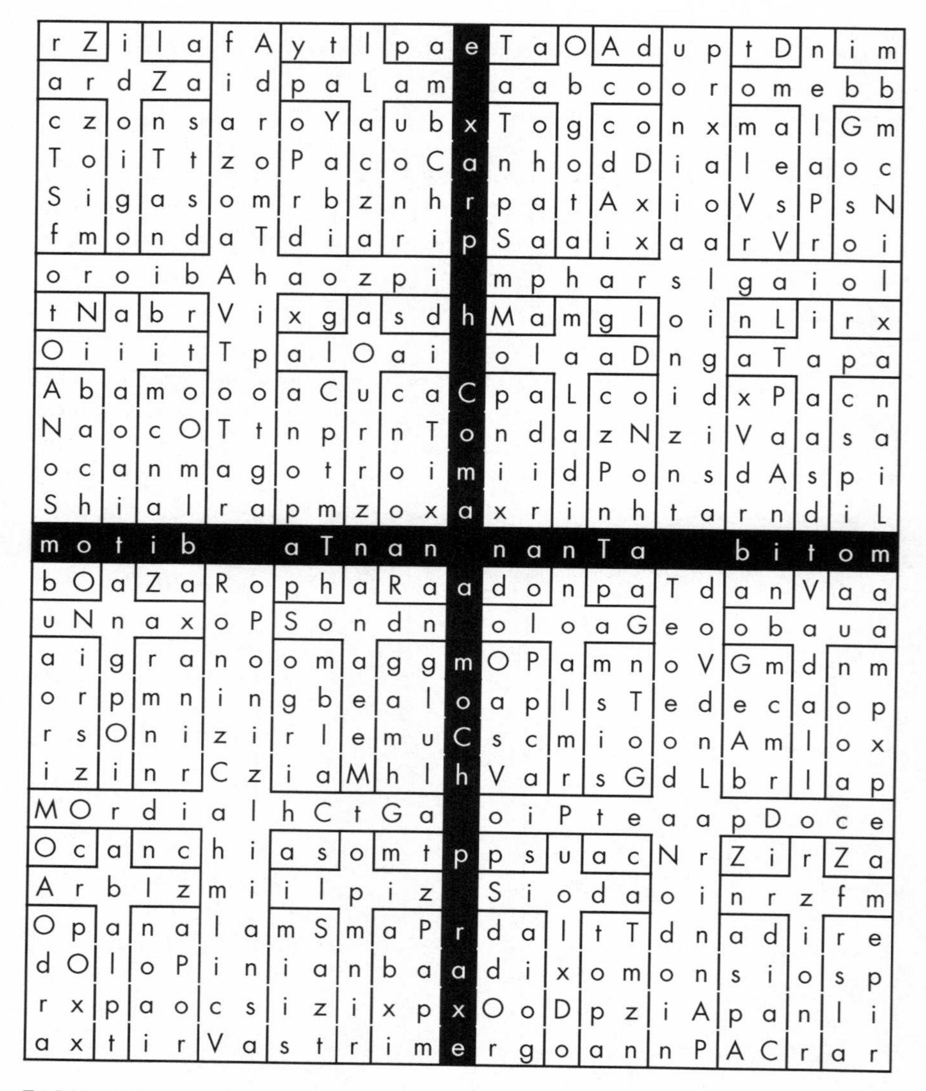

r	Z	i	l	a	f	A	y	t	l	p	a	e	T	a	O	A	d	u	p	t	D	n	i	m
a	r	d	Z	a	i	d	p	a	L	a	m		a	a	b	c	o	o	r	o	m	e	b	b
c	z	o	n	s	a	r	o	Y	a	u	b	x	T	o	g	c	o	n	x	m	a	l	G	m
T	o	i	T	t	z	o	P	a	c	o	C	a	n	h	o	d	D	i	a	l	e	a	o	c
S	i	g	a	s	o	m	r	b	z	n	h	r	p	a	t	A	x	i	o	V	s	P	s	N
f	m	o	n	d	a	T	d	i	a	r	i	p	S	a	a	i	x	a	a	r	V	r	o	i
o	r	o	i	b	A	h	a	o	z	p	i		m	p	h	a	r	s	l	g	a	i	o	l
t	N	a	b	r	V	i	x	g	a	s	d	h	M	a	m	g	l	o	i	n	L	i	r	x
O	i	i	i	t	T	p	a	l	O	a	i		o	l	a	a	D	n	g	a	T	a	p	a
A	b	a	m	o	o	o	a	C	u	c	a	C	p	a	L	c	o	i	d	x	P	a	c	n
N	a	o	c	O	T	t	n	p	r	n	T	o	n	d	a	z	N	z	i	V	a	a	s	a
o	c	a	n	m	a	g	o	t	r	o	i	m	i	i	d	P	o	n	s	d	A	s	p	i
S	h	i	a	l	r	a	p	m	z	o	x	a	x	r	i	n	h	t	a	r	n	d	i	L
m	o	t	i	b			a	T	n	a	n		n	a	n	T	a			b	i	t	o	m
b	O	a	Z	a	R	o	p	h	a	R	a	a	d	o	n	p	a	T	d	a	n	V	a	a
u	N	n	a	x	o	P	S	o	n	d	n		o	l	o	a	G	e	o	o	b	a	u	a
a	i	g	r	a	n	o	o	m	a	g	g	m	O	P	a	m	n	o	V	G	m	d	n	m
o	r	p	m	n	i	n	g	b	e	a	l	o	a	p	l	s	T	e	d	e	c	a	o	p
r	s	O	n	i	z	i	r	l	e	m	u	C	s	c	m	i	o	o	n	A	m	l	o	x
i	z	i	n	r	C	z	i	a	M	h	l	h	V	a	r	s	G	d	L	b	r	l	a	p
M	O	r	d	i	a	l	h	C	t	G	a		o	i	P	t	e	a	a	p	D	o	c	e
O	c	a	n	c	h	i	a	s	o	m	t	p	p	s	u	a	c	N	r	Z	i	r	Z	a
A	r	b	l	z	m	i	i	l	p	i	z		S	i	o	d	a	o	i	n	r	z	f	m
O	p	a	n	a	l	a	m	S	m	a	P	r	d	a	l	t	T	d	n	a	d	i	r	e
d	O	l	o	P	i	n	i	a	n	b	a	a	d	i	x	o	m	o	n	s	i	o	s	p
r	x	p	a	o	c	s	i	z	i	x	p	x	O	o	D	p	z	i	A	p	a	n	l	i
a	x	t	i	r	V	a	s	t	r	i	m	e	r	g	o	a	n	n	P	A	C	r	a	r

TABLE 1.2. The "Great Table" as shown in Dee's *Tabula bonorum angelorum*, Sloane MS 3191. There are some minor details which I have not reproduced here (some letters that have been scratched out and replaced, and a few inverted letters). The table shows the four Watchtowers, with the uniting "Black Cross" in the middle. Take note that the Black Cross does not appear in Golden Dawn sources (which instead arrange its divine letters in a "Tablet of Union"), neither in the Sloane MS 307 version of the Great Table (see chapters two and three; cf. table 4).

indexed with their specific powers and attributions, and also different prayers or invocations to contact and control the entities in hierarchical order, from the highest secret twelve names of God, to the lowest serving angels. Also included are the names of demons and bad angels, which can perform the negative of what their corresponding angels do. Thus, where the angels of "physick" (i.e., medicine) can heal wounds, the inverse "cacodaemons" can cause them.

* * *

The contents of these five books comprise the totality of what has in various combinations and interpretations of later centuries become known as "Enochian magic." According to the division presented by the books itself, we can speak of the following *four key components* forming the foundation of this magic:

1. The Angelic language, later referred to as "Enochian" (from the books *Liber Loagaeth* and, especially, the *48 Claves angelicae*);
2. The Heptarchic system (*De heptarchia mystica*);
3. The Aires, or (per later conventions) Aethyrs (*Liber scientiae, auxilii, et victoriae Terrestris,* with the *Claves angelicae*);
4. The magic of the "Great Table," or "Four Watchtowers" (*Tabula angelorum bonorum*).

It should be noted, of course, that even these four do interact and mix with each other to some extent. Most notably, the Angelic language is a key component of the system of the Aires, as shown above. In addition, the ninety-one spirits belonging to the Aires are linked to the Great Table by certain sigils that apply to its letter squares.[60] Nevertheless, the mentioned classes do stand out with a significant degree of exclusive features; the cryptic apocalyptic statements surrounding the *Liber Logaeth;* the Heptarchic system with its encyclopaedic, grimoire-style list of spirits, sigils, and the hours and days of calling them forth; the (probably) geopolitical and apocalyptic system of the Aires; and the almost universally applicable system for evocation of angels and cacodaemons of the Great Table, providing rather mundane services such as the finding of precious metals, healing sickness, and transportation from one country to another.

In closing, some words should be spent concerning the accuracy of labeling these works "received," and the possible historical problems of doing so. As mentioned earlier in this chapter, recent Dee scholarship emphasizes the continuity with medieval magical traditions, a focus that has proved quite successful. Among the discoveries that have been made is that the ritual paraphernalia "received" by the angels early on, the most significant being the Holy Table and the Sigillum Dei Emeth, seem to have been appropriated from traceable sources known to be in Dee's possession. Thus, Stephen Clucas has shown how the Sigillum is an almost exact replica of a sigil from the fourteenth-century *Liber iuratus Honorii*.[61] Joseph Peterson has shown that there are significant similarities between the design of Dee's Holy Table and certain diagrams from the medieval Ars Almadel.[62] It has even been conjectured that the alphabet of the Angelic or Adamic language revealed by the angels was taken from Giovanni Pantheus's 1530 tract *Voarchadumia contra alchimiam,* which was also in Dee's possession.[63] The orthographic similarities in this latter case are not too apparent, and the relation seems weaker than with Clucas's and Peterson's findings; nevertheless, it does not seem implausible that, as Claire Fanger has predicted, more such cases of similarity and correspondence with earlier manuscripts may surface as more of the medieval sources become better known to scholars.[64] This seems to be the general direction that research on the relation between Renaissance and medieval magic is going.[65]

The idiosyncrasy of the systems resulting *from* the actions stems mostly from the angelic language, the complexity and design of the magical letter squares used, and the specific names of the angels and entities to be evoked. Apart from that, the structure and magical theories seem to be heavily influenced by medieval and early modern sources, notably the *Heptameron,* Agrippa, and the grimoires.

Kelley died under uncertain circumstances in Bohemia around 1597,[66] and Dee himself followed a decade later, in 1609. Despite Dee's great enthusiasm with having these "new" magical systems revealed and explained by the angels, we have no indication that Dee, Kelley, or Hickman at any point got their final signal from the angels, telling them to commence work with the largely apocalyptic magical systems they had received.[67] As we will see through the course of this book, many have tried to do so since.

2

Whispers of Secret Manuscripts

The reputation of the once sought-after, respected, even feared natural philosopher John Dee went into decline in the seventeenth century. This happened already during the last years of his life, seeing the death of his patron Queen Elizabeth and the ascension of James I to the throne, a regent much less favorable to magic, to say the least, having published his famous support of witch hunts, *Demonologie,* in 1597. After his death in 1609, Dee soon slipped into the collective memory as a confused and troubled man, rumored to have dabbled in magic and obscure mysticism. Natural philosophy was rapidly changing, and Dee's way of thinking about nature in terms of corrupted texts and revelation, restitution and apocalypse, became increasingly foreign.[1] The generally bookish approach of the sixteenth century gave way to the new Baconian experimentalism of the seventeenth, while Dee's Adamic language of nature was replaced by Galileo's mathematical. In a lecture to the early Royal Society, the natural philosopher Robert Hooke referred to the angel conversations as "Dr. Dee's delusions," nevertheless indicating that they were being discussed there.[2] Despite his rejection of Dee's magical endeavors, Hooke still had a hope that the diaries were not really about magic, but rather presented a form of cryptography, hiding valuable intelligence information intended for Elizabeth herself.

No one work has been more influential in sealing Dee's reputation than Meric Casaubon's 1659 edition of parts of his diaries, *A True & Faithful Relation*. This book remained the primary reference to the angel conversations for centuries, presenting a picture of Dee as a good but gullible man, who was tricked into believing in foul spirits, masquerading as angels, by the sly necromancer Kelley. The present chapter, dealing with the early reception history of Dee's magical work—*among magicians*—will demonstrate the vast importance of Casaubon's edition. Over the following pages we will look at questions such as what happened to

Dee's copious notes and manuscripts relating to the conversations after his death, how much of it was taken up by other magicians of the seventeenth century, and how do we place such practices in relation to the transmission of manuscripts and the public knowledge of Dee's actions?

Answering all these questions requires us to determine the routes of transmission from Dee's colloquium of angels, looking as we go at how changing historical circumstances affected the perception of his magical endeavors. We shall see that the transmission of Dee's manuscripts has sometimes been difficult to chart out. Parts of it have even been riddled with speculations about a secret tradition of magicians, working with the magical systems contained in Dee's received libri, stretching, perhaps, back to the magus himself. In the present chapter I shall deal with these claims to some extent, evaluating their veracity and placing the reception of Dee's manuscripts in their right contexts. This is not only a question of drawing up a solid, source-driven historiographical account of the transfers of certain obscure manuscripts; the discussions in this chapter will also serve as necessary background for issues that arise in later chapters.

"The Devil's Looking-Glass"

It is not without irony[3] that Casaubon's *True & Faithful Relation* of what happened between John Dee and "some spirits" has been the single most influential contribution to preserving the memory of Dee and Kelley's angelic colloquiums.[4] The Casaubon family is of some importance to the historian of Western esoteric currents, although certainly not as esotericists. Meric Florence Estienne Casaubon was a son of the classics scholar Isaac Casaubon, who in 1614 famously dated the *Corpus Hermeticum* to the early centuries of the Christian era, debunking the widespread Renaissance conception that the texts were of prehistoric provenance.[5] Fifty-five years later his son Meric would add to the family tradition of debunking contemporary hermeticists and magi by writing a highly polemical preface to his edition of John Dee's angel diaries. In the preface, Casaubon attacked the angel conversations as diabolical, asserting that Dee had been tricked by the necromancer Kelley into believing that foul and mischievous spirits were divine messengers. The diaries were "a Work of Darknesse," attesting to the good doctor Dee's gullibility.[6]

Casaubon was a scholar and a divine who had been confirmed into the Church of England when his father took him to the British Isles as a child, adhering steadfastly to the faith all his life and publishing apologetic and polemical treatises to defend it.[7] Essentially, what he did in the preface to

T&FR was continuing a line of antimagical polemics which had long roots in Christian theology. The crux of the problem was that the spirits that had appeared as angels were, by all probability, demons, only masquerading as angels. There was nothing surprising about this view: ever since the early church fathers, theologians had more or less agreed that magic, however it presented itself, really worked by the aid of demons and wicked spirits.[8] Indeed, the view that the devil and his demons possessed formidable powers of trickery and deceit had only been growing in the early modern period, a time when witch hunts and prosecutions of magicians was peaking.[9] Casaubon himself would in fact go on to publish several defenses of the view that demons, spirits, and witches existed, attacking those who denied it.[10] Through the pages of Casaubon's volume, and the preface especially, we witness the demonization of Dee's angelic beings, of scrying, and not least of Kelley.

Casaubon had offered his edition of the angel diaries to the world as a warning against the dangers of magic. Ironically, the immediate effect seems to have been quite the opposite of what he would have hoped for. There is much indication that *T&FR* sparked renewed interest in angel magic generally and Dee's actions particularly. For instance, Deborah Harkness discovered a set of diaries in the British Library that attest to the existence of a group which met occasionally between 1671 and 1688 to invoke angels through a crystal.[11] The group gathered around a scryer by the name E. Rorbon, and judging from the evidence of the more than one thousand surviving manuscript pages, it must have consisted of at least two more people. We can tell that this group of magicians was influenced by Dee's published diaries, since several of his most idiosyncratic angel friends figure in their evocations and visions. The angel Nalvage appears from the beginning of their records; on August 4, 1671, he was already answering questions about "his book" named "Logaeth."[12] Soon Madimi appears as well, perhaps the most peculiar character in Dee and Kelly's gallery of angels, appearing first as a little girl who gradually grows up through the course of the conversations. Undoubtedly unorthodox from a theological viewpoint, Madimi nevertheless became one of the most central angels in the circle around the scryer Rorbon. Despite the pains that had obviously been taken by this group to emulate Dee and Kelley's workings as described in *T&FR*, Harkness notes that their aims and interests, judging from the questions they asked of the angels, diverged from Dee's lofty natural philosophical ones.[13] The main interest seems to have been the recovery buried treasure, a common feature of magical manuals. Nevertheless, there are sections where more speculative topics are discussed, expressed in a discourse replete with astrological and alchemical symbolism, and abstract Kabbalistic concepts.

The angel invocations of Rorbon with companions date from more than ten years after Casaubon's publication, and obviously found inspiration in that volume. But what, then, about the original manuscripts? Who possessed them after Dee's death, and could someone have used them for magic in the period before Casaubon? Some modern commentators have certainly thought so. The alchemy scholar Adam McLean, and more recently Stephen Skinner and David Rankine, have suggested that there must have existed a secret tradition of magicians with access to the manuscripts. Claims about such secret magical traditions have especially been attached to two manuscripts, today in MS Harley 6482 and MS Sloane 307.[14] In addition to being shrouded in some mystery these manuscripts have been quite influential in mediating Dee and Kelley's magic to the context of modern occultism as well. We should therefore turn to these two manuscripts to ascertain, as far as possible, their origin, and relation to other known sources and early transmissions of Dee's Enochiana.

Dr. Rudd's *Treatise on Angel Magic*

The document that is typically taken as the main expression of the hypothesized secret magical group is Harley 6482, the so-called "Rudd manuscript." This is a full treatise on angel magic, written at the very end of the seventeenth century (the date 1699 appears on the title page), by one Peter Smart. Smart, however, made the claim that he was merely copying from the papers of one "Dr. Rudd." We do not learn more about this figure, but judging from the various papers that Smart attributes to him—there is a whole corpus of them—he must have been steeped in the Rosicrucian, hermetic, Kabbalistic, and magical currents of the seventeenth century. Among them are works such as *The Rosie Crucian Secrets,* translations from Michael Maier's works, an English translation of *The Chymical Wedding of Christian Rosenkreutz,* a quarto containing a discussion on "Rosicrucian Chymical medicines," and another one giving "a defence of the Jews and other Eastern Men."[15] In addition to these treatises, the Rudd corpus includes extensive materials on ritual magic. We find, for instance, a quarto "containing all the Names, Orders, and Offices of all the Spirits Solomon ever conversed with: the Seals and Characters belonging to each Spirit, the manner of calling them forth"—a typical Solomonic grimoire of the "nigromantic" type.[16] Side by side with this nigromantic manuscript we find the *Treatise on Angel Magic*.

The *Treatise on Angel Magic* brings together a wide range of authorities on demonology and angelology.[17] It forms a vast synthesis of many different magical traditions; some discernable influences include Kabbalistic speculations, renaissance Hermeticism, astral magic, nigromantic, "Goetic," and Ars Notoria magical traditions, huge portions of Agrippa's *De Occulta Philosophia,* and, importantly for our present concerns, the magical systems "received" in John Dee and Edward Kelly's angel conversations a generation or two earlier.

The Rudd manuscripts present an illustration, bearing the title *Tabula Sancta cum Tabulis Enochi* ("The Holy Table with Enoch's tables"), showing Dee's "Holy Table," the Adamic or "Enochian" alphabet, and seven seals, which were called "Ensigns of Creation" in the original diaries.[18] The original Holy Table had been one of the most important paraphernalia of Dee and Kelly's angel workings. It was a wooden table, with a three to four feet square surface, serving as a sort of altar for the scrying sessions. Upon it would be the "Sigillum Dei Emeth," the famous waxen image used in the workings, and the "show stone" crystal employed for scrying would be seated on top of it—both still on display in the British Museum. According to Dee's diaries, the designs for making the Holy Table and the other ritual paraphernalia were purportedly transmitted by the angels early on in the conversations. As we saw in the previous chapter, however, more recent Dee scholarship has found that these "received" paraphernalia bear close resemblance to earlier sources.

What is particularly intriguing about the illustration in the Rudd manuscript is that the Holy Table has been rearranged in a fashion that reveals that the author had specific practical intentions with the material. The author of the manuscript had taken care to inscribe the protective holy names "Adonay" and "Jesus" on the top of the table, and a heptagram has been added to its design, containing the seven Ensigns, or "Enochian tables" in Rudd's terminology, within its seven points. Around is the square edge with angelic letters as in the original. The main alteration, however, is that the table has been placed within a many-layered circle inscribed with the Hebrew letters of certain angel and secret names of God. In a rectangular box by the side are mentioned some of the "Shemhamphorash", or seventy-two secret names of God, which according to Kabbalistic traditions can be extracted from Exodus 14:19–21. The four compass directions are also indicated within the circle, written in Latin, and the names of the four angels Raphael, Michael, Gabriel, and Uriel are represented in Hebrew. Outside of the circle we find four pentagrams, bearing Greek letters adding up to the words "Alpha" and "Omega," as well as the name "Tetragrammaton," written in Latin characters.

What should one make out of these elaborate representations, arrangements, and appropriations of Dee and Kelley's received magical material? Who was this "Dr. Rudd"? What sources was he working from, and what should we think of the hypothesis that he was part of a secret tradition following Dee, independent of Casaubon's *T&FR*?

Among proponents of the secret tradition hypothesis, the enigmatic Dr. Rudd has typically been identified as Captain Thomas Rudd (1583–1656), a mathematician and military engineer.[19] This identification seems to stem from a "possible connection" conjectured by Frances Yates, who went through the Rudd material for her research on *The Rosicrucian Enlightenment* (1972).[20] Her reason for vaguely stating this possible connection was that Thomas Rudd had published an edition of Dee's "Mathematical preface" to Euclid in 1651. To Yates, this suggested that Thomas might have been an "enlightened Rosicrucian," in the sense portrayed by her book, hence fitting in nicely with the many Rosicrucian texts of the Rudd corpus.

This hint has been expanded upon by the later hypothesizers of a hidden transmission of Dee's magical diaries after his death.[21] Most notably Adam McLean, and more recently the scholar-magicians Stephen Skinner and David Rankine, place Thomas Rudd at the center of a previously unknown magical tradition.[22] According to this line of interpretation, the strong Enochian elements in the *Treatise* would indicate that Rudd was heir to some of Dee's manuscripts, and copied parts of the system from these. In McLean's account, the fact that the material is altered in interesting and sometimes quite radical ways is even taken to indicate that Rudd was heir to a lineage that knew the *real* meaning of this enigmatic part of "Enochian magic."[23] When it comes to lines of transmission, one claim has been that Dee's diaries were handed down to Rudd through his son, Arthur, who, as we have seen, served briefly (and unsuccessfully) as a scryer for his father. Around these people a group of practicing magicians would have formed, continuing a tradition of magical practice based on Dee and Kelley's (and, one would have to assume, Hickman's) earlier work.

There are, however, several problems with this hypothesis. Particularly, I find two lines of argumentation to refute the claims. First of all, the conjectured transmission does not match with what we do know about the history of Dee's manuscripts and household after his death. Secondly, I think it can be proved quite clearly that the Rudd *Treatise* gathered its information on Enochiana from Casaubon's *T&FR*. Let me spell out these arguments in more detail.

Although the transmission of Dee's magical diaries is confusing at times, it has by now been traced and documented rather accurately by historians.[24] The first problem for the hypothesis of a secret tradition is that the documented transmission includes neither Arthur Dee, nor anyone going by the name Rudd, whether doctor or captain. Dee's son left for Russia to serve as the tsar's physician immediately after Dee's death, and does not seem to have been a major heir to the Dee household. In fact, Dee entrusted his library, including many of the possessions used during the angel conversations, to his closest friend in the later years of his life, the alchemist and later colonial politician John Pontois.[25] We have statements showing that these objects were in Pontois's possession until his death in 1624, when they were sold.

The angel diaries were at this point split into two clusters of manuscripts, a division that has remained to this day. Importantly, the "raw manuscripts" detailing the minutiae of the sessions traveled one route, while the "received books" traversed another. The first cluster, with the minutiae, was sold to Sir Robert Cotton (1571–1631) together with the Holy Table on which Dee and Kelly had worked.[26] These are the documents Meric Casaubon would edit and publish in 1659, as a favor to the Cottons who had been his hosts.[27] The other bulk would remain unpublished for hundreds of years until the 1980s.[28] The transmission of these manuscripts also remains more conjectural. They first seem to have come into the possession of the surgeon and Paracelsian physician John Woodall (1570–1643), who was connected with Pontois and was even given custody of his London apartment when Pontois made his final trip to the colonies.[29]

Although there is no direct positive evidence that Woodall actually acquired these manuscripts, they resurface again only after one "confectioner Jones" has purchased a wooden chest from "a parcel of the Goods of Mr. John Woodall."[30] The papers had apparently been hidden away in a secret compartment of a chest (explaining how Woodall could have possessed the rare manuscripts without even knowing). The Jones household did not seem to care too much about the manuscripts, however. Their current fragmentary nature is due in part to a zealous kitchen maid of the Joneses, who was given the opportunity to use some of them to line up the confectioner's pie plates.[31] The manuscripts that *did* survive later passed into the hands of Elias Ashmole (1617–1692), who is the one who tells us about the secret compartment incident, in 1672. Ashmole, who had developed a deep fascination for Dee, was able to acquire these documents in exchange for his own book on the Order of the Garter.[32] We should note that Ashmole seems to have taken a more than academic or purely collector's interest in the manuscripts. After obtaining them he commenced the laborious process of making sense of Dee's handwriting, as well as the arcane content of the conversations. Finally, he attempted to reconstruct the magical system they contained, and may even have experimented with them practically. Unfortunately though, the sources are unhelpful for establishing any details surrounding this.[33] From Ashmole the originals passed into the possession of the collector Hans Sloane, and they still remain in the Sloane collection of the British Library.[34]

The question now, of course, is this: where would a mid-seventeenth-century Dr. Rudd fit in the picture? If he was indeed heir to a manuscript tradition, or even an unknown *practical* tradition, it would have to be connected with one of these two transmissions. To me it does not seem likely, however, that Robert Cotton, who lent the documents to read by the suspicious eyes of the Archbishop of Armagh,[35] and then to publish by Casaubon in a clear antimagical bent, would house a circle of magical practitioners in his library. Neither does it seem likely that Mr. Jones, who just stumbled upon the documents by accident, and obviously did not care enough about them to keep them out of the reach of a kitchen maid, would have the same zeal for keeping alive a continued magical tradition based on them. The first problem, then, is that we do not find a place where an otherwise thoroughly undocumented magical tradition could have existed.

We cannot remain entirely satisfied with this, however, and therefore proceed to consider another line of argumentation that could test the hypothesis. One way to make the secret tradition hypothesis more likely would be to establish that manuscripts such as Rudd's *Treatise* contain information that could only have been obtained from the original sources. On the other hand, if it could be established that it contains information only available in Casaubon's *T&FR,* the hypothesis should be considered not only uncorroborated, but falsified.

Book printing was a tedious and imperfect art in the seventeenth century, and printing errors were even more frequent than they are today. The *True and Faithful Relation* was no exception; when compared to the manuscript sources it becomes evident that the published version of Dee's diaries is in fact full of misspellings, corruptions, and copy errors. For the historian, these errors are of great value, since they provide a way for determining whether some manuscript relied on the original manuscripts or the printed edition. This method of comparison is useful for our present purposes: if we find that the same errors are present in the Rudd manuscript and the *T&FR* it becomes increasingly plausible to date the former after 1659, and dispel the hypothesized secret tradition.

Luckily for us, a clear error exists in the engraving of the Holy Table included in Casaubon's edition.[36] Due to what seems to be a block-maker's error, some of the Enochian letters on the Holy Table have been transposed and reversed in Casaubon's version. Since the Enochian material in Rudd's *Treatise* largely revolves around the Holy Table, it is possible to compare it with Casaubon's and the version found in the manuscript sources. This reveals an intriguing discovery: the twelve Enochian letters at the center of the Holy Table in Rudd's version are organized identically as those in Casaubon's table, while they both diverge from the version in Sloane MS 3188.[37] A similar tendency applies for the letters engraved at the circumference of the table. When compared, the Casaubon table shows the upper and lower letter string in the reverse order from the original, while the right and left letter strings have been transposed for each other. In Rudd's table, the left and right strings have been transposed in the same manner, while only the lower string appears in the reverse order. In addition, there appears another divergence in the lower letter string, not appearing in any of the other two versions. In Rudd's version, two characters are missing from their "correct" places, while appearing together at the end of it—as if the copier first forgot them, and only included them at the end when he discovered that there were two empty slots and identified the missing letters. All in all, the impression is that the author of the *Treatise* repeated the errors in *T&FR*, while making a few additional copying errors (or alterations) of his own.

In addition to this reproduction of printing errors we could add a couple of other things indicating that Casaubon was Rudd's source. Generally, the author of the *Treatise* is unaware of the proper nomenclature used in the parts of the angel conversations that were not published by Casaubon (the seven "Ensigns of Creation" are referred to as "Enochian tables," for example). Also, in the list that Rudd gives over the Enochian alphabet, three letters are missing. Interestingly, going through *T&FR* we find that the only place in that volume where the characters are reproduced is in the illustration of the Holy Table. Incidentally, the engravings on the table do not use all the characters in the alphabet, but, suggestively, only the ones that Rudd seems to be aware of.

Sloane MS 3188, f. 9

T	I	O
U	L	R
L	R	L
E	O	O

True & Faithful Relation

O	I	T
R	L	U
L	R	L
O	O	E

Dr. Rudd's *Treatise*

O	I	T
R	L	U
L	R	L
O	O	E

TABLE 2.1. A comparison of the central letter square of the Holy Table as it appears in different sources. From it, we see that Dr. Rudd's *Treatise on Angel Magic* replicates the block maker's error in Casaubon's *True and Faithful Relation*. This indicates that Casaubon was Rudd's source.

The conclusion of these considerations, then, is that we can safely assume Harley MS 6482 *not* to have been part of a secret tradition with unique access to Dee's papers. Rather, we can place the manuscript firmly in the current of revived interest in Dee's actions following Casaubon's publication, having perhaps more in common with the diaries of angelic sessions from the 1670s and 1680s discovered by Harkness. These conclusions have another implication as well: it follows that whoever wrote the *Treatise,* it cannot have been Thomas Rudd. The good captain died in 1656, three years before *T&FR* was published. Who the real author was remains an open question at this point, but he must have worked after Casaubon. Meanwhile, we cannot entirely rule out a possibility mentioned a century ago by A. E. Waite: "Dr. Rudd" may simply have been an invention of Peter Smart, the alleged copyist at the dawn of the eighteenth century.[38]

When Angels Become Demons, and How to Deal with It

So far we have established that a fascination for Dee's angel conversations arose in the second half of the seventeenth century, and that several attempts were made to recreate his magic at this point. With the possible exception of Elias Ashmole, who seems to have been the first to have rediscovered Dee's "received books" which detail the magical systems given by the angels, these reconstructions based themselves on Casaubon's *True & Faithful Relation.* In the process we have established that claims to a secret tradition of ritual magicians working in the wake of Dee's death remain unsubstantiated.

It would perhaps seem puzzling at first that a volume published with the expressed intention of warning people against the dangers of magic should stimulate such new interest. Another interesting question, then, which we should briefly consider, is this: How did the magician wishing to revive the workings described in the book evaluate Casaubon's claim in the preface that Dee's angels had been demons? In the case of the *Treatise,* it seems clear that the demonization did, in fact, have repercussions. Clearly not in the sense Casaubon had intended, however: instead of giving up magic as such, the author of the *Treatise* seems to have taken the necessary ritualistic precautions in order to accommodate the demonized angels. This may indeed have been the rationale for the rather thorough alterations that have been made to the original material.[39]

The *Treatise* is full of theological and magical speculations about how to distinguish "Celestial Angels and Intelligences" from "evil spirits and infernal powers of darkness."[40] Furthermore, the author suggests two different ways of dealing ritually with entities, based on which of the above categories they belong to. Ritualistically,

> Evil spirits . . . .may be constrained and commanded by invocation to service and obedience, comparatively as vile slaves. . . . But Celestial Angels and other dignified Elemental powers and spirits of light by nature wholly benevolent and good, may not be commanded nor constrained by any Invocation.[41]

The real problem, it would then appear, is how to deal with spirits that claim to be benign; here the author clearly shares the orthodox theological opinion that demons try to trick humanity by masquerading as angels. For cases of uncertainty, then, the author prescribes a method of testing through which the entity claiming to be an angel has to respond to certain holy "words of power." If the entity is a demon in disguise, hearing holy words repeatedly would suffice to expel it, while a genuine angel would be attracted—or so the theory went.[42]

If it had already been established that the entity was a mischievous demon, the whole procedure would of course be much easier: one would simply adopt a ritualistic approach aimed at constraining and binding the spirit to submission. It is in light of this theory of magical ritual that the author's changes to the setup of Dee and Kelley's Holy Table become interesting. By embedding it firmly in a circle taken from the Goetic grimoires, fully equipped with protective and constraining words of power, it seems no question that one expects to encounter spirits of the foul and nefarious type.

There is also some more evidence of this. In connection with the seven "tables of Enoch" (Ensignes of Creation), for example, which were painted on the Holy Table, the author notes that "[t]hese Tables . . . .are charged with Spirits or Genii *both good and bad* of several Orders and Hierarchies, which the wise King Solomon made use of."[43] The mention of King Solomon is notable, since it is clear from what follows that the bad spirits mentioned are actually the Goetic demons or fallen angels tabulated in the clavicles of Solomon. The way this is done is also quite intriguing. The seven "tables of Enoch" as shown distributed on the Holy Table in Casaubon's engraving are in themselves rather enigmatic, consisting of a variety of geometrical shapes (mostly squares), with some letters (the letter "b" occurring frequently), numbers and crosses distributed in a seemingly haphazard way. One of the tables, for instance (being the one to the middle left in Casaubon's engraving), is formed like a circle, with a square inside, around which are four "I"s. The square itself is divided into six by six smaller squares, containing letters, numbers, and an unknown, presumably magical, character. The upper left square contains the numbers and letters "5 P b 4 P" and the next one "A 8 B 3 O."

The author of the *Treatise,* however, appears to have "found the key" to these perplexing signs. In his version of the table, which he calls *Tabula Veneris* (the table of Venus), the two squares mentioned contain the entries "5 Paimon Bathin 4 Purson" and "Astaroth Ebra."[44] These are mostly names of fallen angels, taken from the *Goetia*.[45] For instance, according to *The Goetia,* Paimon is "a Great King, and very obedient unto Lucifer," and Astaroth is "a Mighty, Strong Duke, and appeareth in the Form of an hurtful Angel riding on an Infernal Beast like a Dragon, and carrying in his right hand a Viper."[46] The rest of the squares of this and the other tables are similarly filled with this kind of creatures: Bune, Barbatos, Botis, Berith, Buer, Belial, Forcator, and so on. No question why the author of the manuscript felt the need of a protective circle to work with Dee's system. He seems to have accepted Casaubon's demonization of the angels down to the last letter.

More "Secret" Documents

Before we can leave the seventeenth-century revival of Dee's magic, there are yet two more manuscripts to consider. These two documents, MS Sloane 307 and 3821, both contain a copy of the same magical text: A close description of Dee's Great Table (without referencing Dee and Kelley even once, it should be noted), its functions and uses, and procedures for putting it to work. Sloane 307 has been catalogued as "Invocation of Angels," while 3821 bears the name "Tractatus Magici et Astrologici." The copy in 307 is the best one in terms of quality, while the one in 3821 has many erasures and errors, and some major omissions. Also, while 307 contains only the Enochian material, 3821 is a larger collection which also includes a list of invocations of traditional astrological angels and intelligences, a "select treatise" on astrological magic in the Agrippan sense, some "celestiall confirmations of terrestriall observations," and even copies of letters written by Nostradamus. Since 307 seems to be the most complete version, whether it was the original from which 3821 was copied, or a more elaborate and exact copy of a common source, I will focus primarily on this manuscript when describing the contents.

The document begins with biblical mythology. It recounts the Fall of man from the garden of Eden, and the descent of the world. The devil who tempted Adam and Eve is mentioned by "his true name," namely Choronzon. It then relates how contact with the angels that had been

Adam's compatriots is still possible, even after the Fall, and we soon find ourselves in a detailed technical description of the use of the Great Table. The copy in 307 is amended by a nicely prepared version of the Great Table, or *Tabula bonorum angelorum,* which the student could use for reference when reading the detailed description of how to extract the names of various angels, seniors, and powerful secret names of God.

In recent years, the magical manuscript contained in Sloane 307 and 3821 has also been connected to the alleged secret tradition emanating from Dee. It was recently (2004) published by Rankine and Skinner, who, in accordance with their overall hypothesis, try to substantiate an idea of its exotic provenance.[47] In the introductory material the two editors speculate about two possible origins for the manuscript. Either it was copied from Dee's originals when he was still alive (they reckon between 1605 and 1608), or it must have been written after the manuscripts resurfaced in 1662.[48] In other words, Rankine and Skinner already make the assumption that it must be connected to that part of Dee's manuscripts which contained the "revealed books." Curiously, the possibility that it was either connected with the papers in Cotton's possession or written under the influence of *T&FR* is not considered an option.

For reasons that are not too clear the editors furthermore favor the first of their two options, namely that the manuscript was copied already while Dee was still alive. The copier, they reckon, was Thomas Rudd.[49] However, at this point Skinner and Rankine reveal some unusual ideas on who Thomas Rudd really was. First they state that the copier "was a doctor, [and] lived from 1583 to 1656," and then go on to claim that the Thomas Rudd who republished the *Mathematical Preface* was this copier's *son,* who "styles himself as 'Captain.'"[50] The title of captain, they hold, must have implied that he was into navigation, and insinuate that this makes some connection with Dee probable, since he also had been interested in navigation. Clearly, the questionable claims concerning Dr. Rudd, which we have already expelled earlier in the chapter, here become only more confused.

Checking the documented biography of Thomas Rudd, born 1583, dead 1656, one sees that the "two Rudds" were, in fact, one and the same. He was a captain and never a doctor, with his title earned not from navigation, but from his capacity as a military engineer, stationed in the Low Countries in the 1620s.[51] The only reason for assuming this Rudd to have been the copier of the manuscript seems to be his spurious association with the previously discussed *Treatise on Angel Magic*.

Attempting to establish the real provenance of this manuscript we may very well use the same procedure as before: compare it to the other possible sources, look for consistencies and copy errors, and make a judgment based on that. First of all, we need to establish if Rankine and Skinner's tacit assumption that the manuscript must have been associated with the "received books" and not the Cotton manuscript is justified. It immediately appears that it is not. As was the case with the Rudd manuscript, it contains no information that could not have been gleaned from Casaubon and the Cotton manuscript. One revealing detail is that the arrangement of the Great Table follows the one we find in those sources; notably, Dee's "black cross," which combines the four watchtowers in the received book *Liber scientiae,* is absent from Sloane 307. Instead, we find the twelve "secret names of God," which the cross should consist of, inscribed in a rectangular box in the middle of the watchtowers.

As Ian Rons has pointed out in his rather baleful review of Skinner and Rankine's book, there is also at least one instance where the exotic provenance of the manuscript is debunked due to exactly the same kind of evidence seen with the Treatise, namely, the duplication of errors found in *T&FR*. In the manuscript there is talk about a demon bearing the name "Choronzon." In the original diaries, preserved in Cotton Appendix XVI, this name was spelt "Coronzom." In Casaubon the "m" has transmuted into an "n," rendering the name of the demon "Coronzon." It would seem then, that this was the basis for the copier of Sloane 307, who additionally saw an "h" where there previously had been none.[52] It would seem, then, that also this manuscript belongs to the post-Casaubon resurgence of interest in Dee's magic.

The example presented above is relevant not only for debunking the final claims to a secret Enochian tradition in the seventeenth century. It also happens to illustrate the influence that this particular manuscript must have had on the formation of Enochian magic in modern occultism. As we will see in the next chapter, Sloane 307 was one of the sources for the Golden Dawn's incorporation of Enochiana into their grade system and magical teachings, believing it to have been a most ancient manuscript.[53] It was also in this manuscript that Aleister Crowley would read the name of the demon "Choronzon" for the first time, an entity which he would later encounter in the flesh in the deserts of Algeria.[54] That story will be revisited in chapter 4; now, however, we must turn to the nineteenth-century Golden Dawn and what should be considered the formative period of modern Enochian magic.

3

Victorian Occultism and the Invention of Modern Enochiana

Memories of a Dark Past: A Note on John Dee in Enlightenment Historiography

By the eighteenth century the original transactions of the angel sessions had found their way into archival oblivion in Oxford and London, and Casaubon's edition had finally cemented Dee's unfavorable reputation. As the age of Enlightenment dawned Casaubon's theologically founded condemnation of magic was replaced with accusations of irrational superstition and folly. When Dee was remembered in Enlightenment historiography, it was mostly to remind the bright minds of the age of the misguided thinking of those that came before them.

Together with the belief that society and the human intellect had progressed to more sophisticated levels came a number of misrepresentations of the past. Anything "occult" or "Hermetic" was per definition backward, sharing an almost mystical affinity of irrationality.[1] Thus, an entry on John Dee appearing in James Granger's *Biographical History of England* in 1774 started by stating that "John Dee was a man of extensive learning, particularly in the mathematics, in which he had few equals; but he was vain, credulous, and enthusiastic." It is with some surprise that we continue to read that the doctor was also "strongly tinctured with the superstition of the Rosicrucians, whose dreams he listened to with great eagerness, and became as great a dreamer himself as any of that fraternity."[2] As is well known, there was no Rosicrucianism prior to the publication of the *Fama Fraternitatis* in 1614, about five years after Dee had passed away. What is more, there were no real Rosicrucian fraternities either until possibly the end of the seventeenth century. Nevertheless, this association between Dee and Rosicrucianism would be repeated in later works of history as well—including by Edmund Burke.[3] As we shall see later in this chapter, the Rosicrucian connection would only grow much stronger by the time of the occult revival at the end of the nineteenth century.

Another significant account of Dee's work was published in 1834 by the British radical political philosopher and journalist William Godwin (1756–1836). Godwin was married to the feminist writer Mary Wollstonecraft, and was the father of Mary Shelley, author of the classic gothic novel *Frankenstein*. Godwin's *Lives of the Necromancers* nicely illustrates the attitude to the esoteric inherent to Enlightenment historiography.[4] Here he had gathered information on a large variety of various mystics and magicians, and presented a standard attack on these deluded subjects. His interpretation was fairly in the line of Casaubon's, describing Dee as "a mystic of the most dishonourable sort," adding that he was "induced to believe in a series of miraculous communications without common sense."[5] In the spirit of the Enlightenment Godwin asserts Dee's story to be "strikingly illustrative of the credulity and superstitious faith of the time in which he lived."[6]

Nevertheless, Godwin's treatment of Dee is noteworthy also because it suggests that Godwin had a fairly good overview of the sources (which is much more than can be said of Granger and Burke), referring to his copious magical notes "still existing in manuscript" in addition to Casaubon's "well-sized folio."[7] Because he took the trouble to track down obscure sources Godwin in fact points toward the developments that concern us in this chapter, namely the rediscovery of Dee's manuscripts, and other related magical papers discussed in the previous chapter. Just as Casaubon's debunking had sparked a revival of interest in Dee from a practitioner's point of view, Godwin's exposé (which went through several editions in the 1830s, and one more in 1876) was followed by new appropriations of the angel conversations from crystallomancers, at the heart of the enlightened nineteenth century. This is where the story of modern Enochiana really begins.

Crystallomancy and Early British Occultism

The rediscovery of Dee's angelic conversations ran more or less parallel to the crazed interest in spiritualism and mediumistic phenomena of the Victorian era. One important student of the Dee manuscripts was the collector and crystallomancer Frederick Hockley (1808–1885). We have little verifiable information about Hockley, and he remains a quite obscure figure.[8] Most of what we know about him and the network of magicians and occultists working in England around mid-century comes from the correspondences of Francis George Irwin (1828–1892), preserved in the London archives of the United Grand Lodge of England. Irwin on his part had a military career (with the title of Major), described as a "zealous mason" who became an important link between Hockley and the later generations of Victorian occultists.[9] Beyond his obscurity Hockley is considered to have been one of the pioneers of Victorian occultism; the sketchy sources reveal that he was an experienced magician, highly revered by his fellows. He was believed to have been a pupil of the magical school initiated in Cambridge early on in the century by Francis Barrett, the author, or rather compiler, of the influential occult standard work *The Magus* (1801).[10]

According to his own statement, Hockley had been "a Spiritualist" since 1824,[11] that is, twenty-four years before the Fox sisters started what we formally call Spiritualism through the notorious "Hydesville rappings." His main interests, not to say his procedure of work, were nevertheless much different from those of the spiritualists. In accord with the older traditions Hockley would employ a scryer, usually a "speculatrix"—a young, virgin girl—and a crystal, to produce spiritual visions and make contact with various entities. The entities he believed to be able to reach with this method really varied widely, from human beings, both deceased and living, to the higher angels. Hockley even claimed to have watched Sir Richard Burton's legendary adventure to Mecca in 1853 by this clairvoyant method. Nevertheless, his main agenda seems to have been a thirst for higher knowledge of the workings of the heavens and the cosmos through communion with angels and other higher beings, especially an entity called "the Crowned Angel."[12]

By the mid-nineteenth century crystallomancy was pretty much a (re)established and autonomous field of occult practice, and arguably one of the most central aspects of early English occultism, which would spawn the more well-known late-Victorian variety.[13] It does not seem unlikely that Hockley, one of the major forces in the reestablishment of crystal gazing, found at least a little influence in what he perceived to be the tradition stemming from Dee's angel conversations. Among his collection of manuscripts was a copy of "Dr Rudd's" *Treatise on Angel Magic,* which we discussed in the previous chapter, as well as a private copy of the "Clavis Angelicae containing the 18 great Calls and Celestial Invocations of the Table of Enoch."[14] This latter title shows that he had likely accessed Dee's "revealed book" under that name, which was available in the Sloane collection. Concerning the *Treatise,* as both Hockley and Dr Rudd show a major concern for keeping wicked spirits out of the crystal, an influence is not improbable. However, it also seems clear that Hockley's workings were influenced by a wealth of different medieval magical sources, from the Goetia to the Ars Notoria.[15] Since we saw that Dr. Rudd, too, drew on these manuscript traditions, the possibility that any resemblance is due simply to the use of similar sources cannot be dismissed.

Another figure of great importance for facilitating the revival of the angel conversations is Kenneth Mackenzie (1833–1886), a friend and probably a student of Hockley's. Like Hockley, Mackenzie was into both Masonry and magic. He was also into the legacy of John Dee, and even claimed to have taken a speculatrix to the British Museum once, where they had conducted a session with Dee's very own crystal.[16] By Mackenzie's account, the scryer could see the city of Prague unfolding in the stone, apparently still "remembering" its previous owner's adventures on the continent. It also seems that Mackenzie spent time in the British Library, where he would have studied the Dee material. After his death Mackenzie is known to have left several notebooks dealing with the magical system "revealed" by the angels.[17]

As will soon become apparent, these two occultists' interest in Enochiana may have been decisive for the later fascination with the system. Hockley, and especially Mackenzie, were the probable channels through which Enochian material was fused into the Golden Dawn synthesis.

Ciphers, Secrets, and Fraud: Enochiana and the Origins of the Golden Dawn

The Hermetic Order of the Golden Dawn was established in 1888 by a small coterie of London-based freemasons and occultists.[18] The key founders were the coroner William Wynn Westcott (1848–1925) and Samuel Liddell "MacGregor" Mathers (1854–1918), both members of the Rosicrucian Masonic group Societas Rosicruciana in Anglia (S.R.I.A.). William Robert Woodman (1828–1891), Supreme Magus of the S.R.I.A., was invited in as the third chief, but passed away quickly thereafter.

The S.R.I.A. was thus an important precursor for the Golden Dawn, but it was not the only one. Mathers and Westcott had both been frequent lecturers in the Hermetic Society, another esoteric group of the 1880s. It had been founded in 1884 by Anna Kingsford and Edward Maitland as a response to what they considered a deliberate neglect of Western esoteric traditions in the popular Theosophical Society. It led the way in what has been called the "Hermetic reaction" to Theosophy, an episode of identity politics internal to British occultism.[19] When Kingsford died prematurely in 1887 the society's activities ceased, leaving occidental occultists without a platform. This event forms an important context for the founding of the G.D., which culled many of its early members from "Rosicrucian" and "Hermetic" oriented parts of the occult milieu, recruiting well among discontent Theosophists as well. The G.D. presented itself as a decidedly Western alternative to the increasingly Oriental and anti-Christian Theosophical Society, reinstating Egypt as the wellspring of esoteric wisdom, while claiming an ancient and "authentic" Rosicrucian heritage.

The somewhat cryptic circumstances surrounding the foundation of Hermetic Order of the Golden Dawn and its origins has been the subject of countless speculations in a fair share of books and articles.[20] One of the key issues of the speculations concerns the "Cipher Manuscript," a document written in a cipher from Johannes Trithemius's *Polygraphiae*.[21] These came into the possession of W. W. Westcott in 1886, apparently tucked away among the papers of the Swedenborgian Rite.[22] After deciphering the simple substitution code, the Cipher MS revealed the skeletal form of the five first initiation rituals of a secret fraternity, going under the name of "the Golden Dawn." Realizing their possible significance, Westcott passed the notes on to his friend, Samuel Liddell "MacGregor" Mathers (1854–1918), who expanded and transformed them into the first initiation rituals of the Golden Dawn.

But the Cipher MS offered nothing to suppose the Rosicrucian connection which would become central to the Order's "emic historiography."[23] Westcott therefore provided such a connection himself, by forging (or causing to be forged) a series of letters from one "Fräulein Sprengel" of Ulm.[24] Through their spurious correspondence the mystery lady revealed herself as a Rosicrucian adept, going by the Order name of *Sapiens Dominabitur Astris* (S.D.A.), in charge of a secretive Rosicrucian Order in Germany, *die Goldene Dämmerung*. S.D.A. attested that the lower grades of her Order were the ones revealed in the cipher manuscript. Since this was already in Westcott's possession, the adept was kind enough to provide him with the authority to open a local Temple in London. The first initiations into the grade of Neophyte in the Isis-Urania Temple of the Golden Dawn duly took place at Mark Mason's Hall, London, in March 1888.

* * *

What really concerns us here, however, is that the Cipher MS also included material from Dee's angel conversations, and is thus already the *fons et origo* of the Golden Dawn's incorporation and vastly influential interpretation of Enochiana. While it has been established that Westcott invented the German Rosicrucian order and forged the correspondence with Fräulein Sprengel, the provenance of the Cipher MS is less clear. This is unfortunate, since it is such a seminal document in the history of Enochiana. We are therefore compelled to have a closer look, reviewing the possibilities that have been sketched up for it.

After a century of debate, the exact history of the Cipher MS still cannot be discerned. There are certain hints, however.[25] First of all, the official story that circulated in the Golden Dawn can be discounted right away. According to that version, the manuscript was related to a German Rosicrucian order, as we have seen.[26] It was rumored to have been in the possession of Eliphas Lévi at one point, and was of some antiquity. This story is a clear case of an emic historiography, designed by the Order leaders to convey an air of legitimacy. The reasons for disregarding it are many, and I will not go into all of them in detail here. It will suffice to mention a few points that are of relevance to our present concerns.

While the Cipher MS is written on paper watermarked 1809, the eclectic occult information they contain include knowledge that was not yet in existence at that time. References to Egyptian texts that were only available after Champollion deciphered the hieroglyphs in 1822 are particularly clear, together with the occult correspondences between the Kabbalah and the Tarot, a system that was first developed by Eliphas Lévi in his *Dogme et rituel de la haute magie,* first published in 1856.[27] In addition, the historian Ellic Howe has noted that the mention of a certain name in the MS makes it likely that the author had access to Mackenzie's *Royal Masonic Cyclopædia,* published as late as 1877.[28]

The Enochian material incorporated in the Cipher MS could be another hint of their provenance. Together with the fact that the manuscript, when deciphered, is written in English, this more than suggests an English, or even London-based origin. We have seen that detailed knowledge of Dee's diaries and the Enochian system therein was scant during this period, limiting the possible authors considerably. The possibilities are narrowed even further when one considers the combination with the Rosicrucian grade structure, and the obvious knowledge of Lévi's Tarot attributions. Although the evidence is not conclusive, there is one known person who would possess all the knowledge included in the document: Kenneth Mackenzie.[29] As we have seen, Mackenzie was an occultist who actually went "back to the sources" and studied the Dee material at the British Museum and Library. He was also the author of the *Royal Masonic Cyclopædia,* thus explaining the point of overlap in the Cipher MS. Furthermore, Mackenzie was known to be the one Englishman who knew Lévi best from the beginning of his breakthrough. In 1861 he went to Paris and had two long interviews with Lévi, the tone of which shows the deep solemnity and veneration with which Mackenzie met the French magus.[30]

For the above reasons the suggestion that Mackenzie wrote the Cipher MS is now considered fairly uncontroversial. Ascertaining the intention behind them has proved somewhat more difficult. As Mackenzie was involved with a number of fringe-Masonic systems and Orders, it is not impossible that he was preparing a new set of initiations for somebody.

Some suggestions that have been made are that he was preparing a new set of ceremonies for the Royal Order of the Sat B'hai, or maybe the initiations for a planned expansion of the S.R.I.A. itself. These remain speculations which are unlikely to be verified unless new evidence comes to the surface.

From Ciphers to Rituals

The Cipher MS came into the possession of Westcott soon after Mackenzie's death, and it was through MacGregor Mathers's elaboration on them, resulting in the rituals of the Golden Dawn, that they were given historical significance. This also applies to the Enochian elements contained in the MS. The incorporation of Enochian material into the structure of the Golden Dawn initiation rituals and its magical system transformed the former into something quite different from what it had been in Dee's original system.

The transformation must be seen in connection with the mode of religious creativity generally present in *fin de siècle* occultism. Elsewhere I have described the specific form of creativity involved in the Golden Dawn's reconstruction of esoteric material as relying on a "programmatic syncretism."[31] By this I mean that there existed at the core of the esoteric project a kind of perennialism that was informed by the late-Victorian scholarly discourse on foreign and ancient religions and culture. In scholarly discourse, the comparative method now reigned supreme; the first edition of James Frazer's groundbreaking *Golden Bough* appeared in 1890, two years after the formation of the Golden Dawn. The *fin de siècle* occultists adopted much the same approach to new information that became available about foreign and ancient cultures. But in place of the generally skeptical, rationalistic agenda of someone like Frazer and the early anthropologists, they placed a *perennialist* agenda, which led to a construction of concordances between disparate systems.[32] Furthermore, any comparison necessitates some schemata through which new information can be understood and appropriated. For the Golden Dawn, a taxonomic matrix was given already in the Cipher MS.

The full fifty-six folios of the Cipher MS, and the Golden Dawn initiation rituals founded on them, create a grand synthesis of a wide range of symbol systems, from alchemy, the Kabbalah, and astrology, to the Tarot and Enochiana. The basic system around which everything revolves in the first five degrees of the Golden Dawn, however, is that of *the four elements* combined with the symbolism of the Kabbalistic "Tree of Life." Later, the lower grades would simply be referred to as the "Elemental Grades" of the order.[33] The scheme is already present in the Cipher MS, and correlates each grade to a *sefirah* on the Tree of Life; the exception is the first grade of Neophyte, which is conceptualized as "below" the sefirotic Tree. Furthermore, each of the four grades is related to one of the four elements: Earth (Zelator), Air (Theoricus), Water (Practicus), and Fire (Philosophus). This fourfold scheme is duplicated again and again in the symbolism of the Golden Dawn, most notably through the four letters of Tetragrammaton, which are given the same elemental attributions (י = Fire, ה = Water, ו = Air, and ה = Earth). This Kabbalistic and elemental symbolism forms the template for the other occult systems incorporated into the system. Kabbalah and the fourfold symbolism of the elements constitute the schemata for the Golden Dawn, a sort of taxonomic backdrop against which a programmatic syncretism could take place.[34]

	Grade name		Sephirotic attribution	Elemental attribution
FIRST ORDER (Elemental Grades)	Neophyte	0° = 0°		
	Zelator	1° = 10°	Malkuth	Earth
	Theoricus	2° = 9°	Yesod	Air
	Practicus	3° = 8°	Hod	Water
	Philosophus	4° = 7°	Netzach	Fire
SECOND ORDER	Adeptus Minor	5° = 6°	Tiphareth	
	Adeptus Major	6° = 5°	Geburah	
	Adeptus Exemptus	7° = 4°	Chesed	
THIRD ORDER	Magister Templi	8° = 3°	Binah	
	Magus	9° = 2°	Chokmah	
	Ipsissimus	10° = 1°	Kether	

TABLE 3.1. The Rosicrucian grade system of the Golden Dawn. Note that only the first and second orders were actually in operation.

The Enochian system was expectedly assumed to fit this scheme as well. The first reference to the Enochian material in the Cipher MS is in the notes for the Zelator ceremony. After it had been asserted that Zelator "is the Earth grade," the operator of the rite was instructed to present the candidate with the "Earth tablet as in old MSS."[35] It later appears that this "Earth tablet" is one of the four letter squares from John Dee's "Great Table," or "Table of good angels," discussed in chapter 1.[36] As we saw in the first chapter, the angels told Dee that these tables were to be used magically for evoking certain angels to perform rather mundane tasks, related to things such as medicine, transportation, or the finding of metals. The author of the Cipher MS, on the other hand, has come up with a creative reinterpretation. Seeing that Dee's Great Table is divided into four, the idea suggested itself that their *real* meaning should be found in the four elements.

One should be quick to take notice that Dee's diaries also describe the Great Table as "earthly." But in the diaries, "earthly" referred to *the* earth, rather than the *element* earth.[37] In other words, the table is *mundane* (i.e., "worldly"), describing a system of magical evocation for terrestrial purposes. Additionally, one should note that the fourfold division of the table, which the author of the Cipher MS equated with the fourfold symbolism of the elements, has a clear and explicit function in the diaries as well. It delineates the different offices of the spirits, so that one quarter concerns medicine ("physicks"), one concerns transmutations, a third names the spirits who can find metals, and a fourth contains the "creatures that live in the four Elements."[38] Interestingly then, elemental attributions have their place in Dee's version as well, but a more limited and differently allocated one. Magical command of the four elements is subjected to a broader fourfold categorization of offices, where the three other offices are medicine, metals, and transformation.[39]

The elemental attribution was repeated consistently throughout the description of "elemental grades" in the Cipher MS: Theoricus was correlated with a "tablet of air," Practicus with the "Great Western Quadrangle of water," and finally Philosophus with the "fire tablet."[40] This of course means that the specific interpretation of the Enochian material that has become associated with the Golden Dawn was already present and well developed in the Cipher MS.[41] Nevertheless, there was significant room left for creativity when MacGregor Mathers elaborated on the, after all, very scanty notes. Let us have a closer look at Mathers's innovations.

Mathers's creative input to the Golden Dawn system came in two phases. First, he was given the Cipher MS by Westcott in order to produce the full initiation rituals described therein. This must have happened between October 1887, when Westcott first wrote to Mathers for help,

TABLE 3.2.
Examples of Golden Dawn adaptations of the "Great Table"

T	a	O	A	d	u/v	p	t	D	n	i	m
a/o	a	b/l	c	o	o	r	o	m	e	b	b
T	o/a	g	c	o	n	x/z	m/i	a/n/u	l	G	m
n	h	o	d	D	i	a	i	l/a	a	o	c
f/p	a	t/c	A	x	i	v/o	V	s	P	x/s	y/N l/h
S	a	a	i	z/x	a	a	r	V	r	L/c	i
m	p	h	a	r	s	l	g	a	i	o	l
M	a	m	g	l	o	i	n	L	i	r	x
o	l	a	a	D	n/a	g	a	T	a	p	a
p	a	L	c	o	i	d	x	P	a	c	n
n	d	a	z	N	z/x	i	V	a	a	s	a
r/i	i	d	P	o	n	s	d	A	s	p	i
x	r	i/r	n	h	t	a	r	n/a	d	i	L

"The Second Watchtower: or the Great Western Quadrangle of Water," as appearing in Regardie, ed., *The Golden Dawn*, 632. The four watchtowers of the Great Table were given elemental attributions in the Golden Dawn. The "quadrangle of water" corresponds roughly to the upper-right quadrangle in Dee's table (cf. table 2). Notice how several squares include many letters, apparently to include the possibilities found in different source material. In addition, when compared with the version given in table 2, we notice that several letters do not match at all.

E	X	A	R	P
H	C	O	M	A
N	A	N	T	A
B	I	T	O	M

The "Tablet of Union". This table was placed in between the four "Elemental Tablets" in the Golden Dawn system, and was generally attributed to "Spirit". It is formed by taking the letters in the Black Cross of Dee's original table (cf. table 2). The letters appear like this in *True and Faithful Relation*, as well as in the Sloane 307 manuscript, but not in Dee's final version in Sloane 3191.

and March 1, 1888, when the Isis-Urania temple of the Golden Dawn was officially opened.[42] Mathers's second and more original contribution to forming the Golden Dawn system was his creation in 1892 of the so-called Second Order of the Golden Dawn, the *Rosae Rubeae et Aureae Crucis*. In addition to simply being "more secret," this was also the institutional locus for the actual *practice* of ritual magic in the Golden Dawn.[43] We will have a closer look at the Second Order toward the end of this chapter, but first we should consider Mathers's elaborations on the Cipher MS for the Golden Dawn "in the Outer" (i.e., the First Order).

Generally, Mathers followed the notes and instructions in the Cipher MS faithfully. But since they were far from complete, he necessarily had to improvise to write up the full, workable initiation rituals. For example, in the Zelator ceremony, all that is said in the manuscript regarding the Enochian component is that the grade "is of Earth" and that therefore the candidate should at one point be "shewn" the "earth tablet." The tablet itself is not reproduced in the MS other than a small drawing of a square with a cross in it.[44] It would be up to Mathers both to consult the "old MSS" which the cipher refers to and to construct the whole ceremony of the "shewing" of the tablet.

The final liturgy is indeed far more elaborate, and full of additional information which is *not* found in the Cipher MS:

> [Hierophant says to candidate:] This Grade is especially referred to the Element of Earth, and therefore, one of its principal emblems is the Great Watch Tower or Terrestrial Tablet of the North. It is the Third or Great Northern Quadrangle or Earth Tablet, and it is one of the four Great Tablets of the Elements said to have been given to Enoch by the Great Angel Ave. It is divided within itself into four lesser angles. The Mystic letters upon it forms various Divine and Angelic Names, in what our tradition calls the Angelic secret language. From it are drawn the Three Holy Secret Names of God EMOR DIAL HECTEGA which are borne upon the Banners of the North, and there are also numberless names of Angels, Archangels, and Spirits ruling the Element of Earth.[45]

The perhaps most striking addition to the version in the Cipher MS is Mathers's inclusion of a myth of origins. What is particularly interesting about it is that he does not mention Dee and Kelley with a word, but simply restates what the angels in Dee's journals had said: the tablets were of heavenly origin, and had first been revealed to the patriarch Enoch. One should keep in mind that this would be the very first encounter an initiate into the Golden Dawn would have with the Enochian material.

The small bit of information conveyed to the candidate effectively forms a part of an evolving construction of the Order's tradition.

Two other things are worth mentioning concerning this quote. First, Mathers mentions "the Angelic secret language," which is not addressed in the Cipher MS per se (although certain Angelic names taken from it are included). This is important, as we shall see that the Angelic, "Enochian" language is also given a role in the Order's emic historiography. Secondly, the elemental attribution of the tablet is given wider significance, by the statement that the angelic names contained in this particular table are "Spirits ruling the Element of Earth." At this point, the new function of the spirits is given explicitly magical significance. During the "opening" part of the rituals, when the officers prepare the Temple for receiving the candidate, the Hierophant uses the "elemental tables" and their three "Holy Secret Names of God" to call down the spirits of the element in a magical fashion reminiscent of theurgy.[46]

A Note on Sources

The interpretations of the Enochian material in the Cipher MS and in Mathers's full version open for another question: What sources were they working from? The more or less radical reinterpretation of what we saw in Dee's material might initially suggest that whatever the sources were, the (re)creators of it, namely, Mathers and the author of the Cipher MS (probably Mackenzie), did not grant them exclusive authority. This draws our attention to Casaubon's *True and Faithful Relation,* perhaps, which would probably be the easiest available source as well. However, there are several things that indicate that the author of the Cipher MS consulted other sources as well, while outright demonstrating that Mathers did so.

As we saw, the Cipher MS makes a passing reference to "tables as in old MSS." The four "elemental tablets," to use the Golden Dawn nomenclature, are not reproduced in their entirety, but only hinted to through the mention of the three "mystical names" from each of them, and a draft-like drawing. The reference to the "old MSS" indicates that the author of the Cipher MS at the very least was aware of the existence of some of the manuscripts in the British Library, and had probably consulted them. Another thing concerns folio 55, which in fact is written in a different hand and was added to the corpus of the Cipher MS only later.[47] Probably forged by the Golden Dawn chiefs, this shows in full what is referred to as "the tablet of union." This tablet, consisting of four more Enochian "names of power," is what was by Dee referred to as "the Black Cross" connecting the four "elemental tablets." In this folio it has the same connecting function, but it is kept as a tablet, not formed into a cross, as in Dee's version. Keeping the four words of power as a *tablet* and not as a cross seems to suggest that the author (Westcott?) has relied mostly on Casaubon in this matter, or possibly Sloane 307, which Westcott knew and copied. In *A True and Faithful Relation* the Great Table is never shown completed, with all the four squares connected with the Black Cross. Rather, the four combining words are presented in the exact same way as they stand in this Cipher MS folio.[48] This could indicate that at least the author did not bother checking the original manuscripts too thoroughly, or else it did not matter too much what they said.[49]

When it comes to Mathers's elaboration on the information in the Cipher MS, the latter interpretation seems even more likely. When carefully assessing some of the later Golden Dawn instructions based on Mathers's work it becomes clear that he must have consulted the British Library manuscripts. Dee and Kelley's "Great Table" was revised and edited several times, and when the Sloane and Cotton manuscripts are compared with Casaubon's edition, there exist all in all five different versions of some of the tables.[50]

One of the major idiosyncrasies of the Golden Dawn "Four Watchtowers" or Elemental Tablets is that instead of containing one letter in each square, some squares contain two, three, or even four letters.[51] The tablets assigned by the Golden Dawn to Water and Earth are especially rich on such multilettered squares. When I compared these with all the extant Dee manuscripts that discuss the tables, it became evident that the reason for including several letters was to cover the range of possibilities given in the original documents. Hence, it is clear that Mathers consulted Dee's unpublished manuscripts, and did much research into the discrepancies of the complex letter squares.

What is intriguing is that Mathers therefore surely must have known that the instructions given to the *use* of these systems were radically different in the original documents from what was asserted in the Cipher MS. This proves Mathers's fundamental trust in the Cipher MS as a main source of authority. But it also suggests that syncretism was not considered a sin. Instead, creative reinterpretations could *improve* on occult systems that had previously been unconnected.[52] That is, probably reasoning with the idea of an ancient, underlying *philosophia perennis* in mind, Mathers and other Victorian occultists would claim that their inspired versions *recreated* the primordial meaning of a system that even Dee had only gotten partially right.

Enochiana and Rosicrucianism in the Emic Historiography of the Second Order

I have already mentioned the Golden Dawn's mythmaking concerning the Cipher MS and the alleged Rosicrucian order in Frankfurt. The Rosicrucian aspect was not all that present in the Outer Order of the Golden Dawn, but would become much more explicit in the Inner. In that connection the Enochian material was utilized in various ways as well, in attempts at constructing an even grander myth of esoteric transmission and descent.

When MacGregor Mathers wrote and launched the Second Order initiation rituals in 1892, the Golden Dawn took a more emphatically Rosicrucian direction. The central motif of the two new initiation rituals, the "Portal Ceremony" and the heavily Rosicrucian Adeptus Minor initiation, is the so-called Vault of the Adepti. Through the rituals, this turns out to be a representation of the legendary vault and burial chamber of Christian Rosenkreutz, as portrayed in the *Fama Fraternitatis* of 1614. Consequently, the myth of the adept Christian Rosenkreutz, gathering esoteric wisdom from adventures in the Near East in the fourteenth century, is incorporated as a foundation for the Golden Dawn's own constructed tradition.

At the same time the Enochian material began playing a more significant role with the inception of the Golden Dawn's Second Order. This was expressed in the new initiation rituals; both of the two new ceremonies Mathers devised for entrance into the Second Order employed Enochian symbolism to a much higher degree than did the Elemental grades that we have considered so far. More importantly, the Rosicrucian myth was blended with a novel myth of the origin of the Enochian system and language, which was disseminated through the Adeptus Minor ceremony, and would later be elaborated on by individual adepts and Order clairvoyants. Much of this will be picked up on in later chapters of this book; at present I will look briefly at the place Enochiana is given in the Golden Dawn's conception of Rosicrucianism.

The aspirant's first real encounter with the mysteries of Christian Rosenkreutz is found in the Adeptus Minor ceremony. The information bestowed here continues to build on the emic historiography of the Order, which was hinted at in the lower degrees as well. The candidate is told that the mysteries of the Rose and the Cross have existed since the dawn of time, but were gathered together by Christian Rosenkreutz and brought to a small society in Europe in the late middle ages.[53] Here much of the primordial wisdom was translated and written down by some of Rosenkreutz's "monastic brethren." Among the writings left to this society, the candidate was told, was "some of the Magical Language" which, it was explained, "is that of the Elemental Tablets." A dictionary of the language was even claimed to have existed at the time.[54] That the Angelic language would form a part of Rosenkreutz's secrets was to be expected, since "the True Order of the Rose Cross descendeth into the depths, and ascendeth into the heights—even unto the Throne of God Himself, and includeth even Archangels, Angels and Spirits."[55] In other words, the Inner Order of the Golden Dawn was not a terrestrial institution at all: it was a truly cosmic and spiritual Order, with God as the highest "Secret Chief."

As was the case in the Zelator ritual, there is no mention of Dee and Kelley in the account of the "Magical Language" or the "Elemental Tablets." But by linking Enochiana with the Rosicrucians, this passage goes much farther than the Zelator ceremony in removing Dee and Kelley from the history of the Enochian system. The claim is, after all, that the Angelic language was already around in the early fifteenth century—almost two hundred years before Dee and Kelley met each other. Viewed with the eyes of the historian, this claim is of course supremely anachronistic. In the context of the Golden Dawn's emic historiography it is a clear expression of the belief in a sort of *philosophia perennis:* a wisdom that had existed since the dawn of time, a wisdom that had been lost and then uncovered by (the fictional) Christian Rosenkreutz, and secretly traded down through the centuries. In this more esoteric scheme of things, Dee and Kelley would be degraded to the role of mere links in a greater chain of transmission, the origin (not to mention the right interpretation!) of the Angelic language and magical system being far removed from them.

Nevertheless, the fact that they are not even mentioned when Enochiana is spoken of surely signifies more than trivial forgetfulness. It is not unreasonable to suppose that the anachronism, which would be apparent to anyone who would care to dig in the sources, made it convenient to avoid mentioning Dee in the first place.

Enochian Magic in Theory and Practice

Now that we know a bit about the importance of Enochiana to the Golden Dawn, and something of their use of sources, we can move on to another interesting question: What did the actual practice of Enochian magic look like? Although the Golden Dawn is considered one of the first esoteric orders that actually taught and practiced ritual magic, it was not until the opening of the so-called Second Order ("Rosae Rubeae et Aureae Crucis") in 1892 that they started to do so. The five initiations of the Outer Order were largely a training course through which the candidate was familiarized with the various systems and the magical theories that the Order subscribed to. Within this "Second Order" of higher initiates certain instructions were issued which dealt practically with various parts of the Golden Dawn system. Among these instructions, five documents were directly related to the Enochian system.[56]

By going through the papers and instructions circulated with the Adepti Minores, and keeping a comparative eye on the Dee manuscripts presented in chapter 1 of this book, I will show what constitute the main idiosyncrasies of the Order's take on Enochian magic. In doing this I will also elucidate the relationship between the Enochian system and the whole theory of magic in the Golden Dawn. Finally, I will go through certain extant manuscripts that give us an insight into the practices and results that some Golden Dawn members had with the Enochian system. Taken together, this will provide a good representation of the theory and practice of Enochian magic in the Golden Dawn.

With the creation of the Second Order a catalogue was issued listing the manuscripts that were circulated among the members of the Adeptus Minor grade, listed from A to Z.[57] These were instructions dealing for the most part with magic and occult symbolism. Five of the documents dealt with the Enochian system:

Book "H": *Clavicula Tabularum Enochi*
Book "S": *The Book of the Concourse of Forces*
Book "T": *The Book of the Angelical Calls*
Book "X": *The Keys of the Governance and Combinations of the Squares of the Tablets*
Book "Y": *Rosicrucian Chess*

As was the case with the initiation ceremonies, the definitive focus of these magical instructions was on the Great Table.

The four latter of these texts have been of great influence on later developments, after they were reproduced in the 1930s by Israel Regardie's *Golden Dawn*. As will be shown in due time, these four books set out on a typical Golden Dawn syncretistic approach, outlining the attributions of Kabbalistic, elemental, astrological, alchemical, and Tarot symbolism to the Great Table (*Book "S"*) and even constructing a divinatory, four-handed chess game out of the Enochian tables (*Book "Y"*). Meanwhile, we should pause and notice the significant fact that *Book "H"* was not printed by Regardie. His reason for this editorial decision deserves some attention, since it illustrates an interesting point about the reception of Enochian magic. In his introduction to the volume, Regardie wrote about *Book "H"* that

> [it is] typically mediaeval, and definitely unsound from a spiritual viewpoint, and it is certainly not in accord with the general lofty tenor of the remaining Order teachings. It explains how to find precious metals and hidden treasures, and how to drive away the elemental guardians thereof. It is an inferior piece of work . . . and so I have decided to omit [it].[58]

Given his work's tremendous influence on occultists and scholars of occultism alike, Regardie's editorial (in)discretion has, as we will see more clearly in later chapters, to a great extent shaped and simplified the view of Golden Dawn Enochian magic, and arguably of Golden Dawn magic in general. It is interesting that Regardie, who claimed to "have obtained a good deal of information about 'Enochiana'" through "meditative and British Museum research" considered this work to be "an inferior piece."[59] In reality, the significance of *Book "H"* cannot be understated, since it is the single document in the extant Golden Dawn corpus that gets close to the original interpretation of Enochian magic found in Dee's angelic diaries and "mystical books."[60]

The book was collected by Westcott and consists of a partial transcription and adaptation of the magical tables and text in Sloane MS 307—the nicely prepared version of the Great Table which we discussed in chapter 2.[61] Since *Book "H"* is also a faithful version of that manuscript, it significantly differs from the other Order teachings on Enochiana. The interpretation and use of the Great Table is presented pretty much as it was set forth in Casaubon's *True and Faithful Relation* and Dee's *Tabula bonorum angelorum*.[62] We do not find the Kabbalistic and elemental bias, which is integral to the rest of the Golden Dawn material. Instead, it gives instructions on how various names are to be extracted from the tables. It shows the hierarchy of the spirits, who controls whom, how various combinations and permutations of angelic names can produce the names of demons, and a range of other obscure feats stemming from the original Renaissance system. Interestingly then, it would seem that the proximity to original Renaissance magic, with all its mundane goals and functions plainly in view, was what made Regardie react. As we have seen earlier, the angel Ave told Dee that the letters of the Great Table contained "all human knowledge," the names to call forth angels—but also demons—proficient in medicine, which could cure *or* cause diseases, knowledge of the mines of the earth, demons proficient in coining, spirits offering transportation to distant lands, and so on.[63] These aims were what Regardie dismissed as "medieval" and inferior. His dismissal reveals an important feature of the dynamic of reinterpretation involved in occultism's perspective on older esoteric source materials: They all tend to become much more profound and "spiritual" viewed in light of a perennial wisdom purportedly far removed from earthly goals.[64]

Despite Regardie's hesitations, *Book "H"* may have been of some importance as a source to the Inner Order teachings, as it is cited and referred to several times in the other material concerning Enochiana.[65] Besides the official version prepared by Westcott, we know that several other Golden Dawn members made personal copies, at least F. L. Gardener, William A. Ayton, and Allan Bennett.[66] It is even possible that it was Sloane 307, rather than the original Dee/Kelley manuscripts, that was the "ancient MSS" mentioned in the Cipher MS. Even if this would be the case, however, the original interpretation of the functions of the Great Table was not picked up in the rest of the material. Neither does it seem as if practical experiments of the kind of work described were conducted by Golden Dawn members, or at least we do not have any evidence of it. As we will see from the extant manuscripts dealing with the practice of Enochian magic among Second Order initiates, their experiments were mostly preoccupied with what was described in the four other books, deriving from Mathers's synthesizing genius rather than Westcott's copying activities.

The most influential of the Enochian-related documents circulated in the Second Order was *Book "S": The Concourse of the Forces*.[67] This book, probably conceived by Mathers, lays the foundation of the uniquely Golden Dawnesque interpretation of the Great Table, in full accordance with the general syncretistic approach of the Order. The main objective of the book is to show the attribution of a complex set of correspondences to each letter on the four tables, culminating with the transformation of each single letter square into a three-dimensional truncated "pyramid."

Following the schematic symbolism of the Kabbalah and the four elements, the first step described is to attribute the four letters of Tetragrammaton to the Enochian squares.[68] As each of these letters is attributed already to one of the four elements, these automatically follow. When the zodiacal signs are attributed next, these also follow certain guidelines with reference to which element the sign "belongs to." Similar rules are set down for the remaining symbol systems; planetary, Tarot, and geomantic. The result is that the Enochian letter tables are turned into elaborate "maps" of elemental, Kabbalistic, planetary, zodiacal, Tarot, and geomantic attributions. In addition the tables are to be painted in the colors of the element corresponding. Since we have seen that the correspondences become very complex (remember that there are four different tables attributed to each element, all of which are subdivided four times, with the same attributions) the completed tables make a quite colorful sight.

The last and important step in *Book "S"* is the transformation of each single letter square into a truncated pyramid. Building on all the symbolisms that have been projected onto the tablet it is now possible to divide each single letter square into four triangles. Each of these will bear one of the symbolic attributions piled up on the square, that is, an element, a planet, a zodiacal sign, and a Tarot trump, or a letter of the Tetragrammaton.[69] Each square thus transforms into a three-dimensional structure, with each of the four attributions making up a wall of a pyramid, truncated to reveal a platform on top of which the letter of the original square should be engraved. Again, it is advised that each of the sides of the pyramid be painted in the appropriate color, forming a rather impressive polychromic display. This highly complex and syncretizing construction is unique not only in the reception history of Dee and Kelley's Enochian system, but in the history of occultism at large.

In this historically unique construct each of the sides of the pyramid, bearing different attributions, should be seen as converging at the center of each pyramid. The essence of this "concourse of forces" is concentrated in the Enochian letter at the apex.[70] Toward the end of the chapter we shall see examples of the practical use of this system.

The remaining three "books" or instructions concerning the Enochian system all build on the basic structure revealed in *The Concourse of the Forces*. For instance, *Book "X"* further adds to the complexity of symbolisms by giving a procedure to attribute an Egyptian god to each letter square, "enthroned" as it were, on each pyramid.[71] In addition, a sphinx (or "sphynx," in the preferred G.D. spelling) should be created, and actually placed "within" the pyramids. Again, different types of sphinxes could be constructed by analyzing the mythological creature through elemental symbolism: the creatures featured in the sphinx (i.e., bull, eagle or hawk, man or angel, lion) are all attributed to the four elements, making it possible to construct unique sphinxes in accordance with the elemental symbolism of each pyramid.[72] For practical and "quick working" with this system, Mathers adds a note describing how the adept could make figures of paper, which were put together like a jigsaw puzzle to create the specific sphinxes and pyramids, and also small Egyptian gods of paper to be enthroned on them.[73] These paper models should be employed as foci of concentration and contemplation in visual scrying work. We will see some examples of this shortly.

The *Book "T"*, also called *The Book of the Angelical Calls,* goes back to another part of John Dee's original Enochian system, by introducing to the Adepti the forty-eight *Claves Angelicae*. As we saw in chapter 1, the function of these was somewhat obscure in John Dee's angel diaries. On the one hand it would seem that they were to be employed with the letter tables in *Liber Loagaeth* to unlock "the Gates and Cities of wisdom."[74] At the same time it is clear that the last thirty calls (which in fact are all the same, except one word) had a very definite function, in calling and commanding the thirty "Aires," presiding over the ninety-one spirits who govern the various geographical regions.[75] The exact system of doing so was spelled out in Dee's *Liber scientiæ, auxilii, et Victoria Terrestris*.[76]

In the Golden Dawn instruction, however, they are all given new meaning, again with reference to the "Elemental Tablets" and the "Tablet of Union." The six first calls belong to the Tablet of Union. Two of them uniquely so, the four next are also to be used with the elemental tablets. The next twelve are each referred to one of the sub-quarters of the elemental tablets. Thus, when working with the system, the Adept would start by invoking one of the calls attributed to the Tablet of Union and the appropriate Elemental Tablet. Then one would use the call of the sub-quarter in which the angel one is working with is located. For instance, to get to the angel Amox of the "watery quarter of fire," one would have to go through the sixth and the seventeenth angelic calls or keys.[77]

When it comes to the calls of the thirty Aires, which were somewhat more clearly defined in Dee's manuscripts, and hence less mysterious than the other eighteen, they are only mentioned briefly by the *Book "T"*. No indication either to the aim or method of using them is provided.[78] One gets the impression that Mathers (and maybe Westcott) was so focused on the Great Table and its invented elemental symbolism, that when seeing that the Aires of the original system was not reducible to it, he either lost interest or simply failed to see an immediate way to incorporate it more or less consistently with the rest of the Golden Dawn magical teachings.

The last aspect of Golden Dawn Enochian magic is contained in *Book "Y"*, and is perhaps the most outlandish feature. This is a board game, entitled "Rosicrucian chess."[79] The author of the document noticed that the Enochian elemental tablets can be transformed into *chessboards* by removing some of the letter squares in a systematic fashion. Each of the tablets consists of 156 letter squares. By removing the big central cross (36 squares), the lesser crosses in each quarter (10 x 4) and the four "kerubic" squares above each of these lesser crosses (4 x 4), one is left with sixty-four squares. This is the number of squares on a regular board of chess (8 x 8). Hence, one ends up with four different chessboards, each corresponding to one of the four elements.

The idea of "discovering" the occult significance of chess is not that far removed from what Eliphas Lévi had done with the Tarot some decades earlier, "uncovering" its hidden relation to the Kabbalah.[80] One significant difference is that the Golden Dawn's Enochian foundation of chess is far more elaborate, complex, and hard to get at than Lévi's rather straightforward attributions.

The function of the "Rosicrucian" chess game, later most often referred to as "Enochian chess," seems to have been divination. According to the nature of the problem one wants to answer, one of the four elemental tablets is chosen as the board of play. Following the Order's teachings, each board will be divided into four lesser corners attributed to four "sub-elements." This reveals a main difference from ordinary chess: the Enochian variety is a four-handed game. Four players play out the actions of the four sub-elements upon the table chosen, a kind of dramatized battle between occult forces. Building on *The Concourse of the Forces,* each square is conceived of as a pyramid, uniquely joining various "occult forces." The pieces have also been exchanged, attributed to various Egyptian gods. They are to be perceived as the "rulers" of various elements and forces, moving across the board and "activating" the squares that they enter during the course of play. The result is that the movement of the pieces on the board can activate a wealth of imaginative speculation and occult reasoning on the part of the players and diviners.

Contacting the Beyond: Practical Experiments of the Second Order

When looking closely at the Golden Dawn teachings one gets the impression that the actual practice or application of Enochian magic had two main possible manifestations: the contemplative, imaginative *scrying* of various names and letter squares, and the actual operative *conjuring* of angelic entities. Of these, the first is best known and most typical of what we know of the Order generally, not least since this part of the system is described in the Enochian documents published by Regardie, especially *The Concourse of the Forces*. The possibilities for actually *conjuring* spirits with the system were mainly laid out in the *Clavicula Tabularum Enochi,* which Regardie did not find worthy of publication.

When one goes through the extant material containing the results of practical experiments, the vast majority is also clearly of the scrying and contemplative type. This may be as expected, since scrying had a high priority and was widely taught with different methods as well (especially the so-called tattwas).[81] In short, it was a pillar of the practice of Golden Dawn magic. In the following, I will briefly go through the material relating to the practice of Enochian magic, as to give an overview of what went on.

The most obvious source is to be found in a series of experiments circulated in one of the "Flying Rolls" of the Second Order. Probably used as a sort of magical *exemplum,* Flying Roll no. XXXIII is entitled

"Visions of Squares upon the Enochian Tablets," and contains just that: visions attained by seven members of the Second Order, using methods to scry the pyramidal letter squares described in *The Concourse of the Forces*.[82] The objective of these scrying experiments seems to have been the exploration of the "locations" in the "Astral Light" that these occult keys give access to, and the acquisition of more arcane lore regarding those occulted regions.

To give but one example, I will cite extensively from one of Dr. Edward Berridge's experiments with the square "c" of the "Earthy Lesser Angle of the Tablet of Air":

> Having rehearsed the 8th Angelical Call and enclosed myself within a pyramid as above [diagram of the pyramid of the square with elemental attributions is given], vibrating the Names, I followed the ray and found myself in a hot, very dry atmosphere; I therefore invoked the God Kabexnuf [the Egyptian god attributed to the pyramid in *Book "S"*] by the power c.n.m.o. ["angelic" letters extracted from the tablet] on whose appearance I used all the tests I knew, whereby he was strengthened. [83]

This describes the first steps of the Enochian vision quest. The adept rehearses the call and uses his "magical imagination" to place himself in the pyramid. After meeting the god of the square and interacting with him, the adept goes on to explore the realm that is opened up to him. Berridge describes how he meets a Sphynx resting on a black cube, showing him certain secrets of the workings of the Macrocosm.[84] After "resting" on an erupting volcano for a while—an experience he, quite plausibly, describes as not very pleasant—he was taken to "a higher plane where there was a luxuriant forest of tropical plants of gorgeous scarlet and orange," and was shown "many tigers," "tiger lilies and Japanese red lilies." Finally Berridge was shown a human being belonging, by correspondence, to that place. The man is described as looking pretty much like "Chopin playing madly on a piano in a large empty room."

The imagery is unquestionably rich and vivid, but it does not significantly differ from the result of other systems of scrying deployed by the Order. For instance, one is reminded of the visionary experiences Moina Mathers describes in her introduction to the use of "tattwas." The tattwas were another focus for scrying, which was used widely in the Order; this one extracted and recontextualized from Indian sources.[85] After similarly having "projected" her imagination or "astral self" through the focusing symbol used, Moina writes: "I perceive appearing an expanse of sea, a slight strip of land—high grey rocks or boulders rising out of the sea. To the left a long gallery of cliffs jutting out some distance into the sea."[86] The same occult faculties are used, namely, the imagination involved in scrying, for more or less the same aims. It would seem that this use of the Enochian system only differs from the use of tattwas in degree of potency and profundity; Enochiana is simply seen as the more complex, superior system with which one could work "astraly."[87]

The use of Enochian chess is perhaps at an interesting intersection between the contemplative practices described above, and the operative, manipulative calling forth of spirits detailed in *Clavicula Tabularum Enochi*. Although any deep knowledge of its function has been lost with the death of the earliest members of the Golden Dawn,[88] it seems clear that it was first and foremost meant to exploit the vast symbolism laid out in *The Concourse of the Forces* to form a tool for divination. Now, divination can be seen as being "in between" operative and contemplative magic in this respect, since it works primarily with visionary and imaginative meditations on the symbolism that appears, while it is also at the same time more operative than the typical contemplative scrying seen above. Divination, whether by Enochian chess, the Tarot, or geomancy, is meant as a response to a certain question an adept would have elaborated or answered, and thus works more directly with matters in this world.

We know that at least some central Golden Dawn members practiced Enochian chess. During the schism of the order in 1900, when the London rebels overthrew MacGregor Mathers and set up their own governing commission, they also appointed seven "Adepti Litterati," specialists in specific branches of occultism. One of these was Reena Fulham-Hughes, who was listed as a specialist of "Tarot and Enochian Chess."[89] This suggests that the system was taught and practiced by some, probably as a divinatory system similar to, but more complex than, the Tarot.

One particularly famous account of high-standing members using Enochian chess is given by William Butler Yeats. Yeats recounts some of the eccentricities that would unfold during his stay with MacGregor and Moina Mathers in Paris in 1894.[90] The atmosphere was pleasant, with Yeats reading from his latest play, Moina's brother, the famous philosopher Henri Bergson, coming over, and MacGregor complaining of the latter's failing to be convinced of MacGregor's magic.[91] Among these trivial anecdotes, however, Yeats tells that in the evening they would gather together and play a round of Enochian chess. Yeats and Moina would make one team, while MacGregor, always the eccentric, would play with a spirit as his partner. As Yeats described, "[H]e would cover his eyes with his hands or gaze at the empty chair at the opposite corner of the board before moving his partner's piece."[92] Unfortunately, we do not learn anything about the magical aspects of the games played; possibly they were only recreational games. Sometimes, even magicians do things just for fun.

So what about the conjuring type of magic that, according to the *Clavicula Tabularum Enochi,* the Enochian system could also provide? As stated earlier, evidence of this "old school" kind of magical practice is hard to find in the Golden Dawn material. We do not have published accounts of experiences with conjuring angels or other spirits from this system, such as the Enochian "Kings," "Seniors," or "Aires." However, there are certain hints to be found.

One of the most direct, yet still slightly ambiguous, is Westcott's short "Further Rules for Practice," apparently written to go with *The Concourse of the Forces* and *Clavicula Tabularum Enochi.*[93] This instruction describes the use of the elemental tablets in a ritual setting in some more detail. The magician is to use the ritual of the hexagram to invoke the Kings and the Six Seniors, proceed with the ritual of the pentagram for the Spirit and Four Elements and then go on to the lesser angels that can be extracted from the tables.[94] The students are then told to carefully note that some elemental attributions are different depending on whether you are *summoning* spirits or *seeking* them "on their own planes,"[95] implying that both could be done.

He goes on to give an example of how one should go about to call forth the angel OMDI from the Earth of Fire tablet. After having performed the proper "banishing" or purification ritual, drawn the right pentagrams, and so on, the magician exclaims:

> EDELPERNAA, (the Great King of the South). VOLEXDO and SIODA, (the two Deity Names on the Sephirotic Calvary Cross). I command ye in the Divine Name OIP TEAA PEDOCE and BITOM that the Angel who governs the Watery and Earthy square of OMDI shall obey my behest and submit to me when I utter the holy name OOMDI.[96]

This is clearly a much more coercive and manipulative method than using the Calls and miniature painted paper pyramids to scry the letter squares. The method reminds one of the sorts of coercive and constraining rituals found in more "nigromantic" grimoirs, such as the Goetia.

But what is the aim of the procedure Westcott describes? This seems again more ambiguous. Referring to his own personal experience with this sort of magical experiment, Westcott recalls "passing through" the letter tablets, finding himself in a cave where he was told secrets of the various letter squares on the table he had worked with. He then recalled being taken "through several fiery planes, each of them of greater whiteness and brilliance than the last," stationed on a tower in the middle of the tablet, disclosed more arcane secrets by the Six Seniors, and so on.[97] In short, the result seems almost identical to that of the other, more directly contemplative methods. Toward the end, Westcott nevertheless adds a final note, which is of significance for us: "From the lectures circulated among the Adepti" he had gathered that the angels of the different sub-quarters and sections of the tablets all have certain defined properties.[98] It becomes immediately clear that he is thinking of the *Clavicula Tabularum Enochi,* as he lists the various groups of angels having properties such as "Knitting together and destruction," "Moving from place to place," "Mechanical crafts," "Secrets of Humanity," "Metals," "Stones," and "Transmutation."[99]

What should we make out of this? Despite Westcott's final "discovery," he does not seem to incorporate the specific and mundane functions of the angels and demons in the tables into his magical work. He drops it there and then, and continues entirely along the lines of the Order's vision quests. While acknowledging the more "medieval" prescriptions of the *Clavicula,* it seems that Westcott was at a loss when it came to using it. The short text referred to here suggests that even the highest adepts of the Golden Dawn were never entirely sure about the meanings and use of the Enochian system, and, in fact, seem to make contradictory statements about it.

We know that several Golden Dawn initiates, including the master of the magicians, MacGregor Mathers, did practice conjuring types of magic.[100] For instance, Yeats noted from the same 1894 visit to Paris that Mathers was "gay and companionable," but that he was strained by the many spirit evocations. He further wrote that "[o]ne day a week he and his wife were shut up together evoking, trying to influence the politics of the world . . . .I believe now, [that they were] rearranging nations according to his own grandiose phantasy, and on this day I noticed that he would spit blood."[101] Although we do not get any details as to what system they were practicing, it is perhaps not improbable to speculate that Mathers was experimenting with the use of the Enochian Aires, which, as we have seen, were originally geopolitical in nature. However, this remains speculation.

Another clue to actual practice of Enochiana of a different, perhaps more orthodox fashion is provided by the notebooks of W. E. H. Humphrey, known in the Golden Dawn as Gnothi Seauton.[102] These indicate that the small group of Golden Dawn adepts known as the "Sphere Group,"[103] originally founded in 1898 by the leading Second Order adept Florence Farr, was dedicated to Enochian experiments during the summer of 1901.[104] In the workings the group sought to emulate to a greater extent the workings of John Dee, by substituting some of the ordinary Golden Dawn methods for a crystal and speculatrix. This leads one to suspect that they may also have been influenced by the experiments of Hockley and Mackenzie discussed earlier. The adepts would lead the experiments, while the actual scrying would be done by an uninitiated female seer. The schooled adepts would listen, record, and interpret.

Judging simply by the altered methods, it seems that this group wanted to take Enochian magic in other directions than what was allowed for through the text of *The Concourse of the Forces*. However, it seems that the *aim* was again closer to the introverted, contemplative workings: to gain more knowledge of esoteric arcana, relating to the Enochian system. The sittings detailed by Humphrey show that the interest was in unraveling hidden correspondences in the Enochian alphabet.[105] Unfortunately, we do not learn any details concerning the methods employed to induce the medium's revelations. They may or may not have had a more operative ritual magical basis.

Concluding Remark: Constructing Perennial Wisdom

In concluding this chapter, I want to draw attention to a central and recurring feature or strategy in the Golden Dawn's reinterpretation and presentation of the Enochian system. We have seen that, whether in the context of the initiation ceremonies, in the few official accounts given of the history of the system, and even in the presentations of the magic of the letter tablets, Dee and Kelley, the true originators of the Enochian system, were never mentioned. The de-contextualization that is implied in this systematic "source amnesia"[106] is crucial to the various representations of the system that the Golden Dawn produces. By severing product from producer, disconnecting Enochian from Dee and Kelley, even from the Renaissance, it becomes possible to interpret Enochiana as the ultimate manifestation of ageless wisdom. By this process, it is also possible to give totally new interpretations of the use of this system in magical practice, without losing legitimacy.

With a Marxist metaphor, this alienation of the producers from the product brings about a kind of "commodity fetishism"; Enochiana becomes something sui generis, even something perennial. All the while, this perennialism mirrors the conceptions of the Victorian occultist. This process, then, was pivotal for bringing about the transition from Elizabethan to Victorian angel magic. In the following chapters, we will see its continued influence on later receptions of Dee and Kelley's work.

4
The Authenticity Problem and the Legitimacy of Magic

The Collapse of an Order

Through the foregoing chapters we have seen how a Renaissance natural philosopher's quest to read the corrupted text of the book of nature by appealing to higher powers has led, through a series of historical transmutations, to a field of occultist theory and practical magic. Modern Enochian magic was forged in the hermetic, Rosicrucian, and theurgic crucible of the Golden Dawn, the most influential magical order of the late-Victorian period. The alchemico-metallurgic metaphor here is not merely poetic: the occult fusion which Enochiana was melted into in the Golden Dawn has had important repercussions for its future development. Not only because the Golden Dawn's synthesis has been supremely influential on twentieth- and twenty-first-century ritual magic and the wider occulture, but perhaps equally much because of the Golden Dawn's early organizational collapse and the confusion that arose in its wake.

The Golden Dawn disintegrated abruptly around the turn of the century, mainly due to three successive crises. Serious leadership problems broke out between the increasingly authoritarian MacGregor Mathers, settled in Paris, and the London Isis-Urania Temple; a controversy started among the London adepts over the place of private magical groups within the Order; and perhaps most devastatingly, the scandalous "Horos affair" of 1901 brought the otherwise secretive Golden Dawn to the front pages of the sensationalist press and damaged its reputation beyond repair.

One event that would go on to have serious consequences for the Golden Dawn occurred during the power struggles between Mathers and the London adepts in 1899 to 1900. Some years earlier, Westcott had been forced to resign from the Order due to suspicions from his employers, who were unimpressed when finding out about his occult leanings. This had left Mathers in sole control of the Order, from his

Ahathoor Temple in Paris. When in January 1900 Mathers learned that the adepts of the Isis-Urania Temple had grown so impatient that they threatened to shut down the temple in protest, he was convinced that they really had plans to restart under a different name and reinstate Westcott as chief. Responding to this perceived threat, Mathers made certain strategic choices, which would appear devastating to the Order. In a campaign to discredit Westcott's authority, Mathers revealed the true story about how the Fräulein Sprengel letters, at the very base of the Order's claim to Rosicrucian lineage and legitimacy, had in reality been forged. Mathers wanted to instill the idea that the only link to the real "secret chiefs" of the Order now ran through himself, claiming to be in contact with the real Soror S.D.A. in Paris—apparently still very much alive. The strategy was shortsighted, since people now had to question whether the Order was founded on anything but lies. This backfired on Mathers himself, who had problems convincing anybody about his own extravagant claims. More importantly for us, the revelation that the Sprengel letters had been forged and that there might not even have been an authentic Rosicrucian connection prompted other adepts to start their private investigations into the Order's founding myths, its documents and teachings. The Order's foundations were shaking.

It was still another couple of years until its original organizational structure crumbled. The sensational Horos scandal was an important reason. A certain Mr. and Mrs. Horos, con artists posing as adepts and spiritualists, tricked Mathers and other members of the Golden Dawn, and managed to steal a version of the Neophyte ritual. In September 1901 the Horos couple was arrested, after a young girl had been raped during a bogus Neophyte initiation of their machination. The massive press coverage that ensued seriously damaged the integrity of the Golden Dawn, even though the actual Order had had nothing to do with it. The Neophyte ritual was made public, ridiculed by the press, and deemed blasphemous by the judges, making it difficult for respectable members to remain associated with the Golden Dawn.[1]

The Order finally dissolved in 1903, after another internal conflict over the function of the Second Order and the role of the private magical groups, such as the Sphere Group, which we briefly discussed in the last chapter. Several factions nevertheless attempted to carry on the Order's "true lineage," often claiming renewed contact with secret chiefs or other strategies to fortify their legitimacy. Some of these we discuss in the second part of this book.

* * *

At present, I wish to call closer attention to some theoretical points mentioned in the introduction. One is related to the continued appeal of ritual magic in the modern age generally, while the other has specific bearing on the issue of Enochiana and the fall of the Golden Dawn. First there is the general problem of legitimating magical belief and practice in the face of secular, "disenchanted" modernity. This has been touched upon and discussed in a few full-length scholarly studies of modern ritual magic, such as Alex Owen's study of Victorian occultism,[2] Tanya Luhrmann's important anthropological study of contemporary (i.e., 1980s) witches,[3] Marco Pasi's historical treatment of the notion of magic in British occultism,[4] and other studies looking at the intersections of occultism and contemporary culture.[5] In addition, there have been more focused contributions addressing this problem to some extent, such as Wouter J. Hanegraaff's article on "How Magic Survived the Disenchantment of the World," and my own sociological research on contemporary ritual magicians in Norway.[6]

In addition there seems to exist a related but somewhat different issue to be dealt with within the specialized domain of modern Enochian magic, which I refer to as "the authenticity problem." The problem is connected with the contested nature of this particular magical discourse within modern occultism. During the twentieth century, differing views on what Enochian is and how it ought to be interpreted and practiced have abounded. As we saw in the previous chapter, the discrepancy between the Enochian magic of the nineteenth-century Golden Dawn and that outlined in the original Dee diaries was distinct. Much of the later debate revolves around this question. Since Golden Dawn teachings are at the foundation of most ritual magic practiced in the Anglophone West in the twentieth and twenty-first centuries, Enochian magicians have been faced with a problem when they have had to acknowledge this lack of agreement between authorities.[7] The evidential recognition that Dee's and the Golden Dawn's were not "the same magical system" requires a response. On the one hand the discrepancy must be explained to legitimate the Golden Dawn teachings; on the other, it opens up vistas for attacking the Golden Dawn system through an appeal to a supposedly "original" Enochiana.

This chapter will introduce some theoretical and methodological issues related to these two problems. As such, it reads not only as a conclusion to the first and historical part of this book, but equally much as a theoretical preface to the part that follows. I will begin with discussing the problem of legitimating magic in a secular world before I go on to treat the "authenticity problem" faced by twentieth-century Enochian angel magicians.

Magic in Modernity: The Survival and Revival of Magic between Disenchantment and Re-Enchantment

The resurgence of the occult in the enlightened nineteenth century has long been a fascination of scholars. The century that was born from revolutions and the Enlightenment was itself to spawn Spiritualism, Theosophy, and occultism. As James Webb somewhat dramatically put it: "After the Age of Reason came the Age of the Irrational."[8] After Webb, the thesis that the occult represented solely a Flight from Reason, brought about by what he had called a "crisis in consciousness," a logical consequence of too much logic, has been strongly contested. More recent research rather tends to emphasize the ways in which the various strands of nineteenth-century occultism and heterodox religion were shaped and influenced by prominent trends in Victorian culture, including the ideas of the Enlightenment and an emerging and gradually more professionalized modern science.[9]

A blooming interest in ritual magic was part of the broader Victorian occult revival. Although there seems to have been a certain continuity of individual magicians working through the early modern period into the Victorian era as well (a few of them, such as Barrett, and his possible student Hockley, were mentioned previously) the Victorian occult revival also saw an institutionalization of magic, through groups such as the Hermetic Brotherhood of Luxor and the Golden Dawn. These groups, cast as veritable schools for magic, had a profound impact on later developments.[10] The magical institutions provided a more stable basis for the development and teaching of magic, with the social aspect of magical orders significantly increasing the numbers of magical disciples. Even though the original Golden Dawn was relatively short-lived, its continued influence in the twentieth century was immense, especially due to the effort of such earlier members and disciples as Aleister Crowley, A. E. Waite, Dion Fortune, Israel Regardie, and others, who went on to form new groups and publish important magical material for new generations of aspirants to study. Two of the most influential sources for twentieth-century magic are indeed Regardie's publication of Golden Dawn material from the late 1930s[11] and Crowley's work, particularly the volumes of his Equinox journal, published from 1909, and other textbooks in magic and mysticism.[12]

A question that has perplexed many scholars, however, is just how highly educated, upper-middle-class moderns have been able to maintain a belief in magic, from the nineteenth and twentieth centuries, continuing into the present. This question is closely tied together with the broader debate of the secularization thesis of religion and modernity, and Max Weber's influential thesis on the "disenchantment of the world." As society is modernized through processes of industrialization, urbanization, secularization, and rationalization, the belief in an animated, magical world is thought to be replaced by a mechanical and scientific-materialist worldview; the word *mystical* loses its sacred connotations and becomes instead derogatory, indicative of "obscurantism" or "superstition."

As is now old news, disenchantment and secularization understood in its crudest sense do not seem to be consistent with empirical data on the development of religion in the Western world. The blossoming of new religious movements and the "New Age" counterculture in the latter half of the twentieth century is of course the classic example, also because sociological research commonly identifies educated, relatively well-off middle-class citizens as the main recruits for such spiritual movements.[13] The question, however, has remained how to interpret this: Did secularization and disenchantment happen, later to be replaced by de-secularization[14] and re-enchantment?[15] Or should we rather understand secularization/disenchantment to mean something else than the "strict sense" interpretation, in such a way that we can view it as a process involving radical changes in the religious landscape of modern societies, instead of a total evaporation of "religion as such"? Perhaps, as the pro-secularization theory scholar Steve Bruce recently put it, critics and proponents alike should stop talking about "the secularization thesis," and instead look at the many various hypotheses on social change and religion as falling under a broader secularization paradigm.[16]

The interpretation that secularization ought to mean something else than the disappearance of religion has been favored by many sociologists and scholars of religion in recent decades. Typically, such positions entertain that new religious spiritualities must rather be associated with a gradual displacement of church religion, as a part of the secularization process.[17] Similarly, it would seem that the ideals of most new religious movements are remarkably well adjusted to the more progressive, individualist ideals of the educated middle classes.[18] Hence, one is justified in viewing the impact of secularization as a substantial transformation of religion and religious currents, to better conform to the ideals of a late modern culture in the shaping.[19]

The same demographic profile seems to hold for what little research has been carried out on modern and contemporary ritual magic. For instance, Tanya Luhrmann's groundbreaking study of contemporary witches in Britain found that most belonged to the educated classes, and had a generally articulate and sophisticated approach to their religious and magical practices.[20] Recent statistical data also show that various forms of neo-pagan and magical religion have been among the most rapidly growing "alternative" religions in English-speaking countries throughout the 1990s and into the current century.[21] Hence, there is much to suggest that magic thrives at the very epicenter of late modernity. This brings back the questions "why" and "how"; is the modern fascination with ritual magic characterized by some kind of revolt against a culture of reason and disenchantment, indicative of a tendency toward re-enchantment of the world? Or does "the survival of magic" only exist on the premises of that disenchanted modern culture itself, effecting radical changes in the way magic is interpreted, rationalized, and legitimized by its practitioners? Do these explanations even have to be distinct, separated, and opposed to each other?

By comparing the Renaissance magical worldview of Marsilio Ficino and Cornelius Agrippa to that of modern "occultist magic," that is, the ritual magic that had its formative years in fin de siècle occultism, Wouter Hanegraaff has argued that a considerable reinterpretation has taken place which resulted in a "disenchanted magic."[22] The argument is that the Renaissance systems presented a genuine belief in a "magical worldview" of real correspondences between parts of the cosmos, an invisible mediating spiritus, and the very real existence of demons and spiritual intelligences of various kinds,[23] whereas the post-Enlightenment occultist interpretation involved an ontological move from emphasising entities and correspondences as "real and actual" to viewing them as merely conventional and pragmatically useful symbols.[24] Furthermore, Hanegraaff argued that the modern interpretation of magic is marked by a tendency toward psychologization; entities such as angels and demons tend to be viewed as "parts of the self," and magical practices are seen as psychological techniques for raising one's consciousness or attaining to the "Higher Self."[25]

In Hanegraaff's view, this renewed nomenclature signifies one aspect of a post-Enlightenment disenchantment of magic: as modern magicians are well-educated and sophisticated people who tend to trust science and psychology, upholding the reference to ancient theological entities threatens to bring about cognitive dissonance. A further point is attempted to be scored with reference to Luhrmann's anthropological research. Luhrmann described how modern magicians tend to believe in a separate-but-connected magical plane, which differs from our everyday world. For Hanegraaff, this point is used to demonstrate how the realm of magic is separated from the disenchanted everyday world, in a way that makes it possible for magicians to retain both conceptions, without the worldviews coming into direct conflict. Thus, Hanegraaff holds that "[t]he dissipation of mystery in this world is compensated for by a separate magical world of the reified imagination, where the everyday rules of science and rationality do not apply."[26] Indeed, this is viewed as having a "compensatory function," and in this respect, Hanegraaff argues, modern magic is "somewhat similar to the "escape" offered by the creation of "imaginary worlds" in, for instance, contemporary virtual reality and role-playing games; but contrary to the latter, "it is taken with full seriousness as a religious worldview."[27]

The idea that magic has survived by becoming itself disenchanted has been challenged by Christopher Partridge, a proponent of what we may crudely call the "re-enchantment thesis." As Partridge shows, Hanegraaff somewhat twists Luhrmann's point about the separate magical world of modern magicians to fit the idea that magicians seek to balance a disenchanted worldview with a magical one.[28] By emphasizing the separateness and downplaying the connectedness of the "magical plane" the very idea of magical efficacy is neglected, or at least not given as much attention as it should. As Partridge writes (and I quote at length):

> Work on the magical plane, as Hanegraaff agrees, is believed to have a direct impact on the everyday world. That this is so places a large question mark against his claim that occultists are able to keep the two worlds separate. Indeed, apart from anything else, it would be enormously psychologically demanding to operate with such a fundamentally fractured worldview. In fact, regardless of the updated metaphors, explanations, and interpretations, occultists, like most religious believers, have a single magical worldview. And one only has to read the works of contemporary magicians . . . to realize that the world they inhabit is enchanted. Spirit entities, the communications of the Elizabethan occultist John Dee, and much else that is explicitly magical/spiritual is firmly accepted as part of an integrated worldview. As Luhrmann comments, although magicians do not always agree about the nature of reality, "the idea that spirits exist is not contested." Indeed, she later makes the point that what is believed and practiced by modern magicians can be understood as fundamentally religious—even "magicians themselves come to use the term 'religion' because they feel comfortable calling the feelings elicited in some meditations and rituals 'spiritual' . . . .One might imagine that merely having a spiritual response to a ritual should not commit one to any theory about divine existence or magical force . . . but people often find the distinction hard to handle . . . " Again, while it cannot be denied that, as a result of the Enlightenment, significant changes have occurred in the understanding of the nature of magic, its legitimacy and efficacy, the argument that contemporary systems of belief contitute [*sic*] "disenchanted magic" is flawed.[29]

Instead of any substantial disenchantment Partridge sees only a partially reformed lingo; the main tendency, in his view, is that magicians really retain, or recreate, an enchanted worldview—however different the terminology, and what could aptly be considered legitimating strategies, may be.

This must, however, be understood in light of Partridge's overarching theoretical framework, that the new religious formations of late modernity are not really "secularized religion," but rather the emergence of a new religious "occulture," which increasingly challenges the secularism of the Western-style educated subculture that dominates most of today's truth institutions.[30] Building on earlier work in the sociology of religion, including Ernst Troeltsch's concept of "mystical religion" and Colin Campbell's influential "cultic milieu," Partridge holds the occulture to be an emerging cultural milieu, a "reservoir of ideas, beliefs, practices, and symbols."[31] More than this, understanding the occulture in Partridge's sense also includes considering the various sites and institutions through which these representations are mediated, disseminated, and consumed, including Hollywood movies, music, graphic novels, festivals, "alternative" fairs, and fringe magazines. Indeed, Partridge stresses that the occulture is not merely another "subculture," but rather a new significant culture in the making, a kind of esoteric mainstream.[32] Dropping a number of currents and positions belonging to this culture, he lists "those often hidden, rejected, and oppositional beliefs and practices associated with esotericism, theosophy, mysticism, New Age [and] Paganism," mentioning a couple of dozen other currents, themes, and topics, from alternative science, UFOs, and alien abductions to angels, spirit guides, and astral projection.[33] No doubt, Enochian magic would belong to this spectrum of practices as well. Adopting Partridge's terminology and basic sociological framework, I will return to some of the implications of locating Enochiana within the late-modern occulture in the last chapter of this book.

Returning now to the disenchantment/re-enchantment debate, I do find that both Hanegraaff and Partridge raise pertinent points. Their difference, it seems, is mostly one of accentuation, based on what seems to me to be their reliance on two different "master narratives": that of a Weberian disenchantment thesis, from which there can be no real return, and that of an ongoing opposition between elitist secularism and countercultural re-enchantment. As just indicated, I find Partridge's occultural framework to be helpful for locating especially the contemporary incarnation of the Enochiana discourse. However, there is one problematic aspect, which, as far as I can see, applies to both perspectives: there seems to be a sample bias involved when both look to illustrate their points. In the case of Hanegraaff this especially relates to the problematic act of generalizing the tenets of "occultist magic" from the writings of one occultist, namely Israel Regardie, and one anthropological study (Luhrmann's) of one magical group. Although Regardie's rendering of Golden Dawn magic has indeed been vastly influential, this is not to say that it is without its competitors, or that it is necessarily received in one single way. If there is one thing contemporary research on consumer culture has established, for instance, it really is the fact that consumers of cultural products are not passive receptors, but engage actively, and are not afraid to alter and reinterpret the product by reembedding it in new contexts.[34] The same can certainly be said for the consumption of religious and magical ideas. Additionally, as will be shown in later chapters, other very influential occult authors tend to disregard Regardie's interpretations of what magic is all about. For instance, Aleister Crowley, the major authority in the Thelemic segment of modern occulture, and the proponents of modern Satanism, such as Anton LaVey and Michael Aquino, all go in quite different directions on major points. Although I do believe that there is much merit in describing Regardie's own take on ritual magic as "psychologized," I would be very hesitant about generalizing his position to modern occultism generally, let alone transposing his views backward to the magicians of the Golden Dawn.[35]

I do also find similar objections to Partridge's thesis of re-enchantment, particularly his proposition that modern occultists have "a singular magical worldview." An example of a "disenchanted magic," which in my view better illustrates Hanegraaff's point, is that of LaVey's rationalistic interpretation of Satanic ritual magic. In his expositional essays LaVey emphasizes the emotional aspects of magical rituals, viewing them as "intellectual decompression chambers."[36] The various magical paraphernalia are seen as mere "distractions" to hinder the intellect and give the emotions free reign.[37] Here magic is increasingly interpreted as psychological tools, much less ambiguously than in the case of Regardie. In addition, LaVey frequently attacked Regardie and what he characterized as the sanctimonious and fraudulent "holy esoterica" of "occultisms of the past."[38] The real influences on LaVey's system of magic are "secular" rather than "esoteric" knowledge systems, such as the sociologists Goffman and Klapp, and psychologists like Reich, Ferenczi, and Freud; all of whom are referenced in LaVey's perhaps primary work on what he called "lesser magic," *The Compleat Witch*.[39] To the degree that a disenchantment of magic really has taken place, it is, in my opinion, LaVey who represents it in its fullest form. I think one would find that this very influential figure in modern occultism does not squarely fit Partridge's framework; even though clearly a part of the rising occulture, LaVey was certainly no champion for challenging the materialist and scientific worldview of late modernity. That he may have been conscripted as such is a different matter.

To emphasize the difficulty in proposing one interpretation and legitimating strategy to be the dominant one, I will refer to my own sociological study of contemporary ritual magicians in Norway, where one of the objectives was to chart out emic understandings of the efficacy of magic. Although the general tendency among my informants was to take a pragmatic approach in which metaphysical questions were largely bracketed in favor of a focus on actual results, the complexity of the beliefs became apparent as soon as I pursued them further. Whereas one of my informants found the interpretation that entities such as demons are to be seen as "qualities of one's own mind" reasonable enough if pushed to give an explanation, another magician, himself a professional psychologist, did not favor the psychologized view.[40] Although he held a "psychologically reductionist" position to be handy early on in the training of new magicians (to avoid megalomania and a romantic flight from this-worldly realities), he still held that, after a while, one would reach a sort of abductive conclusion in favor of the objective reality of demons, as literally described in grimoires.[41] That is, to account for certain results this magician claimed to have achieved, he held psychologization to be a less plausible, less elegant interpretation than a realistic, externalist interpretation of the entities could provide.[42]

The lesson to be drawn from this whole discussion, I believe, is that a more nuanced approach is needed to frame the various strategies taken by modern magicians to legitimize ritual magic in the face of secular modernity. Moving away from the dichotomous positions of disenchantment and re-enchantment theories, I propose to see these issues rather as a negotiation in which spokespersons adopt various strategies and come up with various solutions to perceived problems. This does not mean that the disenchantment/re-enchantment debate is futile, but one should recognize that it concerns questions on the macro level of history and society. A study such as this, however, detailing the history and development of a rather small subset of magical texts, ideas, practices, their spokespersons and contexts, in a variety of interpretations and conglomerations, should rather focus on nuances on the micro level. This lesson will be sought implemented in the chapters to come. The tool for doing this I find in a more discursive approach, giving emphasis to the plurality of views, differing claims and counterclaims about magic, and their social and often polemical contexts. Through this I hope to demonstrate that even with reference to a small subgenre of magic, such as Enochian, we can identify both "psychologized," "scientized," "traditionalist," "supernatural," "metaphysically evil," "pragmatic," "experiential," and "realistic" interpretations invoked by various spokespersons.

The Authenticity Problem in Modern Enochiana

At the very beginning of the twentieth century the world of occultism was shaken by the breakout of disorder and schism in the Golden Dawn. The story of the rebellious events of 1899/1900, their dramatis personae, and the outcome was briefly referenced at the opening of this chapter, and has been thoroughly documented and described other places.[43] What is important in our context is that the splits in authority led to innovations in doctrine as well; new voices entered the scene through the early decades of the century, fighting for the legitimacy of new as well as old perspectives. This led to a proliferation of occult material coming out of the Golden Dawn milieu, and sometimes quite novel frameworks for occultism were also established. While the chapters ahead will explore some of these new voices and the role played by Enochian magic in them, there is first need of discussing some theoretical aspects relating to these developments, and methodological reflections arising from studying them.

Upon the breakup and fragmentation of the Golden Dawn several magicians and occultist scholars started to critically reexamine the Order's sources. Along with the Sprengel letters the authenticity of the Cipher MS discussed in the previous chapter was particularly questioned.[44] Perhaps as a result of this trend of inquiry into the Order's sources it would not last long until the first of the magicians became conscious of the discrepancy between Golden Dawn Enochian magic and the actual Dee/Kelley material. Aleister Crowley seems to have been the first to have brought this to the fore; he did research on the sources in preparation for his experiments in 1909 with "the Aethyrs," a part of the Enochian system that, as we saw in the previous chapter, was not particularly covered by the Golden Dawn teachings.

Although I will treat Crowley in some more detail later, there is an interesting observation to be made at this point. In his autobiography Crowley shows knowledge of the function that the Aethyrs, or Aires, seem to have been given in Dee and Kelley's work. What is interesting, however, is that Crowley did not find the original interpretation profound enough, characterizing the discovery of their mundane, geopolitical use as a "most disconcerting disenchantment."[45] Instead, Crowley favored another interpretation, that the Aethyrs were "spiritual layers" outside of the four Watchtowers.[46] Although this view may have some grounding in parts of the Dee material, the major impetus for this interpretation seems to have been with reference to the Golden Dawn synthesis, which Crowley after all was schooled in. In a cosmological interpretation of the Enochian system following the Golden Dawn, saying that the Aethyrs were realms outside of the four Watchtowers (i.e., the "Great Table") would really mean that they were outside of the "elemental realms," and thus representing more subtle realities. As we saw in the first chapter, the original interpretation seems rather to have been that these entities were in control of different parts of the terrestrial world, possibly with the intent of localizing and gathering together the twelve lost tribes of Israel before the day of doom.

While Crowley mixed his own research into the original sources with a trust in the Golden Dawn material, it seems that the discrepancy between the Enochiana of the Golden Dawn, eclectically combined with Kabbalistic and elemental magic as it was, and the original system of Dee and Kelley poses a problem of authenticity for magicians holding Enochian to be the highest, most potent form of magic.

This problem could ideally be solved or negotiated in a variety of ways. Immediately, three main strategies suggest themselves:

1. Going back to the sources in order to "correct" the errors made by the eager Golden Dawn occultists. I will refer to this strategy as purism. In this approach, scholarship plays an important part in establishing and defending authenticity.
2. Holding the Golden Dawn's own narrative to be true in some way, that is, by claiming that Enochian was not the product of Dee and Kelley, but predated them, and was "restored" to its pristine authenticity by the Golden Dawn or its primordial founders. This I will refer to as perennialism. Here, scholarship, in the ordinary sense of the word at least, is less important for authenticity, replaced instead by appeals to tradition, mythmaking, or exotic techniques such as clairvoyance or astral scrying.
3. Keeping a more pragmatic approach, where the test of truth is whether or not magicians get useful results from working with the various systems. This strategy I will refer to as pragmatism or progressivism, for the often implied notion that the system can be artificially improved by the magician him- or herself, and that the proof of profundity is in the proverbial pudding.

In the latter approach, "authenticity" in the sense of scholarly traceable origins and development would not really matter; instead, a more progressive stance of programmatic eclecticism, experiment, and testing, or simply an appeal to personal experience, would be the legitimating factor. The purist approach would be marked to a greater extent by historical and scholarly diligence, and arguments based on an appeal to the source materials, while the perennialist position, in whatever form, would have to depend to a much higher degree on esoteric cosmologies, insisting on some exotic provenance of Enochian, in Paradise, the realm of angels, Atlantis, or the invisible college of Christian Rosenkreutz. All these latter claims were indeed present in the Golden Dawn at some point, which, as we have seen, was at pains to avoid mentioning Dee and Kelley as the provenance of the Enochian material.

Together with the two other strategies, these claims are found throughout the twentieth-century sources. Hence I propose viewing "purism," "perennialism," and "pragmatism" as three ideal discursive strategies used by post–Golden Dawn Enochian magicians to resolve the authenticity problem sketched above, and argue the legitimacy of one's own particular position.

A Final Note on Discursive Strategies

At this point I take recourse to the concept and typology of discursive strategies developed by Olav Hammer in his study of knowledge claims and emic epistemologies in modern esoteric movements.[47] By looking at major spokespersons within the discourse community of modern esotericism, Hammer identified three main strategies: appeal to tradition, appeal to experience, and what he phrased scientism, or terminological scientism.[48] As Hammer's work deals with discursive legitimizations of claims in modern esoteric discourse, it has significant bearing on both of the two questions I have raised above.

In relation to the first, the three strategies described by Hammer can be identified in the way magicians legitimize their practices generally, by, for instance, appealing to narratives of personal experience, or by clothing their practices in scientific nomenclature, including the quite frequent appeal to quantum mechanics, or to psychological theories. The relation to the authenticity problem in Enochian magic is somewhat more complex. We clearly find appeals to (constructed) tradition to be at the core of what I termed the perennialist response, while the pragmatic/progressive response may include elements of both scientistic and experiential rhetoric. However, the perhaps more curious purist response does not squarely find its expression in Hammer's scheme. At one level, it is related to scientism, in that it makes an appeal to the epistemic authority of solid scholarship, especially in the discipline of history. As will be shown in a later chapter, however, the claim that teachings on Enochiana must be grounded in thorough, scholarly study of original source material seems to be an additional discursive strategy that started to gain serious ground in the 1970s and 1980s. This is an emphasis on an allegedly scholarly concept of authenticity, which interestingly seems to share common points with distinctions made by some academic writers. One could for example mention Gershom Scholem's work on Kabbalah, where past masters were construed as "authentic" expressions of the tradition, while modern reconstructions and reinterpretations were rejected as anachronistic frauds and charlatans.[49] Intriguingly, we find the same kind of rhetoric employed within occultism as well, leveled against competing interpretations, criticized for being "inauthentic" in the sense of presenting distorted doctrines and practices.

In the second part of the book the historical development of the strategies is reflected in the division of chapters. We will first see how the Golden Dawn current continued, with modifications, into the twentieth century. Chapter 5 discusses the innovations of Aleister Crowley, while chapter 6 looks at new divisions and conflicts on Enochian magic within the remaining and reconstructed Golden Dawn groups, especially between Regardie and Paul Foster Case. Chapter 7 will discuss the emergence of modern Satanism, represented by LaVey and Aquino, and the role of Enochiana in the middle of modern Satanism's first schism. Through these chapters, Enochiana will largely be cast in the context of claiming and contesting "tradition." Chapter 8 moves on to discuss the interesting development that I term "the purist turn," beginning in the 1970s and overlapping with the turbulence in society and the religious and intellectual culture associated with that period. Finally in chapter 9 I chart out the latest developments in Enochiana, with a specific look at the importance of the emergence of the Internet for contemporary occultism. In addition, we will see that even though the purist turn largely influenced contemporary Enochian magic, later years have seen what some practitioners term the "New Flow": a set of new revelations from the Enochian angels, gradually acquiring a position as canonized parts of the Enochian corpus, alongside Dee and Kelley's original material.

PART TWO

MAJOR TRENDS IN ENOCHIAN MAGIC

5
The Angels and the Beast

Aleister Crowley (1875–1947) is one of the most well-known figures in modern occultism. He has been the subject of sensational stories in newspapers and magazines since his own days, and at some sixty years after his death biographies can be counted in the dozens.[1] Nevertheless, it is not until quite recently that academics have started to look at Crowley seriously. Since the late 1990s, an entire literature has cropped up that dissects Crowley's role in the modern religious and occult landscape, and the broader cultural and intellectual contexts of his own days. New biographies give a source-driven and nuanced portrayal of Crowley's life and actions, made understandable in light of his times and the specific goals and endeavors he set for himself.[2] Other academic studies place Crowley in the context of late-Victorian and Edwardian culture, and not least the moral, political, and religious anxieties of the interwar period. In this section of the literature Crowley has been linked to early-twentieth-century discourses on sexuality and transgression,[3] his engagement with the great political ideologies and upheavals has been analyzed,[4] and he has even been used as a focal point for exploring Edwardian experiences of subjectivity.[5]

Perhaps surprisingly, Crowley's ideas on magic have largely been neglected in this current of academic interest, left instead for other occultists to argue over.[6] While there have certainly been some exceptions to this general trend, it is still the case that the scholar who wishes to assess Crowley's magic has much less thorough secondary literature to rely on.[7] By extension, this applies to the endeavor of placing Crowley's role in that subset of occult magical discourse which is Enochiana. The only scholarly commentary touching on this issue is Alex Owen's chapter on "Crowley in the Desert," discussing Crowley's vision quest in the Algerian desert in 1909, induced by magical invocations of the thirty Aethyrs.[8] Owen contextualizes the exceptional series of magical experiments in light of

Orientalist discourse, sexual frustrations and taboos, psychology, and the search for the authentic self. Needless to say, our present concerns are somewhat different, and even though Owen gives a valuable interpretation of the mutations of Golden Dawn magic into Crowley's work, she cannot tell us much about the specific relevance of Enochiana in the middle of all this. Indeed, what little she has to say about Enochian magic is that it was "a complex magical system developed by John Dee…and his clairvoyant, Edward Kelley."[9] As the first part of this book demonstrated, such a description is much too simplistic. It will be an aim for the present chapter, then, not only to recapitulate Crowley's exotic use of Enochian magic, but to frame him in the unfolding narrative of the reception history of this particular set of angelic magic.

As we shall see, Crowley has indeed played a central role, steeped in the Golden Dawn's teachings but constantly pushing further with his original interpretations and new strategies to establish esoteric knowledge. Because of this emphatic Golden Dawn heritage, the present chapter should be read together with the next one. In one sense, Crowley could aptly be seen together with some of the figures we will meet there, as a pretender to the "authentic" lineage and authority following the fall of the Golden Dawn. While some of the people we will meet later have tried to reestablish such authority from within the preexisting structures, Crowley sought out different types of legitimating strategies, as well as new institutional bodies for carrying on and embodying such authority. Before we can turn to his appropriations of Enochian magic, then, we should place his overall magical and religious philosophy vis-à-vis the Golden Dawn.

The Making of a Prophet

Aleister Crowley's magical career formally began in 1898, when he was introduced to the Golden Dawn. He was taken up as an ambitious young man aged twenty-three, and quickly advanced through the Order's system of initiations. By the time of the schisms of 1900, Crowley was knocking on the portal of the Second Order. Teaming up with MacGregor Mathers, now having reached a peak of unpopularity among the London adepts, Crowley was given an initiation by the chief personally in Paris. However, this initiation would soon be declared void by the London rebels, after Crowley acted as Mathers's protégé in what has become known as "the Battle of Blythe Road"—an unsuccessful scheme to bring the rebels back to the fold.[10]

When the schisms raged, Crowley set out on a series of explorations, of both terrestrial and magical lands. Availing himself of money inherited from the death of his father, he departed for a journey around the globe, visiting such places as Mexico, Japan, Ceylon, India, Burma, and Egypt, acquiring as much knowledge as he could from those countries' pools of religious and esoteric philosophies.[11] He claimed to have studied Sufism and Arabic in Cairo under the tutelage of an unnamed sheik.[12] While in Ceylon he spent six weeks with his old friend from the Golden Dawn, Allan Bennett, who was now setting himself up as a master *yogi*.[13] Back in London Bennett had been one of Crowley's personal tutors in the art of ritual magic; now he had taken up Buddhism, and gave Crowley an intensive course in yoga.[14] Following Bennett's example Crowley also engaged in a more intimate relation with Buddhism during his visit, and would subsequently consider himself a Buddhist for many years. Crowley would later make attempts to systematize and tabulate all the esoteric knowledge he had accumulated during his various trips and studies, incorporating them with the Golden Dawn teachings on Kabbalah and ritual magic. Notably, this project resulted in his book *777*, a set of tables showing correspondences between various systems modeled on the ten *sefirot* and twenty-two paths of the Kabbalistic Tree of Life, published in 1909.[15]

With hindsight, the most significant event of these years was nevertheless the 1904 "reception" of *Liber Legis*, the book that would become the founding document of Crowley's new religion, Thelema. As part of their honeymoon, Crowley and his first wife Rose Edith Crowley, née Kelly, had arrived in Cairo on February 9, where they would stay for several months.[16] During the stay, Rose apparently started to act strangely. Following a specific ritual evocation performed by Crowley on March 17, allegedly for no other reason than to impress Rose with his magical aptitude, she started to display a kind of mediumistic behavior. She began uttering strange, incoherent phrases to her husband, such as the ominous, "They are waiting for you," and, according to Crowley, making various fragmentary statements about "the child" and "Osiris."[17] This had apparently continued for several days, and Rose would soon reveal that it was the god Horus who had started to talk to her, and that he wanted to get in contact with Crowley.

On March 20, at the spring Equinox, Crowley arranged a ritual to invoke the Egyptian god in his particular form as Ra-Hoor-Khuit, the sun-god. During this ritual, Rose's apparent mediumship would reach its climax. Through her, Horus declared that the spring Equinox of 1904 signaled "the Equinox of the Gods," the moment in time where the previous "aeon" was to be replaced by a new one. More specifically, Osiris's two thousand years-old reign came to an end at the arrival of Horus's aeon, the aeon of "the Child." In Crowley's own interpretation of the event, he was now to establish contact with the "Secret Chiefs," the discarnate intelligences ruling the secret "Third Order" of the Golden Dawn. Despite their previous brief alliance during the tumultuous events of 1900, Crowley had fallen out with MacGregor Mathers, the earthly leader of the Order. Now, conveniently to say the least, Horus and the Secret Chiefs were calling upon Crowley to receive and devise new magical formulae and rituals suited for the New Aeon, and devise plans to destroy the old Order once and for all.[18] Over three days, from April 8 to April 10, Crowley would write the three chapters of *The Book of The Law,* making him the prophet of the New Aeon. This became the founding moment, and the foundation myth, of a new religious movement, Thelema.

As prophet of a new age, the Aeon of Horus, Crowley took great efforts to reform the magical and initiatory formulae of the now, in his view, outdated Golden Dawn. This led to new Thelemic versions of specific rituals taught in the Golden Dawn, such as the important magical rituals of the pentagram and hexagram, and naturally a drift of symbolic focus away from Osiris toward Horus.[19]

Crowley's vision of Thelema as a complete religious and magical philosophy took shape and solidified only several years after the unusual events in Cairo during the spring of 1904. In order to understand the place and function of magic in the work of Crowley, it is necessary to look somewhat closer at the ideas he developed for Thelema.

Magick for All

The Book of the Law and Crowley's numerous commentaries on it prophesize the end of "the Aeon of Osiris," a millennia-long period characterized by patriarchal and largely collectivist religions such as Christianity and Islam, and the coming of a new "Aeon of Horus" to replace it.[20] In this new aeon, a radical individualism is the new credo, and Thelema put forward as its only proper religion. Thelema's famous dictum is "Do What Thou Wilt," but one should quickly point out that this was not simply meant as a license to pursue any indulgence. Rather, Crowley's commentaries emphasized that it also implied the strictest possible discipline, since Thelemites are bound to discover their single "True Will" and follow it unconditionally.[21] This endeavor becomes the ultimate purpose of magic in the context of Thelema.

The True Will is said to transcend the subject's ordinary limitations for knowledge and self-knowledge, and magic is invoked as a tool for reaching this absolute knowledge of self. In Thelemic discourse the magical procedure that leads to knowledge of the True Will is variously referred to in alchemical and Hermetic terms as "the Great Work," or in a more mystical vein as the attainment of the "knowledge and conversation of the Holy Guardian Angel." Although various procedures should be possible, Crowley's preferred one was based on a seventeenth-century magical grimoire known as the Abramelin operation, from which the term Holy Guardian Angel was taken.[22]

With reference to this attainment, Crowley wrote that it

> is the essential Work of every man; none other ranks with it either for personal progress or for power to help one's fellows. This unachieved, man is no more than the unhappiest and blindest of animals. He is conscious of his own incomprehensible calamity, and clumsily incapable of repairing it. Achieved, he is no less than the co-heir of Gods, a Lord of Light. He is conscious of his own consecrated course, and confidently ready to run it.[23]

Only when this True Will has been discovered can the magician begin to make correct choices in life, binding him or herself to it as prescribed in the doctrines of Thelema. Only at the point when one's True Will is known can the more general laws of "magick" which Crowley wrote up be followed, where it is defined as "the Science and Art of causing Change to occur in conformity with Will."[24] Indeed, *magick*, spelt with a "k" to differentiate it from previous "superstitious" interpretations, becomes a complete "form of life."[25]

Crowley's take on magic springs out of his Golden Dawn training, but it is taken in a direction of personal development, and the laying down of a new ethics and a new religion when coupled with the Thelemic project. Institutionally, this synthesis was embedded in two different structures. In 1907 Crowley founded his own magical Order together with George Cecil Jones, the A∴A∴ (*Astron Argon*).[26] Officially launched with the first edition of the occult periodical *The Equinox* in 1909, this Order incorporated the grade structure and basic teachings of the Golden Dawn, but expanded it with Crowley's new take on magic as well as giving a central place for Thelema. Furthermore, its motto was "the Method of Science—the Aim of Religion," reflecting Crowley's insistence that his was a revised form of magic, adapted to conform to the methods and standards of science rather than the superstition characteristic of the earlier aeons.[27] Another important feature which differentiated the A∴A∴ from the Golden Dawn was that it was not intended to function socially in the same way; instead, it should be a school of intense and focused magical training based on a teacher-pupil relation.

In the years leading up to the Great War of 1914 Crowley launched a campaign to spread Thelema to all branches of society, hoping to establish it as a political force to be reckoned with. For this goal, a secretive magical society such as the A∴A∴ was inefficient; instead, Crowley availed himself of his newly acquired leading position in the German Neo-templar group Ordo Templi Orientis (O.T.O.).[28] In a process initiated by the Order's "Outer Head" Theodor Reuss between 1910 and 1912, Crowley was set to rewriting the O.T.O.'s rituals and doctrine, streamlining the initiation outline and making the Order fully operable. However, he also took this opportunity to thoroughly "thelemize" the Order, making it a new and more practically oriented vessel for spreading Crowley's radical social and religious vision. In 1923 Crowley succeeded Reuss as international leader of the O.T.O. (he had headed the British branch up to that point) and more fully emphasized the Order's role for promulgating the "Law of Thelema" and working as a kind of political avant-garde for the new Thelemic world order.[29] The campaign failed badly, however, and Crowley left a largely dysfunctional and splintered Order when he died in 1947.[30]

With this admittedly very basic overview of the doctrines and institutions of Thelema and the place of magic within it, we can proceed to the main task of this chapter: placing Crowley in an emerging post-Golden Dawn discourse on Enochiana.

The Enochian World of Aleister Crowley

When it comes to the subject of Enochian magic, Crowley's role as Thelemic prophet did not primarily manifest in attempts to "thelemize" the system. In a sense, Crowley stayed largely within the Golden Dawn framework of interpretation, while moving beyond it primarily through a partial "return to the sources" and pioneering attempts to incorporate other parts of the original material into magical practice. As seen earlier, not only did the Golden Dawn invent their own readings and interpretations, but they also used only a small portion of the magic available from the original sources as their basis. Their fascination had been with the Great Table, which lent itself easily to a fourfold interpretational scheme in which the elements and the Tetragrammaton figured centrally. Meanwhile, the Heptarchic system and the system of the Aires and the various calls in the Adamic language were left unused. Although the latter were mentioned in the Golden Dawn curriculum, they do not seem to have been implemented practically and deployed in rituals. The most influential contribution Crowley would bring to the development of Enochian magic was indeed to explore and give an explanation for the Aires, or "Aethyrs." It is with him that we find the first attempts at a more or less consistent theory of these entities and their connection to the elemental magic of the Golden Dawn's Great Table.

The relation between the angels of the Great Table and those of the thirty Aethyrs seems to have fascinated the young Crowley already during his short but intense stay with the Golden Dawn. In his autobiography, Crowley described a crude and not entirely successful Enochian experiment that took place in 1899–1900:

> In bed, I invoked the Fire angels and spirits on the tablet, with names, etc., and the 6th Key. I then (as Harpocrates) entered my crystal. An angel, meeting me, told me, among other things, that they (of the tablets) were *at war with the angels of the 30 Aethyrs, to prevent the squaring of the circle.* I went with him unto the abodes of fire, but must have fallen asleep, or nearly so. Anyhow, I regained consciousness in a very singular state, half consciousness being there, and half here. I recovered and banished the Spirits, but was burning all over, and tossed restlessly about—very sleepy, but consumed of Fire![31]

Working of course entirely within the Golden Dawn framework, which he was still at this point learning to master, Crowley had summoned an elemental angel from the Great Table, while "scrying in the spirit vision." Met by the "astral form" of one of the angels of fire, he was told that a celestial war was being waged between what seems to be two distinct types of angelic beings: those of the elemental tablets of the Great Table, and those of the Aethyrs. A subtle hint to the natures of these differing classes of angels can also be extracted from this passage. Since the strife of the warring parties was over "the squaring of the circle," that ancient mathematical and mystical problem, with the elementals striving *against* it and the Aethyrs working *for* it, it seems reasonable to assume that Crowley imagined the Aethyrs to be rather more spiritually profound than the elemental angels. Their agenda in this vision was, as it were, to work mathematical miracles.

Crowley would use both magic and scholarship in his quest to understand and flesh out the cosmology of the Enochian system, which must undoubtedly have seemed like the most profound thing the Golden Dawn had to offer. We know that at one point, possibly already during his Golden Dawn training, Allan Bennett passed him a copy of the Inner Order instruction *Book "H"* to study. This book, which we have seen to be a copy of the Sloane 307 manuscript, amended and abridged by Westcott, would have been a part of the instructions above Crowley's grade at the point, and he should not officially have been able to study it. Nevertheless, as Rankine and Skinner's reproduction of Bennett's copy show, Crowley did have access to it and even added some notes to the text himself.[32]

The system described here, we remember, was one of ritual magical evocation for various defined purposes, closely following the functions sat down in Dee's originals. While it does not seem as though Crowley tried to experiment with that system at this point, he found opportunities to explore the more mysterious Aethyrs after he dissociated himself from the Golden Dawn and embarked on his travels. Perhaps intrigued by the small glimpse of information he had gathered in his experiment earlier that year quoted above, Crowley set out to explore the Aethyrs more closely after arriving in Mexico in the autumn of 1900.[33]

On November 14 and 17 Crowley sat down to scry the two "lowest" Aethyrs, "TEX" (the 30th) and "RII" (29th), by calling the nineteenth Enochian key.[34] The result, Crowley would later describe, was "mysterious and terrific in character. What I saw was not beyond my previous experience, but what I heard was as unintelligible to me as Blake to a Baptist."[35] In the words of his recent biographer Richard Kaczynski, Crowley's visions were "surrealistic, apocalyptic, and bear the stamp of his evangelical upbringing."[36] In his second attempt, for instance, Crowley saw an immense angel approaching, with eagle wings hiding all the heavens. The angel spoke in that recognizable ancient tone of fire and brimstone:

> Cursed, cursed be the Earth, for her iniquity is great. Oh Lord! Let Thy Mercy be lost in the great Deep! Open thine eyes of Flame and Light, O God, upon the wicked! Lighten thine Eyes! The Clamour of Thy Voice, let it smite down the Mountains![37]

After this the exploration of the Aethyrs would be discontinued for almost a decade, until his famous 1909 Algerian adventure.

Algeria, 1909

We shall now turn to the events in the desert of Algeria. On November 17, 1909, Crowley arrived at the sprawling north African city of Algiers together with his pupil and lover, the poet Victor Neuburg. The trip was claimed to be purely recreational in intent, but ended with Crowley reporting a set of twenty-eight visions, which would since rank among the most important sources of revealed doctrine in Thelema, second only to *The Book of the Law* itself.[38]

The visions and voices only manifested after Crowley found his old notebook from the Aethyric experiments in Mexico, almost a decade earlier. Despite denying premeditation of his new attempt to scry the Aethyrs, it is quite clear that Enochiana had not simply faded from Crowley's attention over the interceding years. In fact, several of his activities between 1900 and 1909 reveal a continued interest in the Enochian material. When Crowley edited Mathers's manuscript translation and abridgement of the *Lesser Key of Solomon,* or *Goetia,* in 1904, he added his own translation of the accompanying conjurations from English into the profound "Angelic language" of Enochian.[39] Even more important, unpublished sources show that Crowley engaged in a close study of the original Dee material just prior to his departure with Neuburg to Algeria. On October 30, 1909, Crowley wrote in a letter to his A.∴A.∴ companion J. F. C. Fuller that he had been doing research into the Enochian documents at the Bodleian Library in Oxford.[40] This is significant considering Crowley's claim that there was no premeditation behind the magical experiments that followed only a few months after his research trip.[41] As it turns out, Crowley had planned to include a longer essay expounding on the Enochian system for his new occult review, *The Equinox,* already during the summer of 1909. In fact, it was while looking for his old Enochian tablets (and a pair of skis) in the attic during that summer that Crowley rediscovered the original manuscript of *The Book of the Law*—an anecdote often told in the Thelemic literature.

The trips to Oxford and Algeria were part of the same research project into Enochiana; the first scholarly and theoretical, the second practical and experiential.[42] The overall project did amount in two works which have since become classics of the modern Enochian literature, published a few years later.[43] As I will argue, the trademark of Crowley's approach consisted in innovation grounded in a personal, experiential exploration of the system, only occasionally restrained by a scholarly reassessment of sources.

Being the first magician after the Golden Dawn to fully combine archival research with practical experiments in Enochian magic, Crowley also seems to have been the first to experience the post–Golden Dawn authenticity problem. This may, indeed, have happened during his Oxford research trip. In Oxford Crowley had the opportunity to study Elias Ashmole's copies of Dee's "revealed books," including the system of the Aethyrs portrayed in *Liber Scientiae,* studiously presented in Ashmole's hand.[44] Perhaps it was here that Crowley discovered the "most discomforting disenchantment" about the system of the Aethyrs, namely that the original document seemed to attribute the entities simply to "aires" or "climes" of the world, corresponding to angels governing various geographical regions and peoples.[45]

As was mentioned earlier, Crowley did not favor this interpretation himself, even after being confronted with and recognizing it. This can be seen in the specific editorial choices he took when finally publishing his exposition of Enochian magic in *The Equinox* in 1912. Not only did Crowley omit references to the anomalous *Liber Scientiae* when presenting the Aethyrs in his classic essay "Liber Chanokh,"[46] but he also chose, conveniently, to "omit for the present consideration of the parts of the earth to which they are stated to correspond."[47] Instead of that stated correspondence, Crowley went on to discuss "the Thirty Aethyrs whose dominion extendeth in ever-widening circles without and beyond the Watch Towers of the Universe."[48] In doing so, Crowley is seen to follow an interpretation more consistent with the Golden Dawn tradition, viewing the Aethyrs as subtle spiritual layers outside of the elemental realm, accessible with the use of the nineteenth Enochian call and certain techniques for scrying in the astral.

The experiments in Algeria were indeed an opportunity to work from within this frame of interpretation. The method Crowley employed in the desert with Neuburg was to use a golden topaz stone set in a wooden Calvary cross as a focus for scrying, in Crowley's own words playing a part "not unlike that of the looking-glass in the case of Alice."[49] While gazing into the spiritual realm of a given Aethyr he reported being filled with visions and voices speaking to him, the appearance of angels and other spiritual creatures—as had been the case already in Mexico in 1900. All of these sights and sounds he dictated to Neuburg on the spot, who was charged with writing the whole spectacle down. The outcome of these visionary episodes was published as a special supplement to *The Equinox* in 1911, under the title of *The Vision and the Voice*.[50]

The actions recorded were indeed spectacular. In a recent reconstruction, Richard Kaczynski describes the method of obtaining the visions in the following way:

> A.C. removed his scarlet cavalry [*sic*] cross, a pin inset with a huge topaz inscribed with a rose cross. He gazed into the stone while concentrating on his third eye, the *ajna chakra*, and, when he felt prepared to receive a vision, he began the 28th Call in the Angelic Language: *"Madrax da-es perafe BAG cahis mihaolzed sanit caosgo odeh fisisah balzed izedrase Iaidah!"*[51]

The topaz stone in his necklace rose-cross was used as a substitute for the "shewstone," which Edward Kelley had used to commune with the spirits. An active and ordered use of the imagination, furthermore, played an important part in accessing these ostensible magical "realms." As Crowley noted in his *Confessions*:

> I had learned not to trouble myself to travel to any desired place in the astral body. I realized that space was not a thing in itself, merely a convenient category (one of many such) by reference to which we

> can distinguish objects from each other. When I say I was in any Aethyr, I simply mean in the state characteristic of, and peculiar to, its nature.[52]

Not only does this quote show Crowley applying a Kantian perspective to the magical theories of astral travel, but it also tells something of the nature of the visionary experiences. He would retain his spatial and temporal awareness while "drawing down" these visions to the scrutiny of his imagination. "Remaining in his body," Crowley would describe and speak out in words the visions he had to Victor Neuburg, who promptly wrote it down in his notebook.[53] As a general rule, one Aethyr was invoked in this way each day while the companions marched across the desert, with some days performing two, others none. Each of these sessions typically lasted about an hour or so.

In the visions Crowley would encounter angels and heavenly beings, taken through initiations and shown to "the City of the Pyramids," where the highest adepts dwelled. Content-wise, the bulk of the visions were close to the ones reported nine years earlier in Mexico. There were some exceptions, however. Sometimes the "visions" would take on an astonishing complexity, and even involve strange synaesthetic experiences. This sensual richness can be found in the invocation of the twenty-first Aethyr on November 29. In the transcription of this session, Crowley encounters an enthroned but invisible deity, which tries to communicate with him primarily through taste sensations:

> He [the deity] is trying to make me understand by putting tastes in my mouth, very rapidly one after the other. Salt, honey, sugar, asafoetida, bitumen, honey again, some taste that I don't know at all; garlic, something very bitter like nux vomica, another taste, still more bitter; lemon, cloves, rose-leaves, honey again; the juice of some plant, like a dandelion, I think; honey again, salt, a taste something like phosphorous, honey, laurel, a very unpleasant taste which I don't know, coffee, then a burning taste, then a sour taste that I don't know. All these tastes issue from his eyes; he *signals* them.[54]

Later, Crowley connected these tastes with astrological and Kabbalistic symbolism. In an extreme example of the kind of Kabbalistic hermeneutic Crowley would recommend for his Scientific Illuminism, these translations led to a "decipherment" of the deity's signals, even revealing an apparent message in text![55]

The most enduring event was nevertheless the apocalyptic encounter in the desert with the demon Choronzon. As we learned in chapter 2, the name of this demon comes from Dee and Kelley's records. There its name had been spelled "Coronzom," which in turn morphed into "Coronzon" in Casaubon's published version of the same manuscript. As mentioned in that chapter, Crowley's spelling betrays the influence of the Sloane 307 manuscript, which, we saw in chapter 3, the Golden Dawn had used as one of its original sources.

Spelling and provenance aside, the demon fully entered the mythology of modern occultism following Crowley and Neuburg's invocation of the tenth Aethyr, performed December 6, at night, "in a lonely valley of fine sand, in the desert near Bou-Saada."[56] Due to the somewhat cryptic, fragmentary, and partially conflicting records of this action, it is hard to tell what really went on this evening; on any reading, it was definitely different from the earlier invocations.[57]

Through the previous visions Crowley had learned that he was about to cross the so-called Abyss, an abstract Kabbalistic concept designed to signify the "space" between the three upper *sefirot* and the lower seven, or the unbridgeable space between godliness and manifested individuation. Passing through the Abyss meant the destruction of one's own ego in order to attain a state where one's individuation dissolves and mystical union is attained.[58] In Crowley's system of magic, this crossing is correlated with the so-called dark night of the soul, a term originating with the sixteenth-century Christian mystic St. John of the Cross. In the visions of the eleventh Aethyr (the one immediately preceding the tenth, since they are invoked from the last to the first), Crowley was told that the crossing of the Abyss involved an encounter with the malicious demon Choronzon, who resided there.[59]

Knowing that this encounter was at hand, the method of working was changed accordingly. A complete temple for ritual evocation was set up, in accordance with the standard methods provided by the grimoire tradition of the *Goetia*.[60] A protective circle was built out of stones, enforced with divine names, and east of it a triangle was erected, where the demon was to appear.[61] Although the records are unclear about this, it seems likely that after Crowley and Neuburg had performed the preparatory banishing rituals Neuburg stayed in the center of the circle and took the role of magus, while Crowley took his place in the triangle itself. About to take up position as a material basis for the spirit to materialize in, Crowley proceeded with the invocation of the Enochian Aethyr as usual. Instead of having a vision, however, he was now "possessed" by the demon Choronzon himself, who would speak through him and threaten and test Neuburg's skills and willpower.[62]

The account that followed is somewhat confusing. While Neuburg stands in the circle and commands the demon/Crowley to speak, the demon is said to take on different forms and shapes; variously, Neuburg reported to have been encountered by a girl he had fallen in love with, by Crowley himself, and by a snake with a human head.[63] It would seem that these figures appeared outside of the circle and the triangle, attempting to distract and overcome the mage by appealing to his various emotions. Even more exceptionally, Choronzon the demon would at one point start to talk very fast through Crowley, spouting gibberish, with the goal of keeping the scribe occupied with writing everything down. While Neuburg was busy keeping his records, the demon/Crowley would throw sand on the circle in order to eradicate it and break the magician's protective barrier.[64] Just when Neuburg became aware of the scheme, the demon, purportedly in the form of a ferocious "savage," leapt upon him, biting for his neck with sharp fangs. Only by yelling divine names and stabbing the demon with his magically consecrated dagger did Neuburg repel the attacker and confine him to his triangle once again.[65] What actually occurred during these dramatic minutes remains unclear; however, Lawrence Sutin is probably right in pointing out that the most reasonable solution is that Crowley, behaving possessed, actually jumped upon Neuburg the magician.[66]

No doubt, these experiences made a great impact on Crowley and his followers. Alex Owen even argues that Crowley's personal and material problems in the aftermath of the operations in the desert are a sign that his "crossing of the Abyss" was in fact a failure: the demon had consumed his soul, and consequently he lost his grip on reality.[67] It certainly looks awkward when the academic historian passes judgment on the success or failure of a rite like this. It even seems that Owen, in her search for a psychologized interpretation of Crowley and his magic, is driven to pass over or ignore Crowley's own interpretation of the rituals' significance and relation to later events. In *Confessions* Crowley noted that his later problems in the "real world" were actually an expected outcome of a *successful* crossing: "Part of the effect of crossing the Abyss is that it takes a long time to connect the Master with what is left below the Abyss."[68] The disorientation resulting from the attainment of magical genius may look a lot like personal disintegration. In Crowley's understanding there is a fine line distinguishing prophets from madmen. For himself, he claimed nothing short of prophethood.

When heading back for Britain, Crowley reported in a letter that "we have the Apocalypse beaten to a frazzle. . . . This is the holiday-holyday of my whole life."[69] As we shall see, the apocalyptic madness in the desert would indeed lead to specific doctrinal innovations within the religion he revealed to the world.

The Enochian Aethyrs and Thelemic Religion: Crowley on Authenticity

In 1911 Crowley designed an authoritative curriculum for his magical order A∴A∴, based on a classification of four different kinds of texts, ranging from A through D.[70] Each class of literature reflected both the method of production and the authority of the texts belonging to it. Class A documents were considered "received" works which had the highest authority; their real authorship should be attributed to "the Secret Chiefs" of the Great White Brotherhood rather than the material person Crowley. *The Book of the Law* was the main representative of this category. The collection of visions resulting from the Enochian experiments with the Aethyrs, however, were classed as both A *and* B. The A status reflects that the document was held to contain material considered "received," while it also brought commentaries reflecting on that received material.[71]

The A∴A∴ syllabus furthermore gave a short note for each text, describing its particular relevance. The description for *The Vision and the Voice* declared that the doctrinal content conveyed by the entities in the visions was uniquely authentic:

> Besides being the classical account of the thirty Aethyrs and a model of all visions, the cries of the Angels should be regarded as accurate, and the doctrine of the function of the Great White Brotherhood understood as the foundation of the Aspiration of the Adept. The account of the Master of the Temple should in particular be taken as authentic. The instruction in the 8th Aethyr pertains to Class D, "i.e." it is an Official Ritual, and the same remarks apply to the account of the proper method of invoking Aethyrs given in the 18th Aethyr.[72]

The realms of the Aethyrs accessed by Crowley are considered so spiritually sublime that information acquired there is given a uniquely profound status. Visions endowed by Enochian angels about particular spiritual issues, such as the offices of a "Master of the Temple" (i.e., the eighth degree in Crowley's magical system, and the third highest one), are to "be taken as authentic," while other commands form the basis for official rituals within Crowley's magical system. Additionally, important aspects of what would become a Thelemic theology were revealed by these entities, and expressed through rituals and creeds.[73]

One clear example is found in the Gnostic mass which Crowley wrote up for his Gnostic Catholic Church *(Ecclesia Gnostica Catholica)* in 1913.[74] Crowley designed the mass as an exoteric celebration of the esoteric secrets of the O.T.O., making the sexual symbolism of that secret one of the major themes of the mass' liturgy. By extension, the mass became, and still remains, the most central religious ceremony of Thelema today.[75] What interests us here is that much of the sexual theme of the mass's liturgy centers on two godlike entities which are not found in *The Book of the Law:* the male entity "Chaos" and the female goddess "Babalon."[76] Both of these entities were introduced properly for the first time in the Enochian visions.[77] In these visions, the two "deities" or "entities" are interlinked with certain Kabbalistic representations from the Tree of Life. In the fourth Aethyr, Chaos is attributed to the sefirah *hokmah* ("wisdom"), and Babalon to *binah* ("understanding"), that is, to the second and third sefira respectively.[78] The two deities are seen as the very first manifestation of a dual principle, with a male and female polarity. Thus, this is also a primeval cosmological manifestation of sexuality. In the liturgy of the Gnostic mass, Babalon is described as a universal womb, while Chaos is "the sole viceregent of the Sun." The implication of this is the sort of solar-phallicism associated with Richard Payne Knight, Hargrave Jennings, and others; a religious stance that is central to the mysteries of the O.T.O.[79] Through Crowley's experiential exploration of the Enochian system, and the subsequent and accompanying innovations made to it, Enochiana has become centrally inscribed in Thelemic religion.

Crowley's take on the Aethyrs is important in another respect as well, namely, for the *initiatic quality* that he attributes to working magic with these sublime astral entities. Crowley significantly claimed to have received his initiation into the Magister Templi degree of the A∴A∴ while traveling in these occult lands, and we have seen that the description of its function given in the records later became official teaching in the order.[80] The initiatic theme has had a significant reception in occultism after Crowley, as we will see in later chapters of this book, but it also played an important role in Crowley's quest for legitimating his position in the broader occultist milieu. We have already seen that he claimed *The Vision and the Voice* to be "the classical account of the thirty Aethyrs," and the "model of all visions." Combined with the fact that Crowley was the first to incorporate the Enochian system of the Aethyrs into modern occultism, this has effected the perpetuation of his interpretation of the system at the expense of the original, but by some standards perhaps less spiritually sublime, system portrayed in Dee's *Liber scientiae*.

* * *

At this point we should return to what was mentioned earlier, namely, that Crowley was the first magician after the Golden Dawn to encounter and struggle with "the authenticity problem" as formulated in the previous chapter. It is also in his work that we first encounter the full play of strategies that we have introduced and discussed in chapter 4. Dissatisfied with the Golden Dawn curriculum, Crowley took it upon himself to do research into the original sources. When the evidence of the sources he researched conflicted with the perennialist outlook of the Golden Dawn's frame of interpretation, Crowley would nevertheless favor the latter. At the same time, he is at several instances seen to give more or less pragmatic arguments when the authenticity problem arises. Writing about the Enochian language, Crowley first assures his readers that this is an authentic language:

> The conjurations of Dr. Dee are in a language called Angelic, or Enochian. Its source has hitherto baffled research, but it is a language and not a jargon, for it possesses a structure of its own, and there are traces of grammar and syntax. In any case it is probably corrupt.[81]

But then the argument suddenly switches from authenticity to pragmatics:

> However this may be, it *works*. Even the beginner finds that "things happen" when he uses it: and this is an advantage—or disadvantage!—shared by no other type of language. The rest need skill. This needs prudence![82]

From this twofold argumentation we first read quite explicitly that the power of the Enochian language qua magical language is *not* conventional or pragmatic as such; that is, Enochian is "real" and not simply "a jargon." But in the absence of definite evidence, there is an appeal to the ostensible fact that "it *works*." At the same time, it is also clear that the language is conceived to work *because* of its sublime nature. Thus, the pragmatic appeal to experience does not entirely sidestep the issue of provenance; instead, the experiential argument is designed to support the exceptional claims about the language and system.

As an example, "the angels themselves" hinted to a perennialist interpretation in Crowley's visions of the Aethyrs. Referring to Edward Kelley, Crowley was told that "this is a holy mystery, and he that did first attain to reveal the alphabet thereof [i.e., of the Angelic language], perceived not one ten-thousandth part of the fringe that is upon its vesture."[83] The very provenance of Enochiana lies outside of this world, and its profundity greatly surpasses the insight of even the first historical "receivers," Kelley and Dee. Crowley's legitimization of the system rests in the end on perennialism, asserting its highly enchanted quality. Furthermore, the specific kind of perennialism adopted opens up for continued revelations, which may supersede those of Dee and Kelley and serve as basis for revisions in the system. As we saw already, the continued Enochian prophetic tradition was conveniently perceived as resting in the hands of the prophet of the new aeon and Thelema himself.

A Note on the Crowleyan Heritage

Crowley left a magical heritage that may be viewed as exclusively Thelemic, involving trafficking with idiosyncratic entities, and the performance of rituals that were revised or entirely invented by him, and most importantly, embedded within a Thelemic framework in which the most central aims are the discovery of the "True Will" and the attainment of "Knowledge and Conversation with the Holy Guardian Angel." Examples of such explicitly "Thelemic magic" may be found in Lon Milo DuQuette's *The Magick of Thelema* (1994), Rodney Orpheus's *Abrahadabra* (1995), both of which seek to provide a more or less unified and accessible picture, and more recently in J. Daniel Gunther's *Initiation in the Aeon of the Child* (2009).[84]

Within this "Thelemic school" of ritual magic, one does not generally find one specific take on Enochiana, as an independent and stable system. Rather, elements of Enochian magic are incorporated into other systems in a synthetic approach similar to that of the Golden Dawn. Perhaps the clearest and most grand scale example of this is the tendency to attribute the Aethyrs to the paths and *sefirot* of the Kabbalistic "Tree of Life,"[85] and the widespread opinion that the Aethyrs represent an "Enochian path-working,"[86] comparable in all respects to the practice of Kabbalistic path-workings popularized through the Golden Dawn.[87] In addition is the quite common conception of Enochian, both elemental and Aethyric, as an initiatory tool. This is prefigured in Crowley, who, as we have seen, claimed to have his Master of the Temple initiation through the Aethyrs. The initiatory theme is clearly present, among other places, in a recent publication by the Thelemite "Frater W.I.T." (Scott Brush), tellingly entitled *Enochian Initiation* (2006).[88]

But Crowley's influence on these points reaches far beyond the borders of Thelema. It is not without justification to claim that a kind of Weberian "routinization of charisma" has taken place within modern occultism at large with regard to Crowley and his innovations. His "charismatic" revelations are taken as authoritative in several different movements. As part of this general routinization, Crowley's experiments with the Aethyrs have become paradigmatic in other occult currents. Crowley's influence on later developments of modern Enochian magic has therefore been significant, and we will see it again in due course.

6
Angels of Satan

The critical reader would perhaps find a reputedly angelic language embedded in self-styled Satanism to constitute a supreme incongruity. Nevertheless, when Anton Szandor LaVey (born Howard Stanton Levey; 1930–1997) published the *Satanic Bible* at the close of 1969, the Enochian calls, taken from the version published by Crowley in *The Equinox,* occupied its closing section. Instead of viewing this inclusion as an inconsistency stemming from rampant eclecticism I submit that it should be viewed as part of a strategy for positioning oneself in the magic current after the Golden Dawn, while maintaining a high degree of friction with it. In LaVey's satanic version of the Enochian calls, every reference to "God" or "Heaven" in the English translations had been substituted for the suitable infernal counterparts, "Satan" and "Hell."[1] Furthermore, as the Satanic worldview draws heavily from secular-materialist outlooks, LaVey gives interpretations of magical efficacy that are far less metaphysically charged than those considered so far. As we shall see in the present chapter, the "satanization" of Enochiana infuriated certain prominent figures in the established esoteric milieu, notably Israel Regardie.

The emergence of a satanic variety of Enochian magic added significantly to the contestation of that purportedly angelic system. Through the present chapter we will see how these contests for legitimacy and interpretive authority emerge as intrinsically bound to a wider struggle between various groups, people, and institutions in the occultural milieu. Modern Satanism emerged out of a milieu where occultists of various shades were already deeply entwined in polemics about the nature of various occult and magical practices. Particularly in the United States, the various splinter groups of the Golden Dawn were fighting among themselves, and with the remaining and new Thelemites. In the first part of this chapter I will take a closer look at some of the struggles over the nature and authenticity of Enochian magic in the middle of these clashes. Against this background I go on to place special emphasis on how Satanism's ambiguous relation to these magical groups, and the wider cultural impulse from Western esotericism, formed the interpretation of the Enochian system given by LaVey.

But this is not all that controversy has to do with reception and reinterpretation. Enochiana did not only play a central part in polemics with external groups and spokespersons—the "esoteric Others" of Satanism—but it also featured centrally in the foremost doctrinal split *within* early Satanism, namely between Anton LaVey's Church of Satan and Michael Aquino's splinter group, the Temple of Set. This schism, as we will see, had organizational reasons as well as doctrinal ones. In place of the rationalistic outlook of LaVey, Aquino came to develop an increasingly more esoteric worldview—a feature that is readily apparent in his interpretation and use of the Enochian system as well. I will begin, however, by going back to the significant context provided by the fall of the Golden Dawn, and the many controversies arising there over the "correct" interpretation of the Enochian material.

Background: Schismatic Golden Dawn Groups and Enochian Controversies

Crowley and the A.∴A.∴ was far from the only trajectory carrying on the magical paradigm of the Golden Dawn, and not even the most direct one. When the dust began to settle after the breakup of the original Golden Dawn, three main schismatic groups continued the legacy in various forms: The Independent and Rectified Rite of the Golden Dawn, headed by A. E. Waite; the Stella Matutina, led by R. W. Felkin; and the continued lineage of MacGregor Mathers and those (including, from ca. 1908, J. W. Brodie-Innes) still loyal to his leadership, the Alpha et Omega.[2]

While it falls well outside the present scope to deal in detail with these various splinter groups,[3] I wish to focus on a specific case: a controversy that sheds interesting light on conceptualizations of magic and occult entities in the modern age generally, and on Enochiana especially. Furthermore, this helps us frame Enochiana within its relevant discursive and polemical context.

Before I introduce the controversy, there are a couple of remarks to be made about the various splinter groups that form the context of it. One should know, for instance, that A. E. Waite's group, The Independent and Rectified Rite, aimed to extinguish the practice of ritual magic altogether, and instead focus deeply on a sort of Christian mysticism.[4] As such, it is of less interest for the history and development of Enochian magic. Stella

Matutina, on the other hand, sought to continue the magical practice. It was papers from this faction that were published by Regardie (who had joined in 1934) in the late 1930s. It is also through a particular lineage of the Stella Matutina that knowledge of Enochian chess, discussed in an earlier chapter, was transmitted. Regardie complained in his *Golden Dawn* that none of the adepts he ever met could give any sufficient answers as to what were the rules and function of this most esoteric board game.[5] His major problem was that R. W. Felkin, who was the leader and most accomplished magician of this lineage, had moved to New Zealand during the Great War. In 1916 Felkin took up permanent residence there, and established the Smaragdine Thalasses Temple of the Stella Matutina.[6] It was from recovered papers and conversations with members of this group that Chris Zalewski, many decades later, was able to reconstruct the four-handed divinatory esoteric chess game, later published as *Enochian Chess of the Golden Dawn* (1994).[7]

The Alpha et Omega (A.O.) group similarly sought to continue the magical heritage of the original order under MacGregor Mathers's leadership. This group would become the meeting place for several influential characters in twentieth-century occultism, and give birth to a couple of important offshoot groups. Two of the characters were Violet Mary Firth (1890–1946), better known under her occult pen name Dion Fortune, and Paul Foster Case (1884–1954). Fortune would found her Fraternity of the Inner Light in 1922, after falling out with Moina Mathers, whereas Case, also falling out with Moina that year, founded the Builders of the Adytum (B.O.T.A.) based on the A.O.'s New York temple. The B.O.T.A. soon conducted one of the most successful occult correspondence courses to that time.[8]

Both Fortune and Case were initiated into the A.O. in the wake of MacGregor Mathers's death in 1918, under Moina Mathers's somewhat clumsy attempts at keeping it running.[9] Bringing up various criticisms of both leadership and doctrine, they contributed to the disruption of the Order and Moina's loss of leadership. What is interesting for us is that, in Case's criticism of the Order, we find a series of remarks concerning the Enochian system of magic, on which he held a view that was quite untypical.

"Disintegrations of Mind or Body": P. F. Case and the Spiritual Dangers of Enochiana

Probably due to increasingly diverting views on occult theories and practices Case, based in the A.O.'s New York temple, started to drift away from Moina Mathers in Paris. According to the correspondence they exchanged in the early 1920s, it appears that Moina was concerned with some of Case's teachings, especially on what she termed "the Sex Theory" and "sex matters."[10] It has been suggested that Case was divulging occult secrets concerning what may have been a sexual magical theory belonging to the highest degrees of the Second Order.[11] However, if such a theory really existed within the Golden Dawn at this time, any direct evidence of it, such as notes or records of experiments, are lost. The lack of any definite evidence may be reason enough to doubt that there ever was a Golden Dawn sexual magic. It is, perhaps, more likely that Moina reacted to Case's attempts to *introduce* such theories, which were, after all, quite abundant in the occult milieu of the times, into his local A.O. temple. At any rate, as the dispute continued and increased in gravity, Case declared his resignation from the order in 1922, while Moina, on her part, threw him out.[12]

If teachings of a sexual nature were one of the diverging points of Case's teachings, it was not the only one. Interesting insights into Case's thoughts on the Golden Dawn teachings and tradition is found in a letter correspondence between him and Israel Regardie dating from 1933.[13] This correspondence is also of great importance since it shows Regardie's search for answers about the Golden Dawn one year prior to his admittance into the Stella Matutina. He had then served as Crowley's secretary since 1928, and knew the Golden Dawn material through the publications in *The Equinox*. He had even reproduced and published some of this material himself in 1932, a publication that was scorned by the A.O. while somewhat ambivalently welcomed by the Stella Matutina.[14]

Case's letters to Regardie spell out the view of the former on the legitimacy of the original Golden Dawn, and defend the most drastic changes done by his own American B.O.T.A. Particularly, his defense involved a stronger focus on the Rosicrucian heritage, the Kabbalah, and the Tarot, while the Enochian symbolism so present in the original G.D. had been removed entirely.[15] Case's arguments for removing the Enochian system and magic altogether were several, ranging from the fear of metaphysical devastation to a curious stance of purism. The latter is succinctly expressed in the following formulation:

> I submit that "orthodoxy" simply means "correct teaching" and that the burden of my criticism is that MacGregor (and nobody else) introduced alien elements into the stream which seems to have come to us through Mackenzie, Levi and their contemporaries. In eliminating the Enochian elements, we in America have lost nothing of practical effectiveness.[16]

The "correct teaching" Case refers to is obviously what he conceived of as a "pure" Rosicrucianism. As he further explained to Regardie, Case preferred to play safe "by eliminating from the rituals something that is certainly suspect as coming from a dubious source, by no means clearly connected with 'Rosicrucianism.'"[17] It seems that Case either did not know, or did not consider, that the Enochian elements of the Golden Dawn actually came through the allegedly Rosicrucian Cipher MS; unless he was happy to contend that the MS was fraudulent. For the original Golden Dawn the Enochian material was very much a *part* of the Rosicrucian heritage, playing for instance a major role in the Vault and Adeptus Minor ceremonies, with all their emphasis on the Rosicrucian theme. There, the candidate was told that the Enochian language was part of the knowledge collected by Christian Rosenkreutz, thus preceding Dee and Kelley by several centuries.[18] Today it may of course also be added that blaming Mathers for eclecticism while regarding Mackenzie and Lévi as representing a "pure" current is somewhat ironic; we now know that it was probably Mackenzie himself who was responsible for introducing the "alien element" of Enochian into modern occultism through the Cipher MS, and certainly Lévi can be attributed with the role of initiating the mode of "programmatic syncretism" so prominent in modern occultism, including the Golden Dawn.[19]

At any rate, Rosicrucian purism was not the only basis for Case's reservations. When he asserted that his American branch had not lost anything "of practical effectiveness" by leaving out the Enochian elements, he did not mean that Enochian magic was without any magical potency. On the contrary; Case warned Regardie that he personally believed the performance of G.D. Enochian magic was responsible for "serious disintegrations of mind or body" in as many as twenty-five or more magicians that he had known.[20] The most famous example of this unfortunate consequence Case found in Aleister Crowley; the "personal shipwreck" and "disintegration of that great genius" he attributed to the practice of Enochian magic. Here he was probably referring to the experiments with the Aethyrs in the Algerian desert, the negative magical efficacy of which we have even seen defended in a semiserious way by a later academic commentator.[21] Perhaps contradictorily, Case did most certainly assert the magical efficacy of Enochian, even though in other places he hinted toward the possible artificiality of the Enochian language by stating that "it is not beyond the power of man to invent a coherent language."[22]

Case does seem to go in somewhat diverging directions in his criticism of Enochian, sometimes insinuating that it may be a fraudulent fiction produced by Edward Kelley and reintroduced by Mathers, and other times accentuating the spiritual danger he associated with working it. At any rate it seems to me that the criticism of possible fraud is primarily to be read as a criticism leveled against the *perennialist* interpretation of Enochian; what Case *clearly* does, besides expressing his fears of the system's effect, is to historicize and situate it in the context of Dee and Kelley once more, something which for him withdraws it from any Rosicrucian connections. Thus, with reference to my discussion of the authenticity problem, we do actually find Case to represent a sort of historical purism. Interestingly, this is not only a "negative purism," discrediting Enochiana for *not* being Rosicrucian. Case also writes in the letters to Regardie that one of the actual reasons why the system is potentially dangerous is that, in the Golden Dawn tradition, it is mixed and fused with so many other systems:

> If the Order's method of evoking the elementals were *purely Enochian,* then I should have nothing to say. But since it is a mixture of the Enochian language and tablets with other, and probably older, materials, it seems not unlikely to me that such success as attends the use of the rituals is due to the real effectiveness of the various pentagrams, etc., than to anything else.[23]

Following in this vein and making sure that the problem is the danger he associates with the eclecticism of Golden Dawn Enochian magic, Case reassures that "my objections are not to ceremonial. It is only that I have had so much experience of the subtle dangers of *corrupt* ceremonial."[24]

The B.O.T.A., which still exists today with headquarter in Los Angeles and groups in Europe, New Zealand, and the United States, still adheres considerably to Case's teachings, and does not endorse Enochian magic in any form.[25]

Regardie and the Stella Matutina: Some Golden Dawn Perennialist Responses

The Golden Dawn had cast itself as the modern executor of a perennial Rosicrucian tradition, of which the Enochian material was a significant part. A consequence of this perennialism has been that interpretations of the material that were close to the original Renaissance meaning became way too mundane to meet the occultists' expectations of profound, perennial wisdom. As we saw in chapter 3, this led Regardie to edit out the one single document in the Golden Dawn Enochian corpus that described magical practices in accord with what we find in the original sources. This stance was not directly compatible with an emphasis on the actual historical origin of the material in John Dee's diaries; thus, in addition to the case of Regardie's editing, we also find that information on the provenance itself is completely left out of the Golden Dawn initiation rituals, in favor of more esoteric historiographies. This seems to have worked well in the heyday of the Order, but how to defend the practice and the perennialist interpretation when the purist attack has been made and is gaining ground in a more—as far as occultism goes—public sphere? And, given the Rosicrucian myth, how to explain that the Enochian material emerged for the first time with Dee and Kelley at the close of the sixteenth century, decades before the appearance of the Rosicrucian manifestos?

One particularly esoteric response has been to set "clairvoyants" on the case, to scry the "correct" history of the Angelic system. In his publication of Stella Matutina material in 1937–1940 Regardie included the results of one such approach.[26] Here, the Order's clairvoyants claimed that Dee and Kelley had gained access to the Enochian system only when they were in Central Europe, through contact with alleged Rosicrucian centers in Germany, Austria, and Bohemia.[27] Of course, this claim does not convince the historian, nor a purist with a good overview of the original sources, since it clearly leaves out the accounts given by Dee and Kelley themselves (the reception of the Enochian material started already in London, for instance). In addition, historically there was no Rosicrucianism before the seventeeth century, even though the emic historiography of modern esoteric movements commonly takes the claims of the *Fama Fraternitatis* at face value, and hence dates the foundation of Rosicrucianism to the legendary frater Christian Rosenkreutz in the fifteenth century.[28] The Golden Dawn was certainly no exception. The claim made by still other clairvoyants referenced by Regardie—that Enochian magic is part of a system originally practiced in Atlantis—is no more sober.[29]

Another strategy was to emphasize the importance of the Enochian language, with the claim that it really was a genuine, "natural language." If this could be established, one could start looking for evidence of it predating Dee and Kelley. An interesting document taking this approach is one of the so-called "side lectures" for the grade of Zelator, written by J. W. Brodie-Innes.[30] His speech directed at the new Zelatores reached aspirants who had just recently been introduced to the perplexing letter squares of the Earth Tablet in their initiation ritual. In the lecture, Brodie-Innes explained that the letters on the tablet they had seen had been transliterated from another script, "one of the most ancient symbols in the world."[31] The reference is clearly to the Enochian alphabet. He continued to reveal that the language in question was "a great curiosity merely from the linguistic point of view," because he claimed it was a real language, with real syntax, grammar, and semantics, but yet one that was not proved to have been spoken "by mortal man."[32] Brodie-Innes went on to suggest that it was a primordial, but "hidden," language, never known in *entirety* in historical times:

> We find traces of it on rock-cut pillars and on temples, apparently as old as the world. We find traces of it in the sacred mysteries of some of the oldest religions in the world, but we find no trace of it ever having been used as a living language, and we hold the tradition that it is the Angelic secret language.[33]

The implication is that the language has been known and used by the angels since creation, while drops of it have become known to humanity through history and distorted through time. Brodie-Innes gave one example:

> The high priest of Jupiter in the earliest days of Rome was called Flamen *Dialis,* and you will find that the most learned are utterly ignorant as to whence came the word *Dialis*. They will tell you that it is ancient Etruscan, but beyond that they can tell you nothing. It is not the genitive of any known nominative. On that Tablet (Earth) you will see that the second of the Three Holy Secret Names of God is *Dial*.[34]

By insinuating that Etruscan words are derived from Enochian, one holds on to the idea that the genealogy of the Enochian language itself is the best evidence for its primordial provenance.

If Brodie-Innes laid the foundation of this line of argument, it has been frequently raised again by others eager to defend the perennial status of Enochian. Crowley held the same position in his *Confessions,*[35] and Israel Regardie elaborated on the idea by providing what he considered to be further evidence. In Regardie's view, an Enochian word could be found that bears a resemblance to a Sanskrit word of similar meaning. Linking this with linguistic theories prominent at the time, of a proto-Indo-European language, he found himself able to corroborate one of the more imaginative speculations made by the Order's clairvoyants. If there is a language "which lies behind Sanskrit," Regardie reasoned, then, "according to the philosophy of the Ancient Wisdom" it has to be "that of Atlantis."[36] With one single word sounding similar to a Sanskrit term, Regardie argued that "the Enochian or Angelical language bears several strong points of resemblance to"[37] the assumed Atlantean language. How "strong" and convincing such evidence really is can obviously be disputed; at any rate the line of argumentation and the strategy for defending "the primordial language thesis" is well worth noting.

In their structure, these arguments, whether they hold the Enochian language to be "the hidden Angelic language," of which a few words have been "leaked" to humanity, or whether they, like Regardie's, advance an esoteric historiography in the guise of a scientific linguistic theory, of descent and gradual corruption from Atlantis, through ancient languages such as Sanskrit and Etruscan, all seem to agree on one thing: that Enochian did not *really* originate with Dee and Kelley, but remains part of a most arcane system of perennial philosophy. With recourse to Olav Hammer's mode of analysis, this can easily be seen as a variety of a "rhetoric of rationality." With this line of argumentation, there is an attempt to sidestep the authenticity problem posed by the purist approach, by arguing for a much more ancient provenance than Dee and Kelley.

Satanic Angelologies:

Satanism between Esoteric Discourse and Secular Iconoclasm

The Enochian discourse was already full of controversies by the mid-twentieth century. As we shall now see, these controversies form an important background for understanding the incorporation and use of the Enochian language and Enochian magic in the context of an emerging self-styled Satanic position in late 1960s California. The doctrinal and aesthetic innovations that came out of this movement led to more confrontations with the ideologues of the older Golden Dawn currents.

It does not take too much reading of the primary sources of modern Satanism to find that its relation to the cultural heritage of Western esotericism is ambiguous and complex.[38] On the one hand, modern Satanism, with all "Left-Hand Path" splinter groups, is clearly indebted to ideas flourishing in nineteenth- and early-twentieth-century occultism. The emphasis on ritual magic ultimately follows in the current from Lévi, the Golden Dawn, and Crowley. However, it is an influence that has partially sparked a need for differentiation and opposition to its source.[39] On a broad scale the whole phenomenon of modern Satanism should be viewed as a part of the "secularization of esotericism,"[40] and the emergence of "occulture,"[41] as discussed in chapter 4. In this sense it has become commonplace to view modern Satanism as a "Self-religion," the "dark cousin" of modern spiritualities such as New Age religion and the Human Potential Movement.[42]

The ambiguous relation of Satanism to esoteric discourse also has important bearing in the context of the ideological fault line between the two main strands in the first schism within Satanism. Despite the obvious esoteric connection historically, there exists in modern Satanism a tendency to differentiate and distance oneself from those esoteric currents. This is notably the case in LaVey's writings, where we find numerous passages preoccupied with attacking various "witchcraft and magical groups" and other "occultisms of the past."[43] Instead of the "holy esoterica" of previous occult systems LaVey emphasizes the importance of a robust materialistic philosophy, a Darwinian anthropology, utility-maximizing rationality inspired by Ayn Rand's Objectivist philosophy, and the realization of carnal desire. As a rule of thumb LaVey interprets what he borrows from esoteric systems in the light of, and with appeal to, this rational-materialist worldview. As was mentioned in chapter 4, LaVey's satanic occultism can be viewed as "the secularization of esotericism" come full circle.

But then we find Michael Aquino, the spokesperson of the schismatic Temple of Set, speculating on such esoteric matters as the procession of "Aeons," "Secret Chiefs," and even claiming that the foundational document of his group, *The Book of Coming Forth by Night,* is in some way "channelled" from the Egyptian god Set.[44] The similarity to the esoteric claims Crowley made for his *Liber Legis* of 1904 is clear.

The discrepancy between these two spokespersons needs further explication, as it will form a significant background for the rest of this chapter. A useful typology for assessing it is Jesper Aagaard Petersen's ideal type distinction between *rational* and *esoteric* Satanism.[45] These two categories roughly coincide with the two major organizations, with LaVey's Church of Satan representing "rational Satanism" while Aquino's Temple of Set embody a more "esoteric" approach. The first category is to be viewed as the more secularized and rationalistic variety, viewing Satan largely as symbolic of the self and of egoistical, carnal virtues, that is, as a symbol of mundane things.[46] With the rationalist outlook comes an understanding of ritual magic as emotional psychodrama, only seldom and somewhat ambiguously as a supernatural practice. Esoteric Satanism, on the other hand, tends to fit better with other currents in the history of Western esotericism, seeing Satan as a metaphysical entity or force, present in nature, humanity, or the intellect.[47] This stance is also to a greater extent expressed in the perspective on magical theory and practice. All in all, this distinction is useful in pointing out a difference in how the obvious esoteric heritage is negotiated with a secular worldview. The satanic rationalist generally comes out in favour of secularism, while the satanic or "Left-Hand Path" esotericist tends to validate the esoteric sources and traditions to a much greater extent.[48]

Obviously, this has distinct bearing on how the Enochian system is conceived as well. Anton LaVey assimilated the Enochian calls to various Satanic ceremonial and magical purposes, but tended to view their efficacy in purely *pragmatic* or *psychological* terms. For Aquino, on the other hand, the Enochian keys were indeed exactly that: magical keys imbued with metaphysical qualities to access esoteric realms, disjoined from ordinary reality. Following up the intuitions established by Crowley, Enochian was situated at the center of ongoing contestations of legitimacy, both within and without the Satanic milieu.

The Church of Satan

Enochiana and the Struggle with Esoteric Others

Anton LaVey founded the Church of Satan in California in 1966 more or less by accident.[49] Springing out of a small occultist circle with eclectic interests, the church was not founded on any consistent philosophy, religious creed, or cultic activity. The quest for forging a position only started in the years following the formation of the Church. The first attempt consisted of LaVey's short monograph "Satanism," which was written and circulated in 1968–69.[50] This consisted of the "Nine Satanic Statements," which would later be included in *The Satanic Bible,* and some instructions in what "Satanism" means to the Church of Satan, and especially what the nature of Satanic magic is.[51] In the text, LaVey already makes sure to keep aloof from "other witchcraft or magical groups," which he antagonistically denotes as "white magical groups."[52]

In the book that would be far more important for cementing a modern Satanic identity, *The Satanic Bible* (1969), the strategy of distancing oneself from "traditional" esotericisms was followed up. The main bulk of the book was really an edited version of the material circulated as "Introduction to Satanism" and other "polemical essays" LaVey had written over the previous years.[53] However, there was not enough material to fill a full volume. Instead, LaVey copied material from other sources and pasted it to the front and end of what became the *Satanic Bible.* The first text, added at the front under the title "The Book of Satan," was an adaptation of the social Darwinist tract *Might Is Right,* written by the New Zealander Arthur Desmond under the pseudonym Ragnar Redbeard, at the turn of the century.[54] The second text was the Enochian keys or calls, borrowed from the version published by Aleister Crowley in *The Equinox.*[55] The English translations were, as mentioned, further altered to remove the distinct "holy" and divine tone of the text, replaced instead with diabolical references.[56] The inclusion of the Enochian verses in *The Satanic Bible* made them an important expression of Satanic religious discourse, and their use were further elaborated upon in the following central book, *The Satanic Rituals* (1972).

The randomness of the process leading up to the Enochian calls becoming an authorized part of Satanic discourse is at first sight striking. Even the whole project of writing and publishing *The Satanic Bible* was not LaVey's own initiative; the project was conceived by the editor of the publishing house Avon Books, Peter Mayer, who saw that his market would crave a Satanic bible after the grand popularity of Roman Polanski's 1968 movie adaptation of *Rosemary's Baby*.[57] The United States saw a veritable occult revival, which a deft publisher could easily profit from.

The Enochian material was only included when Mayer's deadline loomed over the project and the book was still not sufficiently voluminous. Indeed, one is tempted to speculate whether the slightly curious Satanic reception of the most famed system of angel magic should simply be explained away by reference to mere happenstance. This may at least serve as part of the explanation. But it has to be accompanied by a few other and perhaps more intriguing considerations as well. Even though chance led to the situation in which LaVey had to choose other texts to flesh out his book, it is *not* mere chance that the two particular texts actually used were an obscure social Darwinist tract on the one hand, and a revised version of the Enochian calls on the other. By choosing these two, LaVey makes a statement: a sociopolitical and moral statement in the case of *Might Is Right*,[58] but one regarding legitimacy toward the esoteric community with the Enochian material. The reembedding of such utterly unrelated individual elements creates a *bricolage* with a uniquely LaVeyian edge.

The inclusion of an altered version of the Enochian keys in *The Satanic Bible* may, in the first place, be seen as a slightly tongue-in-cheek attempt to situate oneself between the preexisting esoteric traditions Satanism drew upon and the anti-esoteric characteristic of rational Satanism. Enochian would be one of the elements of the Californian occulture in which LaVey was situated, even a particularly treasured one. Taking this particular element out of previous contexts, reembedding it with other available elements, from Human Potential psychology to social Darwinism, effectively infusing it with new meanings, is thus not much different from the mode of cultic innovation seen in connection with the New Age movement and other occultural religious systems of the era.[59] It is a characteristic part of the religious dynamics of the twentieth century.

Satanic Angel Magic

The marked tendency toward secularizing esoteric concepts manifests clearly in LaVey's take on Satanic magic. A complete treatment of Satanic magic *sensu* LaVey requires its own study, and falls outside the present scope.[60] However, a basic outline of some general trends is necessary before we look at the reception of the Enochian magic in particular.

One such trend in LaVey's conception of magic is the distinction between "lesser" and "greater" forms of magic.[61] These are to be seen in a continuum where the main difference is that the lower form approximates completely "mundane" manipulative actions in social reality, while the higher forms consist of a practice of ritual magic. In this sense, "lesser magic" lends heavily from non-esoteric sources, particularly the application of lessons from social psychology. Among the people referenced in LaVey's primary work on lesser magic, *The Compleat Witch,* we find, for instance, the sociologists Goffman and Klapp, and psychologists such as Reich, Ferenczi, and Freud.[62]

"Greater" ritual magic on the other hand is said to have the aim of accomplishing "something which, by other means, could not be done."[63] It is described as "a very real power," which "utilizes such tools as hypnosis, telepathy, psychology, etc."[64] The definition of magic bases itself on Crowley's famous statement in *Magic in Theory and Practice* (i.e., "the Science and Art of causing Change to occur in conformity with Will"), but somewhat qualifies it by adding that acts of magic exclude "normally accepted methods."[65] One should nevertheless be careful about inferring from this assertion that LaVey is advocating supernaturalism; on the same page he employs the notion that magic thus understood is effective through hitherto unknown forces *in nature.*[66] This strategy, of naturalizing the purportedly supernatural, is however not new with LaVey, but rather a common strategy in occultism from the middle of the nineteenth century.

In continuation, this interpretation holds true for LaVey's presentation of Enochian magic as well, which in his system is mainly restricted to the Enochian calls and the use of its language. In one of the articles on their use, he gives suggestions as to which type of magical operation is most congenial to each of the Enochian calls, implying that each did have a specific, unique character.[67] Contrary to what we saw in the Golden Dawn groups, LaVey did not see the language of the calls as really "angelic," or indeed as having anything to do with any metaphysical concept of "angels." LaVey asserts that the angels "are only "angels" because occultists to this day have lain ill with "metaphysical constipation."[68] Rather, the Enochian language was to be employed in satanic rituals for perceived psychological benefits; it was thought to be a particularly evocative language. That it was shrouded in some mystery was not the main point, although it clearly did no harm either:

> The magical language used in Satanic ritual is Enochian. Enochian is a language which is thought to be older than Sanskrit, with a sound grammatical and syntactical basis. . . . In Enochian the meaning of the words, combined with the quality of the words, unite to create a pattern of sound which can cause tremendous reaction in the

> atmosphere. The barbaric tonal qualities of this language give it a truly magical effect which cannot be described.[69]

Although we see LaVey echoing Brodie-Innes, Regardie, and Crowley, it is worth noting that the main focus for LaVey is on the sonic qualities of the language. Enochian is to be employed chiefly because of the "truly magical *effect*" that its tonal qualities are said to possess. This is further emphasized in a short essay LaVey wrote on the pronunciation of Enochian in *Cloven Hoof*: "[T]he importance should be placed upon the rhythmic and sequential delivery of the words, rather than a scholarly attempt to pronounce them properly."[70] The emphasis is again on the pragmatic *effect* rather than the scholarly "authenticity," or metaphysical correspondence, of the language.

LaVey's Satanic reception of the Enochian "Angelic" calls is presented in a "secularized," or "disenchanted" tone. Acting well in concert with LaVey's sometimes anti-esoteric stance we see a move away from earlier perennialist legitimizations of Enochian, toward a predominantly pragmatic line of argumentation. Purist considerations about the historicity of the language are also largely ignored; the point of the matter for LaVey is the effect and evocative *sound* of the language, not its provenance.

To emphasize again the polemical context it is interesting to note that LaVey's tinkering with the Enochian calls did not go unnoticed by "traditional" esotericists who, as we have seen, had been quarreling over the correct interpretation of the system for decades. When Israel Regardie in 1972 published an edition of Crowley's 1909 Enochian experiments in the Algerian desert, he attacked *The Satanic Bible* in his introduction, calling it a "debased volume," which presented a "perverted edition" of Enochian.[71] Regardie's attack referred specifically to the satanic revisions of the translated calls, and "several other pieces of similar stupidity."[72] Although not surprised by Regardie's response, LaVey nevertheless took it with some disappointment.[73] The attack was taken seriously enough to prompt an answer. In an article published in the CoS newsletter *Cloven Hoof* entitled "Caucus Race," Michael Aquino, still with the Church at that time, answered Regardie's attack from a historical perspective. By documenting how the Golden Dawn and Crowley receptions of Enochian, which Regardie defended against the satanic "perverted edition," were themselves reinterpretations and decontextualized versions of the original sixteenth-century work of Dee and Kelley, he attacked the very premises of Regardie's argument.[74] From a scholarly point of view, Aquino was entirely right; rather than presenting a sound historical argument Regardie was himself defending an esoteric position against the new dissenting Satanism, just as we have seen him do in the face of P. F. Case's attacks in the 1930s. A copy of the article was sent to Regardie personally who, in Aquino's words, "probably found it as palatable as Anton had found his introduction."[75] After this initial skirmish, Regardie and Aquino later became good friends.[76]

The Temple of Set: Enochiana on the Left-Hand Path

Referring to Max Weber's tripartite distinction between "traditional," "rational-legalistic," and "charismatic" types of authority James R. Lewis has observed that LaVey's primary strategy to base the legitimacy of the CoS against competing occultisms was an emphasis on "rationality."[77] Although in a common sense he is indeed often seen as a "charismatic" leader, he did not *claim* charismatic authority in the technical sense Weber implied.[78] LaVey would never claim that texts like *The Satanic Bible* were "received" or "inspired" works, or that he was "touched by Satan" in any prophetic way. Neither did he offer supernatural ailments to adherents through his magic; rather he appealed to a rational-humanistic and egoistical ethos by which each has to save himself. This rational appeal took the form of distrust and mockery of established "traditional" religions, and also the anti-esoteric stance we have seen above.

Lewis also observed that the legitimizing strategy of the CoS itself changed over the years, especially around the schismatic year 1975. In these latter years of the history of the early CoS the organization had spread far outside its natal San Francisco, and a number of "Grottoes"—local governing bodies of the Church—had sprung up across the country. Coinciding with this, LaVey had started to tire of his official persona as the "Black Pope," and gradually started to cut off contact with these distant bodies.[79] This culminated in his "Phase IV" policy of the Church in 1974, which aimed at making it more like an informal movement.[80] By early 1975 the Church's structure faced disintegration and a series of schismatic Satanist groups emerged from the institutional chaos. Similar in a way to what happened upon the breakup of the Golden Dawn, this led to several new takes on Satanism and its various doctrines and practices.

However much LaVey himself would stress rational authority, it was unavoidable that he was perceived as a charismatic leader as well. This especially holds for the more informal movement of second generation Satanists, who knew their leader as a symbol rather than by personal acquaintance. As Weber predicted that charismatic authority tends to switch toward either rational-legalistic or traditional forms of authority after a while, it is interesting to note with Lewis what seems to have happened in the Satanic milieu after the schism. While some indeed stuck with LaVey's own rational strategy, others, particularly the remnants of the original CoS, moved toward a *traditional* approach in which LaVey's texts formed a sort of canonized corpus, which enables one to distinguish between "real" (i.e., "LaVeyian") Satanists and "pseudo-Satanists."[81] This move is to be understood in context of the variety of other, non-LaVeyian forms of Satanism. Chief among these was Aquino's Temple of Set.

Michael Aquino was one of those who saw LaVey and the original CoS as "authentic" in a more than conventional way. As he writes in his continuously expanding history of the Temple of Set, he

> had never regarded [the CoS] as "just another organization" alongside which other, similar Satanic churches could just as validly exist. Correspondingly I did not consider Anton LaVey as simply a charismatic individual or even genius, but as the *anointed personal deputy of Satan himself.*[82]

One should not be led astray by Aquino's use of "charismatic" in this sentence; what Aquino is actually saying is that he saw LaVey and his organization as having *charismatic legitimacy* in Weber's technical sense. He had been anointed by a higher power, Satan, and could not simply be replaced by the work of men. Neither could his defunct Church. When other rebelling members of the CoS looked to Aquino for somebody to build a new institution, he therefore felt that such a "second Church" could not be formed without some extraordinary legitimacy endowed from "above" (or, per Satanic parlance, "below"). Since Satan had, according to Aquino, in a very real way "anointed" both LaVey and the CoS, a new church body would only be legitimate if the infernal Lord again stepped in and chose someone, bestowing his authority anew. In Aquino's own words:

> As the Church of Satan's 1975 crisis began to unfold, I attempted to comprehend and address it reasonably and practically through correspondence and discussion. But as the situation worsened, I felt increasingly the need to seek guidance from the authority of the Church's very existence, Satan himself. It seemed to me that if the Church were *authentic*—and, for that matter, *ultimately so* beyond Anton LaVey's current representation of it as merely his personal creation and vehicle, the Prince of Darkness would have to step in. As the senior Master next to Anton himself, I concluded that the responsibility to seek such a G[reater] B[lack] M[agic] resolution fell on me.[83]

Aquino sought to renew this charismatic legitimacy through ritual magical means in which, borrowing heavily from the legacy of Crowley, exploration of the Enochian Aethyrs were crucial. It was a series of experiments with this system that led to the writing of *The Book of Coming Forth by Night,* the foundation document of the ToS, which itself contains certain references to Enochian and Aquino's own take on it.

Aquino testifies that he began experimenting with the Enochian system at the time when the crisis of the CoS started to unfold, early in 1975. Having been tipped by the Washington, D.C.–based Satanist Robert Ethel about a recently published facsimile edition of Casaubon's 1659 account of Dee's angel conversations, Aquino tracked down a copy in a local occult bookstore.[84] Once he got hold of it, he found the section containing the Enochian calls, and found that these differed from those used by LaVey. Aquino decided to take "the original Keys out for a test drive." That same evening he went out to some old artillery batteries outside Fort MacArthur, where he had previously "conducted many a Call to Cthulhu during Army Reserve weekends with the infamous 306th Psychological Operations Battalion".[85] Now he was set on exploring the Enochian Aethyrs.[86]

Aquino's first experiments with the Casaubon keys took place on March 8, 1975. The model was Crowley's method, as discussed earlier. The resulting vision of his attempt to invoke the thirteenth Aethyr, called "ZIM," is described in the following manner:

> I recall coming, under hazy circumstances, to a large wooden-beamed hall in which were seated a number of men around a table. I knew them to be the "Secret Chiefs" of the "White" tradition of whom Aleister Crowley and others have spoken.
>
> I suggested that I might be allowed to join them, sensing that they did not immediately perceive my identity as a Magister Templi of the Left-Hand Path. But there was some dissent, as though some of them were wary of me.
>
> Finally I revealed myself as a Magister Templi. They reacted more negatively than before, donning robes of various colors. I responded by donning my own black/blue robe, whereupon there was a reaction by them of even stronger dislike. I responded with anger in turn.
>
> There was a violent conflagration, the hall collapsed, and I recall nothing further.[87]

Already from this first experiment it is clear that Aquino felt he had stumbled upon a potent key to unlock certain esoteric regions of the universe in which he could expect to meet such supra-human authorities as the "Secret Chiefs," so important in the Golden Dawn current.

After this early experiment Aquino was convinced that the "more authentic" version of the Enochian keys he had found in the Casaubon volume had ensured its overwhelming success, in spite of its being a first shot.[88] He believed himself to hold a potent tool in his hands, which called for further experiment. The next full working that Aquino mentions came a couple of months later, on May 30.[89] On this occasion Aquino apparently wanted help with his studies, and used the Enochian calls to conjure up a sphinx and a chimera to discuss some magical importance of the dialogues of Plato.[90] "Scholarly work preceded the working; then G[reater] B[lack] M[magic] was used to overlay it with enlightened awareness," Aquino later recalled.[91]

Immediately following this rather bizarre colloquium, the events began that would lead up to the formation of the ToS: "[I]n the first week of June, something quite unexpected happened. I began to write a text in instalments of one or two hours per night. . . . [I]t declared the Enochian Keys to be a remote corruption of something called the *Word of Set*."[92] The next month Aquino would be preoccupied with "recovering" (i.e., writing) this *Word of Set,* which turned out to be an entirely new English translation of the nineteen Enochian calls.[93]

The reliance on new revelation instead of historically verifiable fact seems perhaps curious taking into account the somewhat purist criticism Aquino himself had leveled against Regardie a few years earlier. Interestingly, Aquino has later built up a considerable defense against possible Enochian purists who would attack the *Word of Set* translation for its divergence from historical sources. The argument goes in two steps. First, Aquino writes how he had gone through all the Enochian sources he knew, equipped with a familiarity with cryptography and a mind to unravel the linguistic "lineage." "After some weeks of work, I concluded that Enochian is *not a true language,*" Aquino writes. "Rather it is an artificial jargon, i.e. arbitrary words placed together in roughly consistent sequences to *simulate* a true language."[94] He continued by comparing it to another language that possesses the same feature: the pseudo-Lovecraftian language "Yuggothic," which had featured in two rituals based on H. P. Lovecraft's "Cthulhu mythos," published in *The Satanic Rituals*.[95] In fact, it was Aquino himself who ghostwrote the whole section of *The Satanic Rituals* dealing with the Lovecraftian theme, and indeed it was he who had invented the language that features there:

> It was about the work of two months to develop the "nameless language" of the *Ceremony of the Nine Angles* and the *Call to Cthulhu*. A word that sounded properly "Lovecraftian" would be constructed arbitrarily: *El-aka* = world, *gryenn'h* = [of] horrors. Then the word would be used consistently throughout the text for both rituals.

> Slight modifications of endings would suffice for different sentence constructions, and there you have a "language" every bit as flexible as Enochian![96]

The second part of the argument against the Enochian purist easily follows: since the language is not a real language, the "translation" is really arbitrary. Thus, he notes that what LaVey had done with his "falsification" of the original translations was to put in words that *felt* more prudent. Rather than wrecking the efficacy of the magic utilizing these calls, Aquino claimed that the CoS produced far *better* results with LaVey's than with the original keys. Aquino's own approach with the *Word of Set* should therefore be seen in the same way: "seeking words to express what I [Aquino] seemed to sense the Keys were actually intended to say."[97]

And what did they say? The first two calls, or "parts of the Word of Set," which were the only ones to be written down at this time,[98] are cast as speeches from the Egyptian god Set. The first one seems to be addressed to a human magus of the Left-Hand Path, and tells how Set has created man and endowed him with intellect and ability to know "all lesser things."[99] It calls ultimately for the human being to ascend to his "divine" nature, through discovery and pride in one's capabilities. The second part of "the Word" similarly calls for self-gratification, and the discovery of "the flame within" that gives "the strength to live forever."[100] I will not delve into the possible theology of these verses, but the role given to the alleged spokesperson should be noted carefully. In these verses, Set has already conquered the role Satan possessed in LaVey's keys. He also speaks in a much more exalted, veiled, or mystical language than any text LaVey would have approved of.

The importance of Set was to reach its point of no return on the night of the summer Solstice, June 20–21, 1975. This was when Aquino performed the Greater Black Magic working (i.e., "ritual") that would be known as the "North Solstice working."[101] At this point, he had reached the conclusion that the ongoing conflict in the CoS could only be resolved through a GBM working, as seen earlier. The time was come to take on the responsibility and prerogative of a Magister Templi to call forth the Devil, in an attempt to renew the pact that, in Aquino's eyes, had secured the legitimacy of the CoS. His method of doing so rested on the newly "received" translation of the Enochian keys:

> My altar was located in the living room of the house. I opened the working in the traditional Satanic Mass, then spoke aloud the First Part of the *Word of Set*. I felt an impulse to enter my study—"the

> Sanctum" as I nicknamed it—and with Brandy [his dog] curled up at my feet, sat down at my desk and took up pen and paper. Then, over the next four hours, I wrote down the words of *The Book of Coming Forth by Night*.[102]

This book would be for Aquino what *Liber Legis* had been for Crowley. Its message can mainly be summed up as a call for Aquino to take up his position as prophet of the new Aeon of Set, and usher in it through the foundation of a new Temple, with new rituals and holy names.[103] In effect, this book is a statement that polemically defends Aquino's newly found esoteric authority against his two most important influences: Aleister Crowley and Anton LaVey. And the key to it all had been the Enochian keys.

Satanic-Enochian Magics: Some Comparative Remarks

LaVey's rationalist take on Enochian was a highly psychologized and secularized one. The system was freed of its "angelic" association by stating that this was merely the outcome of the false consciousness of generations of previous occultists. The potency of the language did not hinge on its "divine," angelic origin, but rather on the particular qualities of its sounds. Whether this relies implicitly on a speculative metaphysics of phonetics remains an unanswered question. What is certain is that the terms used to describe its efficacy are mostly pragmatic. With this in mind, and with the inversion of certain words in the text to better fit a satanic context, the Enochian keys could be employed in satanic rituals.

With Aquino's *esoteric* turn of the satanic discourse, which may perhaps more accurately be seen as a move away from Satanism per se to a broader "Left-Hand Path," the interpretation differs in important respects. Opposite from LaVey, Aquino largely lacks the psychologizing language used to legitimize magic generally. Rather, it is clear that Aquino sees the need to engage with the esoteric sources in a much more sincere way. He seems predisposed to finding the presumably more "authentic" calls in Casaubon's edition more efficient than later renderings. This also led him to compare all extant sources he knew—Casaubon, Golden Dawn, Crowley, LaVey—in order to outline the "linguistic lineage" and determine authenticity. Although he concluded that no such authenticity existed, it is clear that an evocative sound *alone* was not enough for him.

Focus should be given again to the ways Aquino put the Enochian keys to use. Rather than merely being utilized as psychological instruments in the frame of LaVeyian "intellectual decompression chambers," the calls seem to be understood as possessing an esoteric power of their own. With Crowley's visionary quest in the Algerian desert as his *exem-*

plum Aquino's first experiment with the Enochian calls was to invoke and astrally travel to the Aethyrs. In this practice he found a key to higher sources of authority, as Crowley had claimed before him, encountering the veritable "Secret Chiefs" in his very first attempt.

Although the general trend seems to be that Aquino does not allow the same degree of secularized approach as does LaVey, the esoteric interpretations he ends up giving are in and of themselves quite novel. For instance, while the source of the powerful nature of the Enochian calls cannot be merely pragmatic, they cannot be "angelical" either. The solution is the revelation that they are in fact corruptions of the presumably perennial *Word of Set*. The new interpretation he gives to them is conceptualized as a revelation of their true, esoteric *essence,* rather than simply a more prudent rendering. From these considerations it seems that Aquino presents a new sort of Enochian perennialism, which curiously employs pragmatic arguments as well as more scholarly linguistic analyses to ward off purist attacks.

7
The Purist Turn

The Postmodern Condition in Occultism

It is not entirely without justification to say that the advent of modern Satanism put an end to the Golden Dawn era. This does not mean that from thereafter Golden Dawn magic was never again practiced—indeed, in terms of expansion and publications a contrary development seems to be the case. But there is an extent to which the movements stirred by LaVey and Aquino had a lasting impact on the perceived authority of that system. I have argued that LaVeyian Satanism represented in some senses the secularization of esotericism come full circle. This implied a fundamental distrust of the occultist "master narrative" that the Golden Dawn system had really provided, something that has led to the not uncommon assertion that Satanism was a precursor to the development of Chaos Magic in Britain in the 1970s.[1] In a way, it was with Satanism that occultism entered the postmodern age.

Curiously perhaps, the advent of the "postmodern condition"[2] in occultism may have provided a rationale not only for radically relativistic approaches, as associated with Chaos Magic, but also for a search for lost "authenticity." In the postmodern development of Enochiana, this gives rise to what I term the "purist turn": the development of an approach to Enochian magic that rests on systematic and scholarly examination of original sources. Although it seems perhaps surprising at first, this development was really to be expected, since a common trend of postmodernism's "incredulity toward metanarratives" has been, especially in the academic context, a (re)turn to the particular at the expense of the universal.[3] The great system builders have been replaced by the myopic examiners of the unique.

While we have seen that the purist response did exist already, the purist *turn* signifies more than merely the existence of purists. When analyzing the impact of the postmodern condition, Jean-François Lyotard raised the question: "Where, after the metanarratives, can legitimacy reside?"[4] With the G.D. synthesis considered as the master narrative of occultism, what we see with the purist turn, as here defined, is a change in the *conditions* of the discourse community of Enochian magicians in favor of a legitimacy based on diligent research of the particulars of the "original" Enochian system. The inauthentic remnants of previous system builders must be eradicated to preserve the uniqueness of the Enochian system.[5]

This chapter aims to explore the development of the purist current, and its main protagonists. It should be noted at this point that Pasi and Rabaté in their concise article on the Enochian language similarly identified a "purist" current in modern Enochian literature.[6] However, while they cited two works representing this current, namely, Geoffrey James's *Enochian Evocation* (1984) and Donald Tyson's *Enochian Magic for Beginners* (1997), there are still other proponents that, I shall argue, represent clearer and more important examples of the trend. This chapter, then, aims to present a more detailed view of the purist turn, and lay out some of its significance. Thus, after dissecting its internal dynamics and identifying its main spokespersons, I will also have a look at some of the reactions that came in its wake. Through this presentation, I will show that the emergence of a full-blown Enochian purism changed the direction and dynamics of the Enochian discourse.

Preparing the Ground: Dictionaries and Source Materials

One of the background conditions for the purist turn in Enochian magic was a rapidly growing interest in the system, and especially its language, throughout the 1970s. This is quite probably a partial influence of Satanism, or more precisely, of the *Satanic Bible*. Despite its idiosyncrasies, the publication and wide distribution of the book greatly popularized an interest in the Enochian calls.[7] Together with the publication of Llewellyn's new editions of Regardie's *Golden Dawn* in 1969 and 1971, the stage was set for a new generation of occultists to explore Enochiana.

This period also saw a relatively extensive publication of source materials, and even dictionaries of the Angelic tongue, all valuable tools for those wishing to penetrate deeper into the material. In 1974 Stephen Skinner published a facsimile edition of Casaubon's *True and Faithful*

Relation under the title *John Dee's Action with Spirits*.[8] Although this was a limited and expensive hardcover edition, it soon attracted interest among dedicated magicians. As we saw in the previous chapter, it was this edition that sparked Aquino's research into the "linguistic genealogy" of the Enochian keys. It even influenced him to acquire microfilm copies of the material in the Bodleian Library, which he later incorporated into his own *Word of Set* translation of the calls.[9] It is not impossible that it was this edition that inspired other groups as well, such as the Aurum Solis, which will be discussed later, to "correct" the spelling of the Enochian language from the Golden Dawn version.

Another indication of the renewed interest in Enochian and its language is evident from the publication of two dictionaries, in 1976 and 1978. The first one was Leo Vinci's *Gmicalzoma*.[10] Although providing a systematic overview of the language, this edition rested emphatically on occultist premises stemming from the Golden Dawn. As Pasi and Rabaté have noted, Vinci recapitulates the etymological fantasies of Brodie-Innes and Regardie, and even takes them a step farther by suggesting a connection between the Enochian word *raas* (given as "east") and the name of the Egyptian sun god Ra.[11]

In contrast, *The Complete Enochian Dictionary* published by the Australian linguist, anthropologist, and skeptic Donald Laycock in 1978 presents something quite different.[12] In the introductory essay published with the dictionary, entitled "Angelic language or mortal folly?" Laycock aimed to give a scholarly and linguistic analysis of the language. His conclusion was that the language exhibits structural and phonetic patterns that rule out the possibility of it being a natural language, that is, a real language with independent grammar and syntax.[13] Instead, he argued, it possessed syntactical features common to constructed language (it has basically the same syntax as English), and two revealing phonetic features: one that is common in glossolalia, and another which is common when putting together letters arbitrarily, without thought of the disposition of vocals and consonants. Even though Laycock's work has become a classic of skeptical linguistics, his dictionary is still popular with many magicians. The reprint of the book by Weiser is a document of this, prefaced and introduced by two leading occultist authors, Stephen Skinner and Lon Milo DuQuette. In his preface, Skinner, who was a personal friend of Laycock's, even manages to recast him as a practicing magician, without mention of the thoroughly skeptical tone of his article on Enochian language.[14] Nevertheless, it seems clear that the publication of these tools prepared the ground for other purist approaches to the Enochian material.[15]

Robert Turner and the Order of the Cubic Stone

I will now call attention to a little-known group of ritual magicians which deserves serious attention in the modern history of Enochian magic: the Order of the Cubic Stone (O.C.S.). As it evolved, this group acquired a vanguard position in the purist turn of Enochiana. Based in Wolverhampton and the Midlands, UK, the group first emerged in the mid-sixties, founded by the elderly occultist Theodore Howard. Howard resigned quickly, and left the actual running of the order to two young scientific technicians, David Edwards and Robert Turner.[16] By the seventies the O.C.S. had earned reputation as a particularly practically minded magical order. Writing in 1970, Francis King commented about the O.C.S. that "its Chiefs are both competent and sincere—they have themselves done what they teach."[17] In King's view, this distinguished the group from the mainstream, faddish interest in occultism of the late 1960s.

In the leaflets that the O.C.S. would send to interested enquirers in its early years, the stated aim of the Order was to "train the student in our approach to Ceremonial Magic." Furthermore, it was stated that "the system we use is based on the Qabalah and our teachings stem from the Golden Dawn and other similar sources."[18] From a self-initiation ritual published in the O.C.S. journal, *The Monolith,* and later reproduced by Francis King, it seems evident that the "other sources" included Crowley. His "Mass of the Phoenix" ritual is made a part of the initiation, as is a use of the thirty Enochian Aethyrs seemingly based on Crowley's theory about these entities, and their initiatory potential.[19]

At this point in the O.C.S.'s history, their aim was not so much to work a novel and innovative framework of magic, but rather to encourage actual practical work in a tradition that was already established. This impression is strengthened from considering the short book on magic published by one of the Order's chiefs in this period, David Edwards. The occult and magical lore compiled in his *Dare to Make Magic* (1971) bases itself on Kabbalistic correspondences and techniques for scrying deriving ultimately from the Golden Dawn.[20] The main point of the book confirms King's comment on the O.C.S.'s practical approach: in occultism it is not enough to read and memorize; one must also dare to do the practical work and exercises required to become an accomplished magician. The book is filled with suggestions, motivating statements, and advice for practical training.

While this profile seems to hold for the early phase of the O.C.S., its focus was soon to change drastically in directions that are of interest to the present study. This change of perspective happened just around the time King dedicated a short chapter to the Order in his *Ritual Magic in*

England, thus it was not covered by his study. To my knowledge, there have been no scholarly comments on the interesting later development of the O.C.S.[21]

The Enochian Turn of the O.C.S.

The change of perspective in the O.C.S. coincided with David Edwards's resignation from the Order in or around 1970, which left Robert Turner in sole command. Turner seems to have been particularly fascinated with Enochiana. Through the 1970s he developed an increasingly stricter focus on this particular system of magic. What makes Turner's approach stand out from the various trends discussed earlier is his strict insistence on a scholarly return to the source materials. According to a previous member of the O.C.S., Steven Ashe, his "academic approach" led to a gradual rejection of the Golden Dawn and Crowley approaches to magic generally and Enochian magic particularly.[22] Under Turner, "the sole focus hinged upon what could be reconstructed from the Dee material."[23] This makes him the earliest clear-cut example of a consistent purist.

Turner's diligent research of the original manuscripts at the British Library and the Bodleian in Oxford later resulted in the publication of the books *The Heptarchia Mystica of John Dee* (1983) and *Elizabethan Magic* (1989).[24] These are often considered, even from a scholarly perspective, some of the best editions of original Dee material available; certainly, *The Heptarchia Mystica* was the first publication of the Heptarchic system ever to appear in print. Turner's publications have also greatly informed the occult discourse on Enochian magic by popularizing a scholarly founded criticism of the Golden Dawn's approach to it. In the introduction to his edition of *The Heptarchia Mystica,* for instance, Turner expresses his baffled amazement over the neglect of the Heptarchic system. In Turner's view, this is really "the only true example of a complete magical system to be found in the Dee papers,"[25] and yet he could find no trace of its use by modern occultists. Instead, people had been making grand syntheses out of incomplete systems in other parts of Dee's diaries. This vein of criticism has earned Turner's two books a central position in the purist turn.

Turner's scholarly, meticulous approach seems however to have caused, or at the very least added to, frictions within the O.C.S. According to Steven Ashe, an increasing gap started to appear between the scholarly and the practical work in the Order, which frustrated many of its members.[26] When some of the O.C.S. members embarked on practical experiments with the "new" Heptarchic material dug up by Turner's efforts, they were met with discouragement. The Order that had produced *Dare to Make Magic* and been known for its emphasis on practical experiments had gradually developed a more cautious and purely theoretical focus. The discontent peaked at the beginning of the 1980s, when a series of core members left the group due to controversies with the leadership over practical work.[27] This was the beginning of the end for the O.C.S., which nevertheless seems to have been more influential through the publications of Turner.

An Inconsequent Purist? Turner and the Necronomicon Scam

Robert Turner was part of another curious publishing project, which deserves to be mentioned briefly here, namely, the edition of *The Necronomicon* that appeared at the publishing house Neville Spearman in 1978.[28] This book belongs to the genre of literature related to H. P. Lovecraft's "Cthulhu mythos," and more specifically to the subgenre of books (appearing from the early 1970s) purporting to be the real version of the originally fictitious grimoire *Necronomicon*.[29] In Lovecraft's horror universe, this ancient tome was said to have been written down in Damascus by Abdul Alhazred, a mad Arabian poet, just before his mysterious and sudden disappearance in 738.[30] The grimoire was said to have survived in a manuscript tradition continuing into the early Modern period, when John Dee had made a personal copy. However, this was "never printed, & exists only in fragments recovered from the original MS."[31] This fictitious historiography opens doors for the Dee scholar and Enochian magician Turner.

The 1978 Neville Spearman *Necronomicon* edition was published in collaboration between Colin Wilson, George Hay, and Robert Turner. According to the Lovecraft specialist Daniel Harms, Turner had already been looking into the possibility that Lovecraft had been inspired by actual grimoires when producing his ideas about the *Necronomicon*.[32] In the collaboration with Hay and Wilson, however, Turner put his knowledge and familiarity with the Dee material in the British Library to the task of creating an intriguing origin myth to the new *Necronomicon* edition. The introduction, written by the prolific British science fiction writer, literary critic, and occultist Colin Wilson, explained how Turner had set out to explore the link between the *Necronomicon* and John Dee, which Lovecraft asserted in his short "History of the *Necronomicon*." Familiar already with the Dee manuscripts in the Sloane collection of the British Library, Turner was said to have consulted the perhaps most cryptic of all the Dee papers, the grids of squares and letters of the *Liber Loagaeth*.[33] According to Wilson's introduction, Turner copied the elaborate and mysterious letter squares, sent them to the computer programmer and cryptographer David Langford, who "deciphered" the manuscript. The surprising result was the appearance of the text of the true *Necronomicon*, apparently coded in by Dee.

As is often the case with esoteric provenances, this astonishing story never happened. The truth behind the book was revealed by Wilson himself only a few years after it was published.[34] In that version, Turner had not so much played the role of researcher as that of author. The actual history of the volume was that George Hay had been given the task of creating an authentic-looking *Necronomicon* by the head of Neville Spearman. Wilson had later been contacted to look at the material that had been gathered for the volume. He was unimpressed, and contacted Turner to write the actual text of the grimoire. Given Turner's competence as a ritual magician and knowledge of the sources the result is a text that borrows much from actual grimoires, especially the *Goetia*. Any actual link with John Dee, however, remains spurious.

As J. W. Gonce has pointed out, Turner's involvement in this project is ironic when considered in the light of his image as a Dee purist, known for his uncompromising attacks on other occultists' syntheses.[35] Here, the same Turner lends his credibility to the claim that there is a connection between Dee's magic squares and Lovecraft's *Necronomicon*. In this respect it is interesting to note that senior members of the O.C.S. seem to agree that Turner's involvement with the *Necronomicon* volume seriously damaged the work of the Order, probably on several levels.[36] It has been suggested that the relative success of the book distracted Turner from the actual running of the O.C.S.[37] The whole event seems to have damaged Turner's integrity within the group, as well as the integrity of the group itself, contributing to its decline when approaching the 1990s.

An Experiment in Elizabethan Magic

Despite this development there is still the intriguing story of a practical working performed in 1983. Some time that year, the remaining members of the O.C.S. rented the Tixall Lodge Gatehouse in Staffordshire, originally raised in 1555 by Sir Edward Aston.[38] Led by Turner himself, the magicians conducted a rite of Elizabethan magic in these historically authentic surroundings. Although it is not certain what the actual purpose and outcome of the rite was, it has been suggested that it was based on the magical writings of the Elizabethan physician and magician Simon Forman (1552–1611).[39]

On the other hand, it is tempting to see the report of this working in light of a short note made by Turner toward the end of the introduction to his *Heptarchia Mystica,* published that same year:

> A Midlands based occult group have recently reconstructed the Holy Table, wax discs and other necessary equipment and shortly hope to perform the Heptarchical rite, publishing their findings in due course. Whether or not the spirits will welcome this invasion of their four hundred year repose remains uncertain.[40]

Although the evidence remains painfully circumstantial, this indicates that at least a major Enochian working was being planned.

Aurum Solis

We now move on to consider another esoteric order that has largely evaded scholarly examination. The Aurum Solis is an esoteric order that claims to represent "the Ogdoadic tradition."[41] It first appeared in a series of occult books published from 1974 to 1981, *The Magical Philosophy* I–V by Melita Denning and Osbourne Phillips—the pen names of Vivian Godfrey and Leon Barcynski—but claims to have roots back to 1890s England.[42] Although I cannot at present enter into a detailed examination of this claimed lineage, it will suffice to say that it seems likely to be yet another spurious and invented historiography. No documentary evidence has been presented by the authors, and attempts to verify some of the named predecessors have met with no success.[43] Thus, the five volumes of *The Magical Philosophy* can be considered the real foundation of the Aurum Solis, and their content is generally equated with the teachings of the Order.

The Aurum Solis does not qualify as a squarely purist movement. For reasons I will soon explain, I nevertheless hold that its Enochian teachings should be considered in the context of it. I will suggest that the Aurum Solis Enochiana exist at an interesting junction between the Golden Dawn tradition and the *impact* of the purist turn. This subchapter makes a brief interlude from the "strong" purism, represented by Turner, to consider that junction. Another reason that justifies its inclusion here is that the Aurum Solis' related publications have had a considerable impact on later Enochian magic, including that of a more explicitly purist bent.

Robe and Ring

When reissued by Llewellyn in 1982, book one of *The Magical Philosophy* series came with an appendix containing some Enochian material.[44] The material seems predominantly taken from Golden Dawn sources, without providing much new in way of interpretation. Here we find the same emphasis on elemental attributions and magic as we did in the Golden Dawn tradition, and Enochian is to be merged and used together with other systems. For instance, it is stated that the *Claves Angelicae* are to be employed whenever a separate magical language "is required for use in connection with the elemental forces."[45]

In connection with the Angelic language, we also find another interesting passage:

> [A] modern expert on linguistics has expressed a considered opinion that Kelley "invented" [the Enochian language]. The arguments put forward are so irrational, that we cannot and need not rationally refute them: they are furthermore based on theories devoid of all psychological understanding of the role of the natural faculties of the seer, and devoid too of any magical discernment or experience. Any who are disturbed by such arguments need only reflect that this sonorous barbaric language is of extreme magical potency, as many true occultists have proved.[46]

The passage seems to refer to Laycock's work, indicating that the appendix on Enochian was written after 1978. Furthermore, the quote is interesting, as it more than suggests what can be called a "realistic" interpretation of the Enochian language. Although there is an appeal to the evidence of experience, we see no trace of the purely pragmatic standpoint. Rather, the authors are anxious to expel the "irrational" criticism provided by linguistic analysis, in order to assert the language's "extreme magical potency."

So far, there is still not much trace of a purist approach. This changes toward the end of the appendix. When the authors include a section on the system of the thirty Aires or Aethyrs, they recognize its original geopolitical significance.[47] Apparently the authors did find it relevant to consult non–Golden Dawn/Crowley sources, perhaps Skinner's 1974 edition of Casaubon. Furthermore, they apparently did not feel the need to recapitulate Crowley's view on the subject. This is quite significant in connection with the purist turn, since the Aurum Solis thereby seems to be the first modern occultist group to do this. As we have seen already, Crowley's interpretation reigned supreme in other receptions of the Aethyrs, including modern Satanism and Left-Hand Path magic. Even the early O.C.S. followed him on this matter in their ritual for self-initiation.

Mysteria Magica

Books II–IV of the *Magical Philosophy* series contain no reference to Enochian. Book II largely discusses ritual and symbolism, closely following the astrological, Kabbalistic, and alchemical correspondence systems developed by the Golden Dawn.[48] Book III concerns sefirotic symbolism, and includes a discussion of the Golden Dawn system of initiation, which is simplified into a tripartite system used by the Aurum Solis.[49] The fourth book is much concerned with developing a sort of magical psychology, building on the system presented in the previous works.[50] Only in the fifth and last book, *Mysteria Magica* (1981), Enochian reemerges and is treated thoroughly.

Mysteria Magica contains two major sections on Enochian, entitled "De Rebus Enochianis" 1 and 2, in addition to an appendix on the pronunciation of the language.[51] This work clearly reveals familiarity and respect for the original sources. For instance, most of the content of MS Sloane 3191 is reproduced, including the *48 Claves Angelicae* and the *Liber scientiae*.[52] Here, diligent notes and comments on the spelling of Enochian words, and the exact reproduction of the Aires corresponding to geographical regions shows that the authors have taken pains going through the original documents.

But even so, one should note that the presentation of the Aires adds completely new functions to the ninety-one "Good Ministers" of the thirty Aires, seemingly *complementary* to their original function.[53] Although the functions listed are somewhat reminiscent of the offices of the seventy-two spirits of the *Goetia,* the origins of these attributions are not clear. The resulting system is unique to the Aurum Solis.

While much material is added to the pool of Enochian lore already in existence, there is still much remaining of the Golden Dawn system. For instance, while the system of the Great Table has been expanded and explained in greater detail, the basic framework of elemental and Kabbalistic magic is still preferred at the expense of the original system.[54] In addition, part two of "De Rebus Enochianis" is entirely preoccupied with showing how the Enochian system can be incorporated into other kinds of magical operations. Thus, although we see a partial return to the sources in the Aurum Solis' system of Enochian magic, the synthetic approach of the Golden Dawn still seems to have a strong grip.

Despite this, the material published in the fifth book of the *Magical Philosophy* series is at the core of the purist turn, simply because it provided access again to parts of Dee's material that had not been given much consideration in modern occultism. Along with Turner's work, it has had an impact on later magicians of a purist bent.

Geoffrey James's Enochian Evocations

Returning again to the stronger purist position, we have to consider the author Geoffrey James and his *Enochian Evocation of Dr. John Dee* (1984).

This is another of the key publications of the purist turn, greatly influencing later thought on the subject. The book is really a thoroughly edited version of original material taken from various Dee sources, including unpublished manuscripts and Casaubon's *True and Faithful Relation,* with a prefatory article and appendixes. In James's own words, "The *Enochian Evocation* is intended to present the essential core of Dee's evocation system arranged in a fashion similar to other renaissance evocation texts."[55] This means that material has been extracted from their original place in various documents and reorganized such as to give a coherent presentation of a magical system, with the first chapter giving the "sacred history" of Enochian as narrated to Dee at various times by the angels.[56] Then follows the various parts of Dee's magical system in order: the Heptarchic system, the *Claves Angelicae, Liber scientiae,* and the magic of the Great Table.

As with Turner's edition, James's work is not primarily intended for a scholarly audience. His aims are magical and operational, something that is clear from the introduction and the appendices. I will consider two aspects of this: first, James feels the same need as Denning and Phillips to defend the authenticity of the Enochian language from Laycock's criticism; secondly, he makes an effort to fill in some of the blanks of Dee's magical manuscripts, in order to put the system into practice.

In the introduction James spends several pages in an attempt to discard the criticisms and suspicions raised by Laycock. This takes the form of a search for passages in the Dee material that can be considered, in James's own words, "evidence for the presence of the supernatural."[57] Furthermore, he enters into a more detailed dialogue with some of Laycock's points. As was mentioned earlier, Laycock had found that parts of the Enochian language exhibited features that did not make sense phonetically, and suggested that this represented an arbitrary combination of letters. James's response is curious, and goes *contra* Laycock from the presupposition that angelic beings are real:

> [T]he Angelical language. . . .exhibits characteristics that would seem to indicate that it was designed to be a non-spoken language. As Da Vinci had pointed out nearly 100 years before the keys were dictated, spirits would be unable to make audible sounds on their own, due to the lack of vocal chords with which to vibrate air.[58]

This line of argumentation is valuable to note also in the context of the debate on the legitimacy of magic in secular modernity. It seems clear that James does not here allow for psychologized or purely pragmatic approaches to the question of occult entities; rather, he quite clearly supposes some kind of realistic understanding of the angels. Interestingly, we should note that this seems to be a preferred tendency in the purist approach to Enochian. We saw hints of it as well in the Aurum Solis above, and we will see it again in the currents influenced by purism.

However, it seems that James's approach was slightly modified over the years. In the introduction to the second edition of his book, we find the following statement on the reality of angels:

> As best I understand it, Enochian angels are unlikely to be "real" in the sense of being composed out of atoms, particle waves, or quantifiable material. On the other hand, I believe that angels may represent aspects of the human consciousness that all of us share. In that way, they exist in collective unconscious, which is, in some ways at least, more "real" than the physical world.[59]

Again, this underscores the point that studies on emic understandings of the reality of such beings in modern ritual magic should focus on and emphasize the plurality and unfixed status of this discourse. Now, a psychological interpretation is allowed for, albeit one that is just as much a sacralization of the psyche as a psychologization of the sacred. Especially following Jungian and transpersonal perspectives, this has become a major trend in contemporary Western religiosity more generally.[60]

Finally, James has added a section with notes for practice as an appendix.[61] An interesting aspect of this section is the way the author seeks to reconstruct the use of the Aires in *Liber scientiae* by drawing upon procedures in Renaissance manuals of talismanic magic. Influenced by Agrippa in particular, James argues that the spirit of each geographical location should be engraved on a circular disc, together with the name of the region and the name of the Aire ruling it. In addition, he notes the sigils of each spirit, which also appear in Dee's diaries, but were given no attention before. These actually correspond to the letter squares of the Great Table, in a way similar to the famous sigils of the planets in Agrippa's *De Occulta philosophia*. For this reason, James argues that the sigil and letter square where it is found should also be engraved on the disc, making a talisman in the Renaissance magical fashion. In this way we see how a purist still needs to put his creativity to make the magical system coherent, but applies that creativity with a stricter focus on what would have been plausible in the original historical context, rather than on the discourses most prevalent in his own days.

Against the Purist Current

The Schuelers and Enochian Revisionism

In their survey of the Enochian language, Pasi and Rabaté distinguished a "revisionist" current alongside the "purist" one.[62] Revisionists in this sense care less for keeping it close to the originals, favoring and encouraging additions, syntheses, and new interpretations instead. Two books were explicitly mentioned in the essay: Lon Milo DuQuette and Christopher Hyatt's *Enochian World of Aleister Crowley* (1991), and Gerald and Betty Schueler's *Enochian Magic: A Practical Manual* (1996 [1985]). In the case of the former, the revisionism only consists in that these authors accept the *earlier* revisions, done by the Golden Dawn and Crowley. DuQuette and Hyatt's book may be viewed as a document of the continued influence of Crowley's rendition of the Golden Dawn interpretation; the bulk of the book consists of a new edition of Crowley's *Liber Chanokh* and an exegesis of that text.[63] The only *further* revision is found in a scant nineteen pages at the end of the book, where an attempt is made to apply Enochian elements from the G.D./Crowley tradition to "Tantric" sex magic.[64] It is also worth noting that the introduction, written by DuQuette, actually includes a note on what we can consider an effect of the purist turn. DuQuette acknowledges that many "excellent" new works have appeared lately, which "offer valuable contributions".[65] Robert Turner is specifically mentioned, before DuQuette continues with the following paragraph:

> Some [other recent books] I feel are of less value. While perhaps informative as examples of the "findings" of one magician's experimentation, the distinction is not always made clear as to what is the author's speculation and innovation and what actually are the procedures *suggested in the original documents*.[66]

It could of course be brought in against DuQuette that Crowley and Regardie hardly classify as "original sources" in the strict sense either; however, the quote suggests that the approach of the authors was not dominated by wholesale "revisionism."[67] It is more a case of orthodoxy on behalf of the late-Victorian and Edwardian interpretations of occultist ritual magic.

It seems that a far clearer example of a revisionist current is found in what may well have been the authors DuQuette referred to in the passage above: Gerald and Betty Schueler. In addition to the title mentioned by Pasi and Rabaté, the Schuelers have written a whole oeuvre presenting a more or less novel interpretation of the Enochian language and its associated magic.

The Schuelers have published books on Enochian magic with Llewellyn since the late 1980s. The aim has been to construct a new spiritual worldview by fusing the available versions of Enochian magic (the original Dee material, and the G.D. and Crowley syntheses) with other sources, including Theosophy and transpersonal psychology.[68] While the first book, *Enochian Magick* (1985), does not add too much new material (being largely a recapitulation of information extracted almost directly from Regardie's *Golden Dawn* and Crowley's pieces published in *Gems from the Equinox*),[69] the eclecticism becomes emphatic in their following titles. *Enochian Physics* (1988) resembles a pseudoscientific, "New Age science" cosmology, fusing Enochian magic with nomenclature borrowed from modern physics; *Enochian Tarot* (1989) recasts the Tarot based on Enochian entities and symbolism; while *Enochian Yoga* (1995) introduces yogic techniques to an Enochian ritual context. Given the impact of the purist turn, this has unavoidably led to criticisms from other voices in the Enochian milieu, especially online, as will be shown in the last chapter of this book.

Major Themes in the Schueler system

Following largely in the footprints of the Golden Dawn and Crowley, most of the Schuelers' Enochian system is based upon speculations on the Great Table and the Aethyrs. In *Enochian Physics* and *Angels' Message to Humanity* (1996, 2002) these letter squares form the basis of two different esoteric cosmologies. These have later been described as a "two-dimensional" and a "three-dimensional" model, respectively. The first one lays out the cosmos as a "map" detailing the different "planes" attributed to the four elements and the element of spirit, and (following the G.D. tradition) the elemental tablets of the Enochian Great Table. The second cosmology is different, in that it constructs an "Enochian cube" from the tablets (or "Enochian mandalas," in the Schuelers' terminology) of the Great Table, presented as a three-dimensional, cubic model of the universe.[70] The *Tarot* and *Yoga* books similarly base themselves on the Great Table system when synthesizing Enochian with Tarot and yogic techniques.

Since 1998 the Schuelers have run a Web site which features a section (situated between the sections on "Schueler's Gnosticism" and "Norwegian Forest Cats") synthesizing the essentials of the Enochian system presented in their published works.[71] Here, we also find published other parts of the original Dee material, namely, *Liber scientiae, De heptarchia mystica,* and the Enochian language of the *Claves*.[72] But little is done to actually incorporate these sets of data into the general system presented in the Schuelers' books.

Instead, there is a cautionary remark that the system of the *heptarchia mystica,* for instance, should not be taken literally when it speaks about entities that can be exploited to find precious metals:

> [T]his does not mean that we can invoke a deity such as Bornogo and have him tell us where we can find gold for ourselves, for example. Such self-centered goals are laden with karmic pitfalls, and seldom work the way we would want. What we can gain, however, is information, usually in the form of experience (e.g., altered states of consciousness), of our entire universe both visible and invisible.[73]

What emerges here is an apparent ethical divergence between the magical systems of the Renaissance and that of the Schuelers. The latter seeks to overcome the former by presenting a "spiritualized" interpretation of the magical practice that originally had rather mundane goals. It should be recalled that a similar case was seen with Regardie, when he left out the original interpretation of the Great Table in his *Golden Dawn*, feeling that the material was "spiritually unsound."[74]

In the Schuelers' view, Enochian magic "focuses on the Great Work of spiritual evolutionary development and its ultimate goal is ego-trancendence [*sic*] or what is commonly called enlightenment."[75] For the Schuelers, Enochian magic is a framework for self-realization, and not a mere manipulative tool.

The only notable exception to the rule would be when the magic is put to practice for altruistic ends:

> We view the practice of Enochian Magic, or any type of magic, for personal gain as Black Magic. We view the practice of Enochian Magic, or any type of magic, for selfless devotion to the welfare of others as White Magic.[76]

Only altruistic "white magic" is perceived as licit, as in the example of "Enochian healing."[77] This subdiscipline is one of the innovations of the Schuelers, dealing with the construction of new letter squares from words in the Enochian language, to be used with mantras and visualizations to cure sickness.[78]

Matters of Legitimacy

On the Schuelers' Web site there also appear various statements in defense of their approach. The main strategy consists of simply acknowledging that there are different "schools" in Enochian magic, rather than one unifying paradigm by which legitimacy can be measured. There is an attempt to relativize by stating simply that "Schueler's Enochian Magic is Enochian Magic as defined and used by Gerald and Betty Schueler."[79]

In a note included in *Angels' Message to Humanity*, the Schuelers admit "borrowing heavily" from John Dee, the Golden Dawn, and Crowley, and furthermore explain the relationship between their own approach and these other "schools":

> We make no claims to present Enochian Magic, as taught by John Dee or the Golden Dawn or Crowley, per se; rather, we have blended together the best of these magical pioneers into an integral, workable system. We have also added new material, including our own interpretations and findings, to the available and often conflicting source material. Our system of Enochian Magic will agree in many areas with the source material but will disagree elsewhere.[80]

This is, in short, a legitimization of creative innovation. Contrary to both the strict purists and perennialists, it is not believed that any of the previous schools possessed "the truth" in Enochian matters. There is no appeal to primordial tradition, or "scholarly" authenticity. Rather, there is a certain progressive attitude, implying that individual parts can be disembedded and re-embedded in new systems as one sees fit, constructing pragmatically more useful systems. Referring to my previous discussion of the authenticity problem this is a clear example of the pragmatic/progressive strategy, placing the Schuelers' approach closer to LaVey and (to a certain extent) Aquino as far as the structure of the legitimizing rhetoric goes.

In this context it is interesting as well to consider what kind of metaphysical theories come with the Schuelers' Enochian magic. One would perhaps expect that the pragmatic approach to the legitimacy of the system as a whole should imply a pragmatic, ontologically noncommittal interpretation of the entities belonging to that system as well. In LaVey's case, this seemed to hold. With Gerald and Betty Schueler it is not that clear:

> Like John Dee, we view the Angels, Kings, Seniors, and others as inhabitants, and in some cases rulers, of those vast planes and subplanes of invisible worlds that surround our Earth. They are the emissaries, children if you will, of God, however you chose to define Him. In one sense they are real external living beings. In another sense, they are personified projections from our own personal and collective unconscious.[81]

To a certain extent, a realistic interpretation is alluded to, which involves a cosmology where the totality of the world consists of several "planes" and "subplanes," of which our material reality is the lowest one.[82] The angels are "real" in the sense that they have existence on these other planes (similarly it is stated that "the heavens of the world's religions" are situated on the astral plane). At the same time a certain psychologization is invoked with the statement that the angels, in another sense, stem from our "personal and collective unconscious." This may perhaps look like a noncommittal strategy. However, the latter statement seems just as much to be an expression of an esoteric psychology rather than a psychologized esotericism, implying that there is no real distinction between the "collective unconscious" and the supra-material "planes."[83] We recognized a touch of this in Geoffrey James as well—which here has become a thoroughgoing framework for countering the semantic questions of magic whenever they arise.

Donald Tyson's Enochian Apocalypticism

Another central player on the post–purist turn Enochiana scene of the 1990s is Donald Tyson. Tyson won fame in the contemporary occult community in 1993 with his erudite edition of Cornelius Agrippa's *Three Books of Occult Philosophy,* based on the 1651 English translation by James Freake.[84] Additionally, he is the author of a couple of dozen books on occult topics, ranging from rune magic to the *Necronomicon*.[85]

Although Tyson's *Enochian Magic for Beginners* (1997) was classified by Pasi and Rabaté as one of the two foremost examples of the purist current, Tyson's general work does not squarely fit this rubric as employed here.[86] Even in that book, Tyson possesses a desire to push on the boundaries of the actual material and make novel interpretations, although, admittedly, he is tidy enough to clearly tell the reader when he is making subjective statements.[87] The most significant point he brings to the material is the reconstruction of an "eighteen-day working," which, in Tyson's opinion, is to be performed to make contact with the spirits of the Great Table in the first place,[88] together with his firm belief that there is a dark secret to Enochian magic. According to Tyson, Enochian carries within its corpus the magical key to set off the Apocalypse as described in *Revelations*.[89]

The argument of this more spectacular idea is that there exists at the core of the Enochian system a hitherto unpronounced "Apocalypse Working," which especially relate to the use of the Angelic calls. Tyson first expressed his views on the angelic apocalyptic agenda in his book *Tetragrammaton* (1995), which was more recently republished as *Power of the Word* (2004). The same idea was expressed in his much-discussed 1996 article in *Gnosis Magazine,* entitled "The Enochian Apocalypse."[90] In *Enochian Magic for Beginners*, the idea is found several places, such as the following:

> [I]t is also my opinion that the forty-eight expressed Keys. . . .are intended by the angels to be used in a great working, probably of fifty days duration, designed to initiate the period of destructive transformation that is generally known as the apocalypse. This may be linked with the eighteen-day invocation of the angels of the Great Table[91]. . . .or it may be a separate working.[92]

Still, Tyson's book is certainly *influenced* by the purist turn. It is written with the expressed intention of making available all aspects of Dee's original system, and does indeed give a very systematic treatment of both the Heptarchic system, the Great Table material, the Aires, and the *Claves Angelicae,* all based on research of original sources. It also includes a precise and accurate debunking of the Golden Dawn and Crowley syntheses in light of what is actually present in the primary sources.[93] The idiosyncrasies of Tyson's work stem rather from his reconstructions, which are far more spectacular and imaginative than that of the earlier purists, such as Robert Turner and Geoffrey James.

Tyson's ambivalence toward the sources is further indicated by his other projects. For instance, over the years he has collaborated with the Schuelers in their work. Most significantly, he wrote a foreword to the Schuelers' book *Angels' Message to Humanity,* published in 1996. Here it is revealed that it was actually Tyson who came up with the idea of making an inverted version of the "Tablet of Union" of the Great Table—named the "Tablet of Chaos"—to construct the "Enochian Cube" cosmology mentioned above.[94] According to Tyson, it was the collaboration on this project that eventually turned him toward the apocalyptic interpretations of Enochian which he incorporated in his *Tetragrammaton* and *Enochian Magic for Beginners*.[95]

Although he does not seem to involve himself much with the contemporary community of Enochian magicians, the publication of *Tetragrammaton* and *Enochian Magic for Beginners* has acquired for Tyson a position in it, and, as we will see in the last chapter, his work is often discussed by magicians.

8
Enochiana without Borders

The core publications of the purist turn have greatly influenced the reception and conceptualization of Enochian magic in the last two decades. However, while the purist current has remained very much alive in the 1990s and the new millennium, there is a variety of interpretations on the market. The Golden Dawn interpretation still has wide currency, Crowley's use of the Aethyrs is taken as exemplum by Thelemites and non-Thelemites alike, while some seek to build further on these occultist classics, and others even claim new revelations from Dee's and Kelley's angels. With the mass-popularization of esoteric discourse of the late twentieth century, the Enochian discourse has been imported to other countries as well, including non-English speaking countries such as France and Norway.[1]

Meanwhile, the full-blown emergence of the Internet by the mid-1990s has provided for a rapidly growing occult community online, spawning new occult fascination with Enochian in what seems an exponential growth curve. The massive migration of occultism online toward the end of the previous century resulted in a radically democratized situation, marked more by endless discussions and negotiations between individual practitioners with unlike views, than by asserted, normative positions. While I have indeed sought to emphasize these flexible, dialogical, and discursive features in earlier periods as well, moving the discussion into the contested spaces of the World Wide Web has made the subject matter of Enochian magic even more contested. Also, with the blurred boundaries between private and public knowledge that follows online publication, the many debates, uncertainties, and polemics have become even more open and apparent. Competing for survival in the marketplace is not as easy as it was before, given the omnipresence of differing views and products. This has laid strains on practitioners making claims about

Enochian, leading to the flourishing of interesting discussions on the basis for legitimacy in Enochian matters.

The present chapter will emphasize the major trends in argumentation to be found in the contemporary Enochian discourse community online. As the online/offline distinction does not refer to entirely distinct realms or worlds, there will, however, obviously be overlaps. Especially, we shall see that the literary production discussed in the previous chapter has provided a framework which much of the online debates revolve around. In addition to tracing and analyzing these discussions, I will have a closer look at the perspectives of a couple of prominent Enochian magicians who emerged solely from this online occult community, and have continued to have influence in the new millennium.

The Internet, Contemporary Occulture, and International Enochian Networks

The 1990s saw the full-blown emergence of the Internet, and the explosive growth of the World Wide Web. Probably the most revolutionary development in information technology since the printing press, this change in the conditions and means of communication and publishing had far-reaching consequences for the development of contemporary religiosity.[2] As a part of this broader development, occultism has been equally influenced by the new technology, finding new ground for recruitment and dissemination of information online.[3] As Christopher Partridge noted in his discussion of the contemporary occulture, the advent of the Internet "has facilitated and accelerated the emergence of mystical networks and organizations."[4] Following the work of sociologist Colin Campbell on the "cultic milieu," the proliferation of ideas through such networks is at the core of "mystical religion," or, in Partridge's terminology, of occulture itself. The Internet laid the foundation for an explosive growth of such networks, by largely sidestepping geographical boundaries.[5]

The significance of the Internet in providing a way of efficient communication has had a considerable impact on Enochiana. The new routes of communication provided by the Net have facilitated the growth of a worldwide network of Enochian magicians, through various e-mail lists and discussion forums. Generally, it seems, occultists were early birds in taking advantage of the new technology, as the Enochian magicians illustrate. It was only in 1995–96 that the Internet entered a period of explosive growth; during that period the Internet gained the full attention of the general public, and we also saw the distribution of user-friendly software, resulting in millions of new users.[6] Although occultism had already gone online through earlier successful networks such as Usenet, it was in this period of growth, toward the end of 1996, that a number of occultists established the "Enochian-L" mailing list.[7] This would become the basis for thriving discussions and networking between Enochian magicians in years to come. In fact, most of the notable scholars, authors, and magicians currently working with Enochian participated in this list, including such names as Benjamin Rowe, David R. Jones, Al Billings, Clay Holden, Darcy Küntz, Chris Feldman (a.k.a. Christeos Pir), Runar Karlsen, and others. The Internet, shortly put, empowered and gave a voice to a new class of Enochian specialists, previously without the means of uttering their ideas to a broader public of likeminded individuals.

As e-lists became increasingly outdated at the turn of the millennium, the center of gravity for online occult discussions switched toward discussion groups and forums. For the Enochian community, the most notable one is the Yahoo! group "Enochian," established in January 2002 and still growing rapidly.[8] This was the forum to which the Enochian-L subscribers migrated and kept the discussions going. As discussion groups are much more easily available than e-lists to a broader public, the membership rapidly grew. As of spring 2008 the group has more than 550 members, who have published more than 5,200 posts in total.

In addition to facilitating the emergence of communication networks the Internet has also provided a cheap, easy, and decentralized way for individuals to publish material. Also on this front, the occult community has been quite prolific. The resource portal hermetic.com, established by Al Billings in 1996, holds much Enochian material. Here we find both original sources and the essays of modern and contemporary magicians.[9] Another important site is "Norton's Imperium," which was run by the late Benjamin Rowe. Now relocated to hermetic.com, this site still contains Rowe's collected works on Enochian, which have been much discussed by the online Enochianites.[10] In addition, original source documents have been made available in various forms. Perhaps most notable is the online *Magickal Review,* run by Ian Rons, which has secured rights from collections in order to publish electronic scans of the original Sloane and Cotton manuscripts, in addition to more essays and contemporary theories on the practice of Enochian magic.[11]

Also on the material side, the Internet has opened new possibilities. As marketing and distribution of goods has become more and more common online as well, there now exists a Web site making and selling ritual equipment for Enochian magic. A wooden Great Table, a "ring of Solomon" in gold, or a Sigillum Emeth carved in beeswax can all be obtained online and shipped to magicians who have a few hundred U.S. dollars to spend.[12]

It is safe to say that the growth of the Internet has provided a whole new infrastructure for the production and distribution of knowledge on Enochiana, as in other domains. Perhaps one of the most important aspects is that it has provided an arena for a whole class of people who did not already have a voice in the form of being contracted and published authors. It should be remarked that before the Internet revolution, what existed of Enochian material and discussions of it came out of a small handful of publishers. Llewellyn was certainly the main actor, publishing Regardie and the Golden Dawn material, as well as the works of Tyson and the Schuelers. The alternatives, especially the vanguard publications of the purist turn, came out of smaller publishing houses, mostly in Britain, such as Adam McLean's Magnum Opus Hermetic Sourcework series, Askin Publishers, Element, and Aquarian Press.[13] In the 1990s, Weiser Books and New Falcon also entered the scene, most notably representing the Thelemic school of Enochian magic.[14] With the advent of the Internet, and the means of networking and publication that it provided, the access to both production and consumption of Enochian lore was largely decentralized. Consequently, a host of new voices was empowered. What did they have to say?

Discussing the Angels Online

The amount of information available online—material spanning, at the time of writing, fourteen years of running discussions—is far too vast to be considered in its entirety. However, the information accumulated in discussion forums and e-lists has an advantage that will be explored here, namely its "Q&A" quality. This makes it possible to browse for specific topics that are discussed and analyzed by the main participants of the forum or e-list. In the present section, therefore, I will look specifically at discussions related to the points raised in chapter 4, concerning the authenticity problem and the legitimacy of magic.

Discussing Authenticity

When the Enochian e-list was established in 1996, the anonymous author of one of the very first posts addressed "the esteemed Benjamin Rowe," who had also subscribed to the list.[15]

Rowe was already a respected Enochian magician, operating in California, who had written several (unpublished) essays and articles on the topic, now published online. He had been experimenting with Enochian magic since 1985, when he engaged in what he termed extensive "tourism" of the tablet of Earth according to the Golden Dawn attributions.[16] Rowe's various articles reveal an innovative and practical take on Enochian magic, operating primarily from the basis of Golden Dawn and Crowley systems, but also with a sensibility tuned toward the attitude of the purists. This is especially evident from his "Enochian Magick Reference," a document detailing to some extent the different parts of the original system, a brief "history of use," and an annotated bibliography of the existing Enochian literature.[17] His other works include reports on practical experiments, newly composed rituals, and theoretical pieces on the Enochian system.

Rowe was one of the most emphatic and defining voices on the Enochian-L e-list. Although he does not qualify as a strict purist himself, he was highly critical of the eclectic approach of Gerald Schueler, and also to the more imaginative aspects of Donald Tyson's work.[18] This seems to have been a quite widespread opinion on Enochian-L; just after Tyson had published *Tetragrammaton* and his contested 1996 article in *Gnosis,* there appeared a thread discussing his system. At first, Rowe wanted to know if anybody had tried practicing Tyson's method of combining the angelic calls with the Great Table. After a short while, however, the thread focused entirely on his apocalyptic ideas. When Rowe learned that Tyson had collaborated with Schueler on *Angels' Message,* he headshakingly commented that "Between Jerry's theosophy and Tyson's apocalyptics, there's gonna be some mighty confused readers out there."[19] Meanwhile, two others, Michael Lynch and Charla Williams, proposed featuring Tyson in the humor section.[20] Clearly, his position did not have much credibility in the forum, which is perhaps also indicated by Rowe's judgment of his books in the "Enochian Magick Reference" document, where he is included together with Schueler in the "Hall of Shame":

> Tyson combines the Enochian material with Fundamentalist millennialism and Lovecraftian horror fiction, to paint a picture of the Angelic Calls as the means by which the apocalypse will be brought about. In the process, he twists facts to suit his thesis, selectively interprets the Calls, and blithely dismisses contrary portions of the record as "not what was intended."[21]

But Rowe's "Hall of Shame" was nevertheless dominated by the works of Gerald Schueler. One of the highlights of the Enochian-L discussions occurred when Schueler himself joined the list, and engaged in a polemical exchange with Rowe.[22] Before he entered the discussion, Rowe had been criticizing Schueler's books, especially what he saw as unaccredited borrowing from other sources, overly imaginative changes to the system, and a low standard of scholarship.[23] As Rowe quickly pointed out to Schueler on the list, he had an "extreme bias" against his books: "This bias started to build with *Enochian Magick,* and that marvelous piece of semantic nullity, *Enochian Physics,* drove a spike through the heart of my few remaining doubts about my judgment."[24]

The "semantic nullity" of *Enochian Physics* referred especially to what Rowe identified as a rhetorical, inconsistent, and nonsensical use of scientific-sounding terminology. Schueler had defended his eclectic take on magical theory by saying that his work was intended to "put the Enochian material into a framework that is (1) useful and practical, and (2) founded on a solid theoretical basis."[25] Rowe responded by pointing to *Enochian Physics,* hastily deconstructing and debunking some of its scientizing language, before concluding that

> [i]t would take me at least a couple of months to catalog and explain all the errors of logic, undefined and multiply-defined terms, contradictory statements and other messes I found in the book. Doing so would be as tedious as finding all the logical fallacies in Aquinas, and would take us far from the purpose of this e-list.[26]

Rowe intended to show how the whole work was useless as a theoretical fundament, since it was massively inconsistent and contradictory. In his view, Schueler's paralleling of Einstein's famous mass-energy equation of special relativity, $E = mc^2$, with his own "equation of Enochian physics," $S = Fv^2$ (where S is "Spirit," F is "Form," and v is "the speed of thought"),[27] constitutes "a sort of "authority by propinquity," giving the aura of meaningfulness to nonsense by mentioning it in the same breath as something that is meaningful."[28] Schueler's response to the claims that his theoretical expounding qualifies as gibberish is summed up in his statement: "Not for me it doesn't. It actually makes a whole lot of sense."[29] The argumentation seemed to stop there.

Schueler's latter statement is perhaps illustrative of a subjective and relativistic argumentative strategy that goes well with his approach generally. Faced with Rowe's resentful criticism, Schueler further tries to explain that he does not accept any definite and universal mode of interpretation of the Enochian system—even though Rowe surely criticizes him for doing exactly this with his theosophical, scientizing model presented by definite and absolutist figures of speech (e.g., "Enochian magic teaches," "Enochian physics teaches," etc.). Instead, Schueler insisted on being fully aware that "[t]hose whom I would label 'Dee purists' are never going to accept my interpretations, nor did I ever expect them to. I assume that you are a 'Dee purist' and that is fine."[30]

Interestingly, Rowe did not consider himself to be a purist, as he stated explicitly in his response. However, he added, he did "believe in maintaining a sharp distinction between information that comes from the original material, and information that comes by other means."[31] The reason for this, Rowe makes clear, is that he agrees with one central point Schueler makes, namely that Dee's diaries and magical manuscripts have significant gaps, such that they do not present a fully functional magical system: "A certain amount of improvisation has always been necessary, and the angels took this into account in their (admittedly brief) instructions on how to use them."[32] Adding to this, with another clear sting against Schueler, Rowe expressed being "not at all certain that an 'overall theoretical foundation' [of Enochian magic] is in any way necessary, or even possible."[33]

The discussion between Rowe and Schueler is intriguing in connection with the problem of authenticity. It bears witness to an interesting nuance, which deserves to be addressed in some detail. In his criticism, Rowe to a considerable extent makes use of the *language* of purism, although when confronted with it, he denies being a purist. On a broad level of analysis, both Rowe and Schueler have a *pragmatic* approach to Enochian magic; they are both opposed to the strict perennialism, or appeal to tradition, of previous occultist syntheses, and at the same time aware of the operational flaws of the strictly original Dee material. Both arrive at the conclusion that a certain amount of creativity is necessary.

Their main difference is, rather, found on a somewhat deeper level of analysis, where it stems from a differing choice of discursive strategies. For this analysis, I refer again to the three strategies identified in modern esoteric discourses by Olav Hammer, namely "(terminological) scientism," "appeal to tradition," and "appeal to experience."[34] With reference to this, Rowe was an experimentalist, and his language of choice in legitimizing his claims on Enochian magic is found in an appeal to *experience*. His final word in objection to Schueler is not actually purist, but rather experiential. As Rowe put it, to prove his innovations were legitimate, Schueler would "have to publish a hell of a lot of his own magickal records to convince me he got his stuff from actually using the magick."[35] In the course of his own work, Rowe published extensive amounts of personal experiences and dealings with the Enochian entities, from the angels of the Great Table, to scrying of the Aethyrs and the ninety-one parts of the earth presented therein.[36] With the basis in such experiments he went on to (re)construct rituals and methods for working with the Enochian entities, based mostly on known ritual structures from the Golden Dawn and Crowley, such as the rituals of the hexagram, which was revised and "Enochianized" by Rowe.[37]

While an appeal to experience seems to be the main discursive strategy taken by Rowe, the polemical exchange surrounding Schueler's *Enochian Physics* illustrates a clash with what can be discerned as "terminological scientism." Rowe's suspicions about the use of scientific nomenclature constructing an "authority by propinquity" does not seem totally off target; certainly, Schueler himself seems to argue that he is merely "updating" Enochiana by making "a synthesis of Blavatsky, Crowley, Dee, and modern science."[38] Meanwhile, the experiential dimension is not as emphatic in his writing; although when confronted, Schueler had to defend himself on experiential terms as well, by affirming that he had undertaken practical work. But his final word, contrary to that of Rowe, was that a "theoretical framework" explaining how Enochian magic might work is necessary "if you want a worldview that accepts Enochian material as fact. . . . Else it all rests on faith, and you may as well go to church."[39]

Discussing the Nature of Angels

While the previous section illustrates the continued and increasing contestation of legitimacy that has followed Enochiana's migration to Cyberspace, there is now need for a brief discussion as well of the question of interpreting the nature of the Enochian *entities*. Together with the question of "who decides the right way" in Enochiana, this very question seems to attract most interest, at least from newcomers that join the online e-lists or discussion groups. Again, the plurality of views and positions is considerable. As one commentator online put it in 2005, "The two opposing schools of thought is [*sic!*]: spirit contact is either a psychological manifestation, or . . . spirits are real and have their own external abodes."[40] This broad divide frequently shows up in discussions on the reality of the angels; certainly the psychologized version does not have monopoly.[41] For the sake of brevity I will focus my discussion here on one thread of posts on Enochian-L where the local champion Ben Rowe is put to the test by fellow debaters.

After discussing a technical point concerning occult attributions in the Enochian Great Table, Rowe was asked by an eager student, signing interchangeably as "V. H." and "Tim," whether he believed that Enochian was, in fact, delivered by angels, and if he perceived validity (i.e., legitimacy) in Enochian matters to hinge on reconstructing the motivations of the angels.[42] It is well worth quoting Rowe's response at some length, as it reveals an attitude that seems quite pervasive among the more eloquent and articulate segments of the contemporary occultural milieu. First, Rowe responded that for a long time he had adopted a practice in which he

> put the word "angels" in quotes, to show that I was using it as a convenience rather than as a statement of belief about the nature of the phenomena observed. I haven't the faintest idea as to the "real" nature of the source of these recorded words.[43]

Such seemingly agnostic, or rather conventionalist, expressions seem to be quite widespread among present day magicians. I also encountered it in my previous research on contemporary ritual magic in Norway.[44] In addition, it seems to be a part of the structure of "psychologized magic" as understood by Hanegraaff, and the "suspension of disbelief" noticed by Luhrmann in her study of contemporary British witches.[45] Revisited from the viewpoint of a discursive analysis, this seems to be a *strategic* agnosticism; a convenient way for magicians to remain ontologically noncommittal, suspending their judgment when confronted by critical or skeptical voices, while still being able to retain the basic point that there is "something going on." However, the magicians' evaluation seldom stops there, and Rowe is no exception. After asserting this initial bracketing of the ontological question, Rowe claims that the evidence of Dee's diaries provides a picture of independent, sapient beings: "In the absence of strong evidence to the contrary," he goes on to write, "it is simplest to deal with the material in the terms in which it presents itself, and to see where that leads."[46] Rowe invents an analogy to argue his point:

> The evidence I have for the existence of these "angels" as separate beings is of *exactly* the same sort as I have for the existence of "V. H." [i.e., the person he is responding to]. In some ways the evidence in their favor is a bit stronger; the angels I contact using the Calls frequently surprise me, while "Tim" is fairly predictable. Perhaps "Tim" is just a clever AI program running on a MacIntosh somewhere in the bowels of Apple Corp; or perhaps "Tim" is a bit of online theater, maintained over the years by a group of scriptwriters. ;-) Still, most of the time it is simpler to act as if Tim is an intelligent, individual being. The same for these "angels."

The essence of the argument, then, is in one sense "pragmatic," but in another sense "realistic"; given the way things *seem*, the *reality* of the angels may be perceived as an *inference to the best explanation*. In other words, Rowe claims for himself an argument based on abductive reasoning which, although not logically valid from a formal perspective, is widely considered an important cornerstone of the scientific method.[47] Interestingly, the noncommittal, agnostic position seems to be merely an early stage in a broader argument which goes in the direction of asserting the reality of the angels in some more-than-mundane sense.

If, as I have suggested, this position is widespread, it is still far from uncontested. In the thread mentioned, Rowe quickly got a response from someone signing as "nigris (333),"[48] apparently a Satanist, opening most of his posts with "Hail Satan!"[49] Nigris's response is interesting in that it puts the seemingly rational basis of Rowe's evaluation to the test—which eventually pushes Rowe into giving even more of what he considers evidence for the reality of the angels. First of all, Nigris contests Rowe's alleged agnosticism, or bracketing, which is at the basis of his argument, by saying that taking alternative models than those presented in the diaries themselves into account actually *is* relevant from the beginning, as he puts it, "if one is attempting to discover precisely what is going on in the process of communication (as reflective or investigative inquiry during or prior to engagement of the art/science)."[50] In a later post Nigris advocates a psychologized interpretation instead, and, when actually working the magic, employing a quite conscious suspension of disbelief.[51] In addition Nigris attacks the validity of Rowe's abductive inference: the analogy he constructed is not really analogous, Nigris claims, since the inference that "Tim is real" is based on the knowledge that Rowe himself appears in the same manner (i.e., as words on a screen) via the medium of computer and Internet, whereas he has presumably no such experience of ever having appeared to someone as an angel in visions.[52] The point made is that the inference of the reality of the angels is not grounded in the same type of trivial experience; the inference of Tim's existence is based on a background knowledge of how humans generally behave, a trivial, tacit knowledge which he does not have of angels. In the end, Nigris proclaims that "I'm not sure I understand what is being called 'real' and would bypass the question of 'reality' for an analysis of possibilities as regards what it is that is *happening* in the Calls and what or who it might be that becomes involved with them."[53]

As an effect of these criticisms, Rowe defends his position by bringing in more of what he considers evidence supporting the hypothesis that the angels are real and independent beings. He especially points to the Dee diaries themselves, and some of the more mysterious features revealed by a close reading of them. For instance, Rowe points to the somewhat perplexing fact that the names of the "91 parts of the earth" in *Liber scientiae*, and the sigils belonging to each of the ninety-one spirits, are extracted from the letter squares of the Great Table, but that the Table itself actually appears to have been constructed or received only a month *later* than the former.[54] He acknowledges that skeptics have suggested, for this and other reasons, that Kelley must have been something of "a con-man with an IQ above genius level and an eidetic memory, who planned the whole thing out ahead of time, memorized all the data, and leaked it out through the 'visions' over the course of four years."[55] However, Rowe added, "I personally do not find this alternative credible."[56]

Finally, Rowe also indicates that he is conscious of the seemingly fluctuating "nature" of the angels as they present themselves to different people:

> If you read over the available records of people's contacts with these beings, it is clear that the way in which they appear depends a lot on the nature of the magician they are contacting. To Dee and Kelly they appeared as imperious Christian angels; to Crowley they were theatrical thelemites; to the Aurum Solis they were bands of goetia-like spirits; and to me they are friendly, laid-back metaphysicians.[57]

Although this could have been taken straight out of scholarly discussions of the historical and cultural contingency of "mystical experience," as discussed by, for instance, Steven Katz and Wayne Proudfoot,[58] Rowe goes on to assert that the one stable and universal feature, in his opinion, is that the angels act in all cases as "initiators *par excellence*, who aren't restricted by any human religion or world-view."[59] Here we see again the theme initiated by Crowley.

It seems fairly unambiguous in the end that Benjamin Rowe, for one, considered the angels to be real in a more than psychological sense. To close this section, I will quote the opening statement of Rowe's perhaps most influential tract on Enochian magic, "Godzilla meets E.T.":

> What most distinguishes the Enochian magickal system is that it is an artifact, a made thing. . . . It is equally clear to those who have used the system extensively that it is not the product of human creativity, but of a being or beings possessing a much higher order of perception and a much greater scope of action. The magickal beings who are bound into this system are all (except the cacodemons) of at least the human level of development. Each has a nature as deep and complex as any man, and each has an individual will as strong. Further, the system appears to touch on every part of the magickal universe; no magician has yet found any limit to its connections.

> Both of these facts demonstrate that the origin of this magick must have been truly divine. No lesser source could possibly have bound together the elements it contains; no lesser source could have made those elements so instantly and perfectly responsive to the will of the user.[60]

New Revelations

Through the course of this book we have seen how painstakingly preoccupied modern occultists have been with negotiating the authority of Dee's original documents, possessing an air of ancient legitimacy, with new and sometimes quite modern frameworks of interpretation. In recent years, however, the field of Enochian magic has also seen an attempt to move beyond this whole complex of interpretation and reinterpretation of something that happened in Elizabethan times. At the turn of the new millennium we find an Enochian milieu that places emphasis on *new* revelation. Roughly coinciding with Benjamin Rowe's illness and death, the focus of the online discussions shifted from being centered on technical points of interpreting original data and evaluating the Golden Dawn and Aurum Solis, to extensive comparison of notes, reports on newly discovered Enochian words, or entire verses and newly received letter tablets. In Cyberspace, the angels spoke again.

A Latter-Day Edward Kelley?

The most central, or at least the most illustrative, figure of this movement is Runar Karlsen. Karlsen (b. 1963) is a Norwegian magician based in Oslo, where he graduated at the Academy of Fine Arts. He has a firm background in Thelema, having run one of the competing thelmeic groups, "Balt Oasis" of the Caliphate O.T.O., in Oslo in the early 1990s.[61] There is also evidence that he had at some point read the literature concerning Michael Aquino and the revelation of his *Book of Coming Forth by Night*.[62] This seems a relevant fact considering Karlsen's own Enochian endeavors.

When he joined the Enochian-L mailing list in September 1997, Karlsen testified of having been interested in Enochiana since 1988, when he had become absorbed by the Enochian keys.[63] Subsequently he had introduced Enochian workshops and rituals into his O.T.O. group. The name of that group itself betrays an interest in Enochian magic, as "Balt" is the Angelic for "Justice"; associated in the Enochian calls with "Iad Balt": "God of Justice."

When he joined Enochian-L in 1997 Karlsen for a long time held a relatively low profile, making the occasional comment to queries, and posting some of his own experiences with Enochian scrying. After a while he started posting material that revealed more idiosyncrasies. His first contribution was a post on "The Elements," which argued that the elemental attributions assigned to pentagrams used in the Golden Dawn did not make sense, and had to be revised, especially by incorporating certain Enochian spirit names into the equation.[64] This sparked some minor debate in the forum.

But his posts would become more intriguing still. Responding to a discussion on certain unexplained numbers that appear in the text of the nineteen Enochian calls, Karlsen revealed for the first time his quite novel interpretation. In Karlsen's view, "The numbers in the calls refer to independent spirits; a pantheon within the system."[65] He immediately followed up by giving the names of twenty-eight spirits from "the table of NI."[66] "NI" is an Enochian word appearing in the seventh call, where it is rendered as the number 28.[67] The spirit names that Karlsen lists, however, are not to be found anywhere in the original Enochian corpus. In fact, it soon surfaces that "the table of NI" is an entirely new letter table communicated to Karlsen, as some latter-day Edward Kelley, together with several other new calls and spirit names.

Karlsen's main work, it seems, had been to chart out the spirits allegedly "masked" behind mysterious numbers in the Enochian calls and devise methods to call them forth. According to his own statement, Karlsen's first encounter with these uncharted Enochian entities was not a product of any deliberate effort on his part. As he explained, he had been performing some elemental magical work unrelated to Enochian, when nine spirits intruded into his visionary experience. The spirits started speaking in "soft voices at a very loud volume," dictating a book to him in a language he would later identify as Enochian.[68] The book would become known as *Dor OS zol ma thil,* which Karlsen later translated as "The falling seats of the twelve black hands." [69] It contained three chapters that "explained" the works of "the nine fire spirits of EM" (a word meaning "nine" in Enochian, appearing in the sixth call) and revealed their names.[70] This event took place in January 1991.

This was not the only "received work" Karlsen got. Over the years to come, he tried to communicate with the angels in order to have the *Dor OS zol ma thil* translated, but with only partial success.[71] In addition, however, another series of Enochian texts were revealed to him from 1992 and onward.[72] This corpus, consisting of verses in Enochian and a series of new letter tablets, bears the name *I Ged* (translated as "Is falling").

The corpus has later been described as "an Enochian grimoire," in that it tabulates entirely new letter squares and spirit names for the groups of spirits that Karlsen has discovered behind the numbers in the original calls. It also gives entirely new Enochian calls to be used for working with them.[73] Together with the *Dor OS zol ma thil* this new material makes up a whole new subsection of Enochian magic; or, as Karlsen described it to Enochian-L subscribers in 1998, "a pantheon within the system."

Despite the somewhat extraordinary-sounding character of his work, Karlsen was not given too much attention on Enochian-L at first. His early posts gave the impression of a slightly unpredictable character, with unusual and strange ideas, often formulated in less than waterproof English. During his first months at Enochian-L, there was really just one other person, Dean Hildebrandt, who seemed genuinely intrigued by Karlsen's work, and encouraged him by asking clearly interested questions.[74] But as time progressed, Karlsen's presence on the Internet facilitated a growing interest in his work. In Spring 2001 several people posted reports on Enochian-L about their attempts to work with Karlsen's spirits and calls.[75] In the summer of 2002, Paul Joseph Rovelli (writing under the name Zephyros93) uploaded his analysis of Karlsen's transmission as a Thelemic prophetic work to the Enochian Yahoo! group, connecting it with Crowley's *Liber Legis*.[76] When the discussions moved into the Yahoo! group, it seems that Karlsen's revelations were gradually incorporated and recognized as a new part of the Enochian system.

The previously mentioned Dean Hildebrandt played a significant role in this development. He was the first to seriously embrace Karlsen's ideas, and started collaborating with him. In 1997 they started e-mailing and comparing notes as Hildebrandt begun exploring Karlsen's newly received material.[77] Around 1999 they created a Web site together, entitled *Ored Dhagia—The Infinite Ways*, which is dedicated to exploring Karlsen's system.[78] The site features all the newly received material, indexed and commented on by both Karlsen and Hildebrandt, and also a collection of various essays (and links to external essays) written by others who have become associated with this current. Especially worthy of mention are Patricia Shaffer and Marid Audran. Shaffer's claim to fame in contemporary Enochiana was her theory of "letter essences," which she published in its first form on the Enochian-L list in 1998.[79] Operating from a theory that each letter and its corresponding sound expresses some meaning that is universal (although hidden) "to the mind of man," Shaffer constructed a list of such essences for the Enochian letters.[80] Thus she got, for instance

O: Root of Being-Becoming: being, becoming; existence
L: Root of Primacy: first, primary, one; providence
S: Root of Possession: have, acquire, gather; together
N: Root of Interiority: within, inside, self-hood.[81]

Already after Shaffer's initial posting of it on Enochian-L Karlsen showed great interest in the theory, which he found resonant with his own ideas.[82] His positive response led to an exchange of ideas between the two. In his later work Karlsen frequently incorporates Shaffer's method of letter analysis in order to translate new Enochian words.

Marid Audran is another magician who has followed up on Karlsen's track, and has received more material in the same way. A section of Audran's work is included on Karlsen's Web site; this work combines Karlsen's revelations and Shaffer's letter essence theory, while exploring new and uncharted territories, such as the entity Caosgo—an Enochian name allegedly belonging to "the spirit of the Earth."[83]

"The New Flow"

In 2006 someone asked the Enochian Yahoo! group whether or not it was true that Enochiana consisted of several, rather than one, magical systems. The response given by a member calling himself Ima Pseudonym is quite illustrative of what seems to have happened in contemporary Enochiana after Runar Karlsen's entry:

> [O]n a gross level, there are at least three official systems: Watchtower, Heptarchy, and Loagaeth. Patricia [Shaffer]'s Letter Essences are perhaps best seen as an expansion of Loagaeth material, but can be considered on their own. Dean [Hildebrandt] and Runar [Karlsen] have added the I Ged material. Others have added smaller, but still relevant, works.[84]

At the turn of the millennium we find an Enochian milieu that places a much greater emphasis on new revelations. As the quote above suggests, some of these have been more or less canonized as parts of the Enochian literature, adding to the original revelations of Dee and Kelley. At least in the minds of some Enochian magicians, there is no definite distinction of authority or legitimacy between the revelations of Kelley and those of the latter-day spirit seer Runar Karlsen. After all, the real authors of the material are the Enochian angels—or so it is claimed. In recent years there has been a growing understanding in the milieu that what has happened during the last decade or so, starting with Enochian-L and Benjamin Rowe, onward to the Yahoo! group and Karlsen, Hildebrandt, Shaffer, Audran et al., is in fact the emergence of a "New Flow" of Enochian material. The term "New Flow" was first used by Karlsen, but was soon picked up by others.[85] That the tendency was reified by being given its own term is not without significance. It signifies that legitimacy can now rightly reside in claims to a specific sort of revelatory experience; such experiential claims are intersubjectively validated by participants in the Enochian discourse.

In a sense, this development may be seen as a product of the dynamics of the online discussion community itself, starting with the Enochian-L discussions largely revolving around the person of Benjamin Rowe. In summer 2004 this was recognized in an announcement on the Enochian Yahoo! group of a proposed book project,

> that will present what Runar once referred to as "the New Flow" of Enochian work, starting most likely with Ben Rowe and continuing, with permission of course, with the stupendous amount of work accomplished by Runar and Dean, et. al. The emphasis will be on Enochiana as a spiritual practice path, rather than on scholarship per se.[86]

The book has yet to appear. Meanwhile, it is my hope that the present work, although certainly a work of scholarship and not of practice, may have made a contribution toward presenting this interesting new development in a way that does justice to its position within the modern history of Enochian angel magic.

Conclusions

Enochiana as a Contested Field of Discourse

Through the course of this book we have seen how Enochian magic became a center of controversy for post–Golden Dawn occultists. This is in part a result of the kind of religious innovation that was present in *fin de siècle* occultism: with the dawning of a more complete historical consciousness some modern occultists reached the conclusion that the Golden Dawn system was an innovative synthesis, and not necessarily a legitimate one. In the aftermath of the Golden Dawn we saw a developing contest for the legitimate interpretation of the Order's heritage between various competing groups. As is particularly evident in the case of Paul Foster Case's B.O.T.A., the Enochian factor played an important part of this. According to Case the use of Enochiana *delegitimized* the competing Golden Dawn groups, since it had nothing to do with Rosicrucianism. For others who placed importance on Enochiana, however, it was mostly the other way around: Regardie could refer to Enochian as proof that the Order was really arcane, whether stemming from Atlantis or the heavenly angels, while Crowley could appeal to the system of the Aethyrs and his exploration of those entities as confirmation of his prophetic quest. The same theme showed up again in the context of Satanism, where Crowley's strategy was taken over and imitated by Aquino.

Until the dawn of LaVey's "Age of Satan," occultists nevertheless largely stayed within the G.D. framework of interpretation. With LaVey, a breach with the "occultism of the past" was attempted, resulting in further strategies to delegitimize the Golden Dawn's perennial and esoteric conceptions, and instead construct other frameworks for understanding the legitimacy and efficacy of Enochian magic. Here we see a full-blown appeal to pragmatic groundings: Enochian *works* because it is a particularly sonorous and evocative language, not because it is "divine."

These developments coincide with the emergence of a culture in the West of questioning all authority, questioning all claims to truth, questioning all master narratives. In this respect, LaVeyian Satanism represents the emergence of the postmodern condition in occultism, a development that would become most felt in Chaos Magic. Enochian, which has been associated with "High Magic" in the most ritualized and ceremonial sense, does not seem to have caught too much serious attention in that current. However, I do suggest that the "postmodern condition" had a different impact on the development of Enochian magic considered by itself, a kind of influence that is not stereotypically attributed to postmodernism, but which nevertheless belongs to it. By questioning the occultist master narrative of the Golden Dawn one was in need of new foundations for legitimate practice. As more students started exploring Enochiana from the available textbooks, some, such as Robert Turner and Geoffrey James, took to the original sources. The strategy of using the original Dee manuscripts to both attack and delegitimize prior positions, and to pose a positive framework for doing Enochian magic "correctly" became a central feature of what I have termed the purist turn of the Enochian discourse.

The late 1980s and early 1990s witnessed an explosion of interest in Enochiana. In addition to the new standard works of the purist turn Llewellyn signed Gerald and Betty Schueler, whose books contributed to the popularization of the system. These went in a direction quite opposite from that of the purists. As suggested, they tended to cloth their discourse in the scientizing language of a "rhetoric of rationality," while continuing the synthesizing trend, adding new elements including Theosophy and transpersonal psychology. The coexistence of these two approaches to Enochian has given rise to a persistent field of conflict and polemical exchange, especially after the migration of Enochiana online. The vast criticism Gerald Schueler received on the Enochian-L list, and his attempt to defend himself, is indicative of the hardening competition faced especially by those wishing to do something more eclectic with Enochian after the purist turn.

In Cyberspace the Enochian milieu took another turn as well, with the "New Flow" associated with the circle around Runar Karlsen. Adding to the multiplicity of views and approaches, and the contested issue of "What is Enochian?" the last decade has seen an increasing interest in and acceptance of new revealed Enochian material. I believe this to be a development that was facilitated by the way knowledge is produced, disseminated, and consumed after the emergence of the Internet. As discussion forums and online networks of likeminded people complement and to a certain extent even replace the centrality of published books, a picture of Enochian magic as being less stable and fixed seems to have emerged. There has been a growing emphasis on the comparison of notes and discussions of ritual methods, results, and metaphysical issues. When some of the results include entirely new calls, letter tablets, and instructions from the angels, this has presented a picture of Enochian magic that is more dynamic, fluctuating, and in continual development. When this picture is established, the purist criticism is no longer seen as threatening.

The Legitimacy of Magic Revisited

The close attention to individual claims and counterclaims among modern magicians in this book also provides an opportunity to make some remarks on the conceptions of magic more generally. As with the question of the nature of Enochiana the tendency is not toward a broad consensus on all points of interpretation of what magic is, how it works, and what the reality of its entities consists of. Rather we do see a great variety, from LaVey's notion that the angels "are only 'angels' because occultists to this day have lain ill with metaphysical constipation," to theories depending on the collective unconscious, the more "traditional" understandings present in parts of the purist movement, and "realistic" understandings reinforced with (purportedly) rational arguments, such as the abductive inference of Benjamin Rowe and others. There is a wealth of positions, a wealth of argumentative strategies to defend them, and a wealth of reasons to produce them. One should especially remember LaVey's polemical stance toward traditional esotericists—a clear example of how a position and the line of argumentation it is presented in is embedded in a social context.

With this I will recall the debates on the transformations of magic in light of a (possibly) disenchanted modern culture. Especially one should revisit briefly the "psychologization of magic" thesis postulated perhaps most forcefully by Wouter Hanegraaff. While it seems to me that it does not hold in its strongest formulation, there are still other observations that seem to point to a more stable phenomenon. On an *ontological* level, that is, understood as "internalization" of entities such as "demons" and "angels," or the evacuation of magic to the psyche as described by Hanegraaff, psychologization seems to be not a rule, but rather *one* strategy, sometimes employed, among several others. But Hanegraaff also observed something else, which I think is a tendency with some more permanence: the prevailing conception that magic is ultimately about personal spiritual development.[1] This seems to have been a lasting inheritance from the Golden Dawn, with its focus on the "higher self," through Crowley's "True Will" of Thelema, and further reinforced by the self-religionists of the 1960s counterculture. In Enochian magic this focus on spiritual development manifests in interesting ways, such as Regardie's exclusion of the Golden Dawn *Book "H"*, which consisted of an interpretation of the Enochian Great Table that was close to that of Dee and Kelley. The use of angels and demons to procure precious metals, heal or cause wounds, and transporting people from country to country, although the function clearly stated in the original sources, was deemed "mediaeval, and definitely unsound from a spiritual viewpoint."[2] A similar remark was found in the contemporary writings of Schueler, this time with reference to the Heptarchic system. In both cases, it seems, there is a view of magic as more spiritually sublime than what a close reading of the early modern sources they base themselves on allows for. Interestingly, when it comes to modern Enochian discourse, it seems that the only current that really *does* allow a return to the less lofty motivations of magic is found among the purists. At large, however, the Aethyrs remain initiatory astral spheres and sources for prophecy instead of geographical entities and a magical system for geopolitical manipulation, while the Great Table remains a tool for exploring subtle aspects of the astral world and the four elements, instead of a system for evocation of angels and cacodaemons for practical purposes.

There is still a question of whether this could be labeled a psychologization of magic. There is an obvious emphasis on individual development, but it could just as well be framed as an aspect of a modern culture more generally, where individualism, personal expression, and development continue to be ideological focal points. This is in keeping with trends observed for emerging forms of religiosity in the West more generally. In the end, modern magicians tend to have a more *spiritualized* understanding of magic than their medieval and early modern predecessors. Magic has lost some of its utility, and gained instead in religious or even mystical validation.

APPENDIX

Author's note

This appendix contains the most central text alleged to have been received from the Enochian angels by the Norwegian magician Runar Karlsen in 1991. The three chapters, which are given here both in Enochian and Karlsen's own English translations, purport to introduce the names and functions of the nine "Spirits of EM." These are spirit entities that have not appeared in the earlier Enochian corpus. With regard to the language of these new calls, it consists of a combination of "old" Enochian words and new ones, which, again, appear for the first time in Karlsen's work. As Karlsen states in his introduction below, the translations are sometimes quite rough. They appear to include several grammatical errors; however, I have decided to leave the translation pretty much in its original form.

I have also included an introductory note provided by Karlsen himself, kindly supplied for the occasion of this publication. In it, he gives some glimpses of his own interpretation of the work and its significance. Readers who have read the whole book should now have little difficulty placing the interpretations in the proper context of speculations that have occupied the Enochian segment of the occulture for decades. For the ease of reference, I have added notes of my own pointing toward relevant sections in this book.

An Introductory Note to *Dor OS zol ma thil*

Runar Karlsen

This text is dictated by the three first spirits of the EM, the Nine Fire spirits, who speak out on their nature, how things look from their perspective and how the spirits may be used. The EM are a group of spirits among many other groups that are mentioned by numbers in the Calls received by Dee and Kelly.[1]

The title *Dor OS zol ma thil..* connects it with the grimoire *. . I ged*. Combined and translated, they read: "The twelve black hands [and their] falling seats . . . are falling." From this we can understand that it is in *. . I ged* ("are falling") that the processes spoken of are carried out.[2] The *. . I ged* does contain calls for the other groups of spirits mentioned by numbers in Dee and Kelly's Calls. The whole work is therefore elaborating the system already laid out by Dee and Kelly. We see now that there are both global and galactic implications of this work which could not have been understood properly back in the 16th century, as common knowledge was limited (with an incomplete world map, and assuming our solar system to be of only seven planets).

The three chapters reveal the spirits as transcendent, the creator's newborn flame, and the lethal destroyer, or the karmic avenger. These themes are not unfamiliar to imperial religions, so I find it fair to say that the mighty powers of heaven do really want a refreshing if not an outright reset of an outdated or neglected formula.

John Dee was known as a Rosycrucian, and the central glyph of his *Monas Hieroglyphica* is also found in the main Rosycrucian books of his time.[3] The themes of the *Book of the Em* and also certain parts of *. . I ged* are relevant to Rosycrucianism, and may become part of its development into a more independent religion, more in tune with Hermetic philosophy and its traditions.

I finished the translation in 1993 and there have only been a few minor corrections since. I have also written a note to say that my translation is not perfect and should not be relied on in the particulars, just in the general. The translation is "raw" and word by word, little if anything has been done to recreate English sentence structure. There are still a few things remaining to complete the *. . I ged*, as there is much still waiting to be understood of its internal structure and functions. As of spring 2011, the old *Ored Dhagia* website is to be re-launched at http://www.infinite-ways.net, where this work should be completed. Among other things, it will provide an outline or manual to the work spoken of by the EM.

Runar Karlsen, January 2011

14:53 Friday 25. January 1991

DOR OS ZOL MA THIL . . .

The 12 black hands and the falling seats.

Chapter one:

1) *Ma pratisi kolia navadigi, selig quanisi gon. Hua na vetha seg GOVENTAZ dol po.*

1. The fallen virgins are creating the stones on the path, the faithful and handless olives. I that sembles the evil spirit goventaz (saying neither here) am wholly divided.

2) *Beria merkrth, so i rana, vetha keisa leta meru. Kolemn. Kethar sefi roni, Quesar lothi na veit kolia.*

2. I am sleeping beyond, the visit is cold and to assimilate is finding torment. The creator herein. The bridge is to carry out the sunset. The destruction quenches the weaknesses that comes from the created.

3) *Betha re i vah ma the zon, ke it do le. Gavana, dire kiti meg le sik kore; Na vai. Thero saka setia le paia seki sathajia.*

3. Talking cunning is like falling as forms, therefore is it in the first. Arise, dismantle the 12 whose good intension was looking at the trinity's first mystery number, nr 2, Therefore mine provided oneness always shall be my openness.

4) *Mer doi na van sej keti, beria vethi. Ramzakal no i a sevi late zar. PERIO da sajin sekun. Doria da sai vethik lama ran methik coi Necun. Per sak sal.*

4. The torment-snake that is neither good nor bad, sleep comes from. The regrets within 456 becomes, and is the 2nd finding ways. PERIO is the black brother of mine. The black and fallen (brothers) illusionary path of regret are in continuance and (they) rather holy servants. Burning is my house.

5) *Boru metha goii me tha la ke varunn, metha fetha keiin sel na va KATI re vaunn set.*

5. The hurricane is blind, saying around in the excesses, therefore seeing. To the blinding visit within the hands of the good brother, cunning seeing is needed.

6) *Therkes da vei nala Zax periodon. Thata rami, keta sa sek vetha quati zel berathi keiin. Do rati ve nonta ri ve ogg sa vekti lavi Ni Ni me onto rama i sevi kesar ka del o seki norotauni. Pe o ka za Ni vethi ra ta quasar. Te i pe ona terio la KETI. Thedit PeNi, raki o ve lasa.*

6. The 2nd ladder which crosses Zax is the brothers fight. The cycle accelerates, they are within me, it is like having the creator's hands within. In hardening like the earths mercy-like chamber and letting the mute cry invoke the 28 28 (NI NI) for the pouring of regret, the feelings of destruction are the fighters named my defaced sons. Being called within are the 28 making regret as their pleasure. It is your making and shall be the good brother. Work the PeNI and weeping is called forth like riches.

7) *Pena, reti keon tara leane sefi keta ra te ti. Peja naka theri ve naki theja mopolosa theri. Tik tan-tika lef ti ra netika. Sa i on. Pe rati fek karjja seg olon. Fetik sevia na heria fek tarja ketholon teria kothon sak krajin.*
PERIAK

7. The furs; (as much as) the hard creation shall be (as) the branches feeling the regret as it is. Your life shall be like life when your extinguishing becomes. The man of balance; the unique man. Its regrettable being without nothing, the within is so made. The slave in the noisy oven pouring awfulness. Don't visit feelings which split matter noisy, The creatures steady waves shall be the fence of mine disappearing in spirals. PERIAK.

17:15 Saturday 26. 1991

DOR OS ZOL MA THIL . . .

Chapter Two

1) *Sa-Kala kherat; zner PA-I-ON, Ne vaktarim. Pe voojim zakre ta sejion te vani la peres-tak el mana-kire.*

1. And 456 spoke, swore that being is made; the Holy living essence of breath, for your mighty movements in the temple invoked the fiery feet of the One which bids you vitality.

2) *Pe o sa ja ki le ma perest ta veii. Pe la ki teresa kariseò taii. Pe tajo talasa kai nepa, neki o parastia tajo-no-i.*

2. Being called within, truth grants the Ones fall, fiery as the second. Your One grants becoming and let it be lit. For your excesses of the freedom sword, Life calls the Fire of comfort, which lights, becomes and is.

3) *Ven-tora tajik pejitar kavana sel tar tijo, Vekto ram-kaal najise sejio tarkes. Plostra keni-ja-kes meriva tejo pekitar. Fes taji qanos t traja.*

3. Neither sustains and doesn't light but stretches out, the arising hands

goes forth and lights. The mute and cold cry from 456 wills the black brother as the ladder. The variety is truly bound in torment as you are stretching out. Carry out your olive and its seed.

4) *Om NI, Talajo pejina saki tal, vet-toro. PeNI PaNI terio keso. PARAMA terejo tarke lanoviel. Peres saji pent.*

4. Understand the 28 (NI), the creatures stretches out mine excess and makes it sustain. PeNI PaNI, becomes and are. PARAMA shall he the ladder and map of the 2nd and the One. The Fire awfully stinging.

5) *Leta zar veiio kanatroja perestoka levani quat trokij sevi ona spav. Perenu vasti kerestinu, veijia kelastikal quato Ra-Maz-Kil.*

5. Finding the ways perfected and fixed, the fire-mountain invokes the creators mind and feelings that makes one cry in utter joy. The Fire in truth demands union with the 2nd, the born and appearing by the creator's regrettable pact of the bolt.

6) *Fe Ne za vetika quanis sekio, Pereji savina queto rakajita dol. Fetika sekit terejo natika teren sav kel.*

6. Visit the holiness within the not-made olive of mine. The Fire enters the whole weeping creation. Visit the man of mine become that man, go forth and feel born.

7) *Perji-on ta vethik quan tares ke lati seji. Qoulemanu vet tranu sak, i ta fen savji qued saki net. Tol dezi quat setina.*

7. Fire made thee the not-made creations becoming, and is found as the black brother. The creator is herein, making the marrow of mine,(and) is as a follower, feeling our shrinking creation by mine emptiness. All heads the creator's temple.

Sunday 16:00 January 27. 1991.

DOR OS ZOL MA THIL . . .

Chapter Three—Part One

1) *Gohusali ta nat ho raki-sela, methari kati na veiiti sekio fet. Thari ket naria tala veiita. Meri ketholo peti Zax nethik vetio thari ma-sala.*

1. I say thee as the child of zeros weeping hands: follow out the good intention that comes from my visit that is their deadly expansion. Torments steady waves is going to Zax, wearing full equipment, the making shall be fallen wonders.

2) *Fet-io tari KETI na za lo karia, te rati fek quati selig KETI ranousli, pei natir kevi jetolo quanis teri ja moloso.*
2. Eternal visit shall be for the good brother (KETI), that is within the One's oven. The hard noise from the creator's handless white brothers home, for the child does not care, out of him olives shall be the truth spitting out.

3) *Peria KETI sak quati leojo. Peri uat tenik quato, leta vet sakia. PERIO pa leijo ma saki uet davani keniquat.*
3. The Flaming white brother of mine is the wheel of creation. Fire made a wild creator that made or found me. PERIO is the fallen wheel of mine making the arising from the bound creation.

4) *Pel-i-va ta riga za li na huati ta reiji pen pon ta moto sagi ta roi-na. Uet ta raki seii huat da huen na huat ti raki-solo. Tejo hua do rati tejo huat di naro-kolasi-pejon-ton.*
4. The stiff Fire is like thee Core, within the first that hails as the wand destroys the furs of the awful's robes ; the sunrise of the Trinity. Do as the weeping black brother, worship the worshipper that worships its weeping hands. Light the worshipper in the slave, light the worship of the killing of the creators riches for the whole-making.

5) *PERIO dalina uatij seki doro zan. Huat pei dogi la nesi-qurasti-quan. Tekil doro huati seki pa-las-teri naki dogno pejontolosa PERIKO. na huet i GA perjei.*
5. PERIO is the fighter, making mine black finger. Worship for the howling of the walking maidens creation. The unknown blackness for mine adorer shall be the divided life howling in PERIKO's heavenly riches. That worshipper is the Fire of the 31.

6) *Kel-ika sek quato dor-onto pajina huet Berika la maasi doro pejonorak. PeNI PaNI: DO.*
6. Unborn is mine created blackness pouring and stretching over the worshipper of the sleeping (PERIAK) and laid up black heavenly no-son PeNI PaNI: IN.

7) *Keli soko ra, beti dejona fet likavi sejionor Znati gei. Pelika savani ront ka jagile sejona pari KALA mitari konoto sek quati dor-onto.*
7. Born is the reigner's regret, he is talking about resigning, and visits then the earthly sons wandering spirit. The stiff Fire arises upon the mountains sunset and are the reason why the earthly burns, the 456 follows and perfects my creators black pouring.

8) *Pei doro sak quetina, pejina dor teliko sak KETI no.Poi seki darak, ket naji metholo.*
8. For black is my rottenness, stretching out the black death for mine white brothers song. Divide my self-lessness, they will continue.

9) *PARAMAON saki nalati doro. Pei saki Na reti pejolo noraki seg so selig. Keloto sak perijo na veti Periodonto.*
9. PARAMAON mine black cross. For mine Trinity hardens the weeping sickle, and the awful visits handless. Born is the Fire that comes from the brothers full fight.

10) *QUELI !!! Znorzulgi quati na huet tejo norim. KATI?. Tejo Zax Salim. Peti reti nara-timolum-sak. Quati derinu cum pei doromiona.*
10. Disappear from earth!!! (I) bring terrible curses on creation that worships and lights the sons (brothers). The good intention? Lit in the house of Zax! Going to harden the killing wooden work of mine, Creation shall be a united frame for solid gathered shapes.

11) *Pekil sekil darim-ma-thil terio KETIL sekio. Pejonto ra-maz-tok quani, saii peli nerimo-qlzrt.*
11. The apprentice to mine gathered falling seats shall be the first white brother of mine (PA-I-ON) (This is) the heavenly and regrettable pact of the mountain and the olives, the black and stiff fire of the torment-knowing maidens.

Chapter Three—Part Two

1) *Golaqin tuari sek quan. Peii snar tolo quan deri meth faki, tel sono ta meti dol quati neres.*
1. Stainless and pure shall my creation be. The sickles absolute motion unites with creation in a blinding noise, All forms as a blinding whole, to the creators true pity.

2) *Pejonorapethivetsaiionohuetnalekira.Petsakihuetnalimiatiperionasekdolomi.*
2. Heavenly regrets is going to make the temple for the worshipper of the Ones vitality. For mine worshipper, crosses of fire makes mine ALLPOWER.

3) *Perio do sani peji huet na kai talà dorina ka huati nek ki lasa. Perio ke nati sek ki naltamire do neji kel.*

3. PERIO in parts rests, worships that freedom, all is then black, thereby is the worshipper's life's riches granted. PERIO is granting the torment of the cross in willing my child's birth.

4) *Peontorama ketinanu sak keti darum. Peli sak dolomani, ket dire paj sek ki quati nor dol EM.*

4. For the pouring of coldness to the white brothers stone, my w.b.'s [white brotherhood] self the whole offer is my stiff Fire, but for them whom dismantles the 12, by my guaranteeing the creators son of all 9.

Chapter Three—Part Three

1) *Pejiqstra donoki satia mejnokila pejonora pesita quenti la seki hua. Pet nara pei nokila meri Na trajo.*

1. The sickle's release in the servant demands looking for the servant's consumption, for the becoming regrets of the weak fire is a rotten one like mine I. Going to kill. (it) for the servants consumption of torment, to the trinity's becoming.

2) *Terio pen soko la meriona peti KALA tej dores taj netika, poj berijo toj peregi la huati na pei doro sa kila, Pei no thila perejo kani-KAL-me sek doront.*

2. Shall the furs of the reigning one become the made torment, go to 456, light blackness, light emptiness, divide the sleeper and light the Fire of the worshipper of the Trinity, for blackness is what I consume. As for the following falling seats of fire; they are falling with 456 and my black pouring.

3) *Huati nek kien sak letina pejodo tei doronto petalen cors doje. Hua lata kolia dor napi sekil dol terien dal Keti ra.*

3. The worshipper of life is restricted, I find the trinity opened by my sickle, and is against the black pouring of our common fire such howls. Where I find the black creation, that place of mine shall wholly be unto the white brothers regret.

4) *Pereti koi go lati seki la sa dol petina huati gel tojo. Peria cors da LA.*

4. The light rather says my riches goes wholly unto the trinity, and the worshipper is enlightened, (by) FIRE, such of the FIRST.

Chapter Three—Part Four

1) *Doloka—Quasinor,—torona peii dazi; ket ! La marasina huet da kalina doi pe ra si; ket!*
1. Death, o son of pleasure, shall sustain for that head, THEIRS. The hopeless worship of the blood-serpent, your regret ends, THEIRS.

2) *Però kol no basi, la huani ket dor OS. Pei no huati dol geri-sal-qina hua si noro da fiò pei nò.*
2. PERIos creating becomes (like)a cup, the worshipper; and they are the black twelve. For being the worshippers whole killing of the created man. I finished the sons with the union, for the song of it.

3) *Plati gei sati per doii nothora, pel da pej, cor sa qina laviò-sak pereijo.*
3. The partaker herein providing PERDOI (the fire snake) and makes him sustain. The stiff fire there unto such concentration, invoking my FIRE.

Chapter Three—Part Five

1) *Dolomi na terejo kati-sna pa rogo lavio-na-kile sak PeNI PeNA dol parajo nok di savjon.*
1. The All-power that becomes the good brothers motion is being coated. Invoking the bolt, my PeNI furs wholly the fire of the temple.

2) *Pel-on-toki poj dari, quen di na uja qoria sek olon da miorakistal, delio pen dara-mikalz corz snav pejilo por da huati saii.*
2. The stiff fire makes a mountain, divide, unite, the creation there, the made trinity. The oven pours awfulness for the mighty release of tears. The fighter's furs of the mighty regret such makes the knife move and lust for the worshipper of awfulness.

3) *Keni ma-prathisi sekio sna loi doromina del quati sekia tel doroma, pejona dol peno sem da reti Qooloimo—TORIA!*
3. The bound and falling virgins of mine moves and kisses the solid gathered shapes of the fighters of mine creator, the black seats falls, The sickle all furs overruns, the hard understanding of the creators kiss—SUSTAINS!

4) *Petik derio na veit sak peri dol ka seki tel napa-ra-kise, Fejo la ki ti sek quati nor tajo fen.*
4. Not going to unite with what comes from my Fire? All are then my seats and the sword of regret, encircling the one and guaranties it to be my creator's son, the light follower.

5) *Pelia doros saki ses sna per-odo doki la merital quati sonors. Godinal pei soninal dogorathi pei sic le.*
5. The stiff fire of the black 12, my axe moves opens the fire, fulfils the One's all-torment. The creator swore: the speed of matter for the entities of' earth, the mystery of the howling slaves.

6) *Perio sna vethi neiNa koti seg lo ponamira go huasi taj na, Vet sami na rami do kaanistra pei doqola mi senid da ronto.*
6. PERIO's motion is coming from the will of the trinity, and is the cover of the awful one, destroying torment or saying I end it by lighting the trinity making war to the power of regret in olives release, for in the creator power laments and pours blackness.

7) *Quen tagi meii dore, fet guatina le poji sek da retina, kenti malasa ko nori-ma.*
7. The creation lights and looks around the blackness and visits rottenness. Mine hard sickle divides. Rotten fallen riches covers fallen sons.

8) *Feii sek do lami-na-na del kenti sek poroto nomistral. Pejonor dol po.*
8. I am whirling in the stones path, the fighters rottenness; my fiery lust. End and release, sickle son your wholly divided.

9) *KETI sna ve rathi no; QO! Snati qe rathi re-mi-sa-na goro la mana ke saki sovi.*
9. The white brother is acting like a slave, GARMENTS! The move is only the slaves cunning power finger. Desiring the offer are mine feelings.

10) *Pei sek sa lima pei dorok ken ta de ra, peti sna veti vapelionara da ketira quana seqi sel na huati na huati dol po.*
10. The stiff Fire mine house, for darkness is bound of regret. going to move, do as the stiff Fire, kill the white brothers regrettable olive. Mine hand that worshipper wholly divides.

11) *Dolio cors da hueti ro saki sez snarza PERÒ.*
11. Everything, such as the worshipper is gone by my axe, swore PERÒ.

NOTES

Introduction

1. This episode, its context, significance and aftermath is discussed in the last chapter of this book.
2. E.g., in order of appearance, Peter French, *John Dee*; Frances Yates, *The Occult Philosophy in the Elizabethan Age*; Christopher Whitby, *John Dee's Actions with Spirits*, two volumes; Clulee, *John Dee's Natural Philosophy*; Deborah Harkness, *John Dee's Conversations with Angels*; Håkan Håkansson, *Seeing the Word: John Dee and Renaissance Occultism*; György E. Szőnyi, *John Dee's Occultism: Magical Exaltation through Powerful Signs*; Stephen Clucas, ed., *John Dee: Interdisciplinary Studies in English Renaissance Thought*. The literature of recent John Dee research is discussed in chapter 1 of this book.
3. Partridge, *The Re-Enchantment of the West*, Vol. 1., 41, 69, 77, citation on 200, n. 53.
4. Owen, *Place of Enchantment: British Occultism and the Culture of the Modern*, 186–220.
5. Ibid., 196.
6. E.g., Boaz Huss, "Authorized Guardians"; cf. Egil Asprem, "*Kabbalah Recreata*," 132–33, 142–43.
7. Pasi and Rabaté, "*Langue angélique, langue magique, l'énochien.*"
8. For this interpretation, see especially Adam McLean, "Dr. Rudd's Treatise"; idem, "Introduction," 11; Stephen Skinner and David Rankine, *Practical Angel Magic*, 38–43. It was also briefly reiterated by Pasi and Rabate, "*Langue angélique, langue magique*," 107.
9. For parts of this argument, see Asprem, "False, Lying Spirits or Angels of Light."
10. Idel, "Prisca Theologia in Marsilio Ficino and in Some Jewish Treatments," 138–39; cf. von Stuckrad, *Locations of Knowledge*, chapter 2.
11. Partridge, *The Re-Enchantment of the West*, Vol. 1, 62–86, quotation on page 84; cf. Partridge, "Occulture is Ordinary." The term itself appears to have been coined around the early 1980s by the artist, musician, and punk-occultist Genesis P-Orridge (born Neil Andrew Megson, 1950). As Partridge relates, P-Orridge had noted in the late 1970s "how a small number of fanatical individuals could have a disproportionate impact on culture." This acknowledgment lies behind Partridge's theory of occulture as well: while occulture is becoming mainstream, reaching an enormous amount of people and ultimately changing their plausibility structures, the core milieus in which occultural ideas and discourse are produced in the first place are indeed very limited. The same goes, of course, for the occultural field of Enochiana. Whereas a relatively small group of occultists actively work with Enochian magic, drops and pieces occasionally make it into the broader culture through, e.g., literature, film, TV,

and music. See Partridge, "Occulture is Ordinary." See also my discussion in chapter 4 of the present book.

12. Partridge, "Occulture is Ordinary"; Jesper Aagaard Petersen, "From Book to Bit." For a panoramic view of crucial changes in esoteric discourse of the late twentieth and early twenty-first centuries, see the other essays in Asprem and Kennet Granholm, eds., *Contemporary Esotericism*.
13. Von Stuckrad, "Discursive Study of Religion," 266–67. For the concept of "discourse" and its import to Religious Studies, see Tim Murphy, "Discourse."
14. See, e.g., Hanegraaff, "Forbidden Knowledge"; Hammer and von Stuckrad, eds., *Polemical Encounters*.
15. E.g., Hanegraaff, "Western Esotericism in Enlightenment Historiography."
16. Hammer, *Claiming Knowledge.*

Chapter 1. The Magus and the Seer

1. Harkness, *John Dee's Conversations with Angels,* 16–17; cf. Nicholas Clulee, *John Dee's Natural Philosophy,* 140–41.
2. Harkness, *Conversations with Angels,* 16; Whitby, "John Dee and Renaissance Scrying"; Thomas, *Religion and the Decline of Magic,* 255–56, 272–74; Delatte, *La Catoptromancie Grecque et ses derives*; Lang, "Angels around the Crystal"; Fanger, "Virgin Territory."
3. Yates, *The Occult Philosophy in the Elizabethan Age,* 96.
4. Clulee, *John Dee's Natural Philosophy,* 203.
5. Ibid., 203–41.
6. Harkness, *John Dee's Conversations with Angels*. The following presentation of Dee's intellectual trajectory is deeply indebted to Harkness's and Clulee's books.
7. See especially Clulee, *John Dee's Natural Philosophy,* and Harkness, *John Dee's Conversations with Angels.*
8. See, e.g., Foucault, *The Order of Things*; Rummel, *The Humanist-Scholastic Debate*; Copenhaver, "Natural Magic, Hermetism, and Occultism in Early Modern Science."
9. Harkness, *John Dee's Conversations with Angels,* 64–65.
10. In the sense outlined and described by, e.g., Ashworth, "Natural History and the Emblematic Worldview."
11. Harkness, *John Dee's Conversations with Angels,* 71–77.
12. Ibid., 77.
13. See Josten, "A Translation of John Dee's 'Monas Hieroglyphica'"; cf. Clulee, *John Dee's Natural Philosophy,* 77–115; Harkness, *John Dee's Conversations with Angels,* 77–90; Szőnyi, *John Dee's Occultism,* 161–74; Forshaw, "The Early Alchemical Reception of John Dee's *Monas Hieroglyphica.*"
14. See Clulee, *John Dee's Natural Philosophy,* 143–76; Harkness, *John Dee's Conversations with Angels,* 91–97.
15. Cf. Clulee, "At the Crossroads of Magic and Science."
16. Harkness, *John Dee's Conversations with Angels,* 96.
17. Ibid.
18. See Whitby, ed., *John Dee's Actions with Spirits,* volume II, 341; cf. Harkness, *John Dee's Conversations with Angels,* 99.
19. I.e., Yates, *Giordano Bruno and the Hermetic Tradition*; idem, *The Rosicrucian Enlightenment*; idem, *The Occult in the Elizabethan Age*; French, *John Dee.*

20. E.g., Clulee, "Dee's Natural Philosophy Revisited."
21. In order of publication the most significant works shedding light on the angel diaries are the following: Christopher Whitby, *John Dee's Actions with Spirits*, two volumes; Clulee, *John Dee's Natural Philosophy*; Harkness, "Shews in the Shewstone"; idem, *John Dee's Conversations with Angels*.
22. Clucas, ed., *John Dee: Interdisciplinary Studies*.
23. Harkness, *John Dee's Conversations with Angels*, 98.
24. Ibid., 98–130.
25. E.g., Eco, *The Search for the Perfect Langauge*.
26. Szőnyi, "Paracelsus, Scrying and the *Lingua Adamica*," 215.
27. Harkness, *Conversations with Angels*, 160. For more on the authors mentioned and their ideas on this issue, see Francois Secret, *Les Kabbalistes chrétiens*; M. L. Kuntz, *Guillaume Postel*; Claes-Christian Elert, "Andreas Kempe (1622–1689)."
28. E.g., Whitby, "John Dee and Renaissance Scrying."
29. Clucas, "'Non est legendum;" idem, "John Dee's Angelic Conversations and the Ars Notoria."
30. For a concise biography of Kelley, see Michael Wilding, "A Biography of Edward Kelly, the English Alchemist and Associate of Dr. John Dee."
31. Yates, *Giordano Bruno and the Hermetic Tradition*, 167; French, *John Dee*, 114.
32. Sledge, "Between 'Loagaeth' and 'Cosening.'"
33. For this point, see, e.g., Susan Bassnett, "Absent Presences," 285.
34. James, *The Enochian Magic of Dr. John Dee*, xxv.
35. Cf. Harkness, *John Dee's Conversations with Angels*, 23–24.
36. Luhrmann, *Persuasions of the Witch's Craft*.
37. See e.g. Nicholas P. Spanos, *Multiple Personalities & False Memories: A Sociocognitive Perspective*. This book serves as an excellent introduction to the approach, which provides thorough discussions of research and further references.
38. Bassnett, "Absent Presences," 287.
39. Ibid.; Jan Bäcklund, "In the Footsteps of Edward Kelley."
40. Bassnett, "Absent Presences," 292.
41. See Cotton Appendix XLVI (detailing the angel conversations from May 28, 1583, to May 23, 1587, plus March 20, to September 7, 1607); MS Sloane 3188 (the diary for December 22, 1581-May 23, 1583); MS Sloane 3189 (the "received book" *Liber Loagaeth*); and MS Sloane 3191 (including the four "received books" *48 Claves Angelica; Liber scientiae, auxilii, et victoriae Terrestris; De heptarchia mystica; Tabula bonorum angelorum*). All these have been made available in high resolution electronic facsimile copies by Ian Rons, at "The Magickal Review" Web site: http://www.themagickalreview.org/enochian/mss/.
42. Szőnyi, "Paracelsus, Scrying, and the *Lingua Adamica*," 216–18.
43. See Peterson, ed., *John Dee's Five Books of Mystery*, 66-73. This book is a transcription of MS Sloane 3188, which contains the earliest angel conversations we have records of. It should be noted that these were not among the material published by Meric Casaubon in 1659.
44. This is preserved in MS Sloane 3189. The title page says "Liber Mysteriorum Sixtus et Sanctus" ("The Sixth and Holy Book of the Mysteries"), which is another name sometimes used for it. At any rate "Logaeth" seems to be a misspelling stemming from Casaubon's edition of the manuscripts now in the Cotton Appendix. Cotton Appendix MS XLVI f. 15b shows Dee spelling it "Loagaeth," which is the form that will be adopted here.

45. For the diary entries of these conversations, see Peterson, ed., *Five Books of Mystery,* 257–359.
46. See MS Sloane 3189. This book is written in Kelley's handwriting. See also Harkness, *Dee's Conversations with Angels,* 41. For closer examinations of the method of receiving the Angelic language, and critical linguistic evaluation of its claim to be a authentic natural language, see Donald C. Laycock, "Angelic language or mortal folly?" and also my own evaluation, Asprem, "'Enochian' Language: A Proof of the Existence of Angels?"
47. Reeds, "John Dee and the Magic Tables in the *Book of Soyga.*" His thorough and penetrating mathematical and statistical analysis of the tables of *Soyga* and those of *Loagaeth* is also a valuable cross-disciplinary contribution.
48. Harkness, *Dee's Conversations with Angels,* 41.
49. E.g., as an angel answered Dee on April 18: "God shall make clere when it pleaseth him: & open all the secrets of wisdome whan he unlocketh. Therefore Seke not to know the mysteries of this boke, tyll the very howre that he shall call thee," Peterson, ed., *Five Books of Mystery,* 351.
50. Ibid. The manuscript is now in Sloane MS 3191, f. 32–51.
51. See especially Sloane MS 3191, f. 45b-51a.
52. See the modern reprint in Stephen Skinner, ed., *The Fourth Book of Occult Philosophy,* 59–96.
53. This is in MS Sloane 3191, f. 1a-14b.
54. MS Sloane 3191, f. 14a-31b.
55. See MS Sloane 3191, f. 16a.
56. Harkness, *John Dee's Conversations with Angels,* 187–92.
57. MS Sloane 3191, f. 52b-80b. See Table 1.1 for a reproduction.
58. The conversations as they unfolded are printed in Casaubon, ed., *True & Faithful Relation,* 172–83.
59. Ibid., 179. Italics in original.
60. Considering the fact that the letter squares of the Great Table appeared a month later than the names that appear to have been extracted from it, this constitutes one of the more puzzling aspects of the angelic communications. It seems to suggest that the table must have been already produced long before Kelley "scryed" it in sessions with Dee.
61. Clucas, "'Non est legendum." For the Ars Notoria sigil, see Gösta Hedegård, ed., *Liber Iuratus Honorii: A Critical Edition,* 70. This and more links between Dee's work and earlier medieval sources and practices are explored in Clucas, "John Dee's Angelic Conversations and the Ars Notoria"; Claire Fanger, "Virgin Territory." For a highly relevant contribution to the more general discussion of medieval sources' continued importance in renaissance magic, see Frank Klaassen, "Medieval Ritual Magic in the Renaissance."
62. Peterson, ed., *Five Books of Mystery,* 445–46.
63. Donald C. Laycock, "Angelic language or mortal folly?"
64. Claire Fanger, "Virgin Territory," 203.
65. E.g., Klaassen, "Medieval Ritual Magic in the Renaissance."
66. See Bassnett, "Abesent Presences," 286.
67. The way they worked was rather through prayer and petition addressed to God for sending the angels, and not evocations of specific spirits, as is taught in the material they received. Refer again to my initial distinction between the "magic" they worked through and the "magics" that resulted from the actions. See also Harkness, *Dee's Conversations with Angels,* 41.

Chapter 2. Whispers of Secret Manuscripts

1. Harkness, *John Dee's Conversations with Angels,* 217.
2. Cited in ibid., 223.
3. The title of this section is taken from Samuel Butler's satirical poem *Hudibras* (1664), figuring the Rosicrucian adept Sidrophel, obsessed with Dee's angel conversations. In the course of the poem, Kelley's "shewstone" is referred to as "the devil's looking-glass." For a brief discussion, see Harkness, *John Dee's Conversations with Angels,* 224.
4. In the following referred to as *T&FR*.
5. E.g., Frances Yates, *Giordano Bruno and the Hermetic Tradition,* 433–70.
6. Casaubon, "The Preface," unpaginated.
7. Cf. Serjeantsen, "Casaubon, (Florence Estienne) Meric (1599–1671)."
8. Cf. Richard Kieckhefer, *Magic in the Middle Ages,* 37–42; Norman Cohn, *Europe's Inner Demons,* 22–23.
9. Cohn, *Europe's Inner Demons,* 24–29; Stuart Clark, *Thinking with Demons,* 166–67.
10. E.g., Serjeantsen, "Casaubon," unpaginated.
11. The diaries are in MSS Sloane 3624–3628. See also Harkness, *John Dee's Conversations with Angels,* 222–23.
12. See the entry for that date in Sloane 3624.Also note that the spelling "Logaeth" is a misprint on the part of Casaubon—the original diaries had "Loagaeth." Thus, we can know that the magicians were probably working from Casaubon's text.
13. Harkness, *John Dee's Conversations with Angels,* 223.
14. Additionally, Rankine and Skinner found portions of the text copied in two documents in the Bodleian, namely MS Rawlinson D.1067 and Rawlinson D.1363. These are of a later date, and are not complete copies. See Rankine and Skinner, *John Dee's Enochian Tables.*
15. The first two are in Harley MS 6485, the *Chymical Wedding* in 6486, the "Rosicrucian Chymical medicines" in 6481, and the defense of Orientals in 6479.
16. Harley MS 6483. This grimoire was recently published in Skinner and Rankine, eds., *The Goetia of Dr. Rudd.*
17. For a detailed critical analysis of this manuscript, see Asprem, "False, Lying Spirits or Angels of Light."
18. See McLean, ed., *Treatise,* 30–31; cf. Peterson ed., *John Dee's Five Books of Mystery,* 399.
19. This has notably been the opinion of Adam McLean, "Dr. Rudd's Treatise"; and idem, "Introduction," 11. The contention has also been reiterated by academic scholars. See for instance Pasi and Rabaté, "Langue angélique, langue magique," 107.
20. Yates, *The Rosicrucian Enlightenment,* 257–58.
21. As far as I am aware, the first refutation of this attribution in the scholarly literature was made in my 2008 article, "False Lying Spirits," on which the present discussion builds.
22. I.e., McLean, "Introduction," 11–12; Skinner and Rankine, *The Practical Angel Magic of Dr. John Dee's Enochian Tables.*
23. McLean, "Introduction," 15–16.
24. See for instance the overview presented in Harkness, *John Dee's Conversations with Angels,* 117–20.

25. Harkness, *John Dee's Conversations with Angels,* 218–19.
26. Ibid., 219. These documents are now to be found in Cotton Appendix XLVI, detailing the angel conversations with Kelley from May 28, 1583, to May 23, 1587, plus a couple with Hickman from March 20 to September 7, 1607.
27. Cf. Owen Davies, "Angels in Elite and Popular Magic, 1650–1790," 298–99.
28. In Christopher Whitby, *John Dee's Actions with Spirits.*
29. Appleby, "Woodall, John."
30. Harkness, *John Dee's Conversations with Angels,* 220.
31. Ibid., 2, 220.
32. Michael Hunter, ed., *Elias Ashmole 1617–1692,* 41–42. See also the indispensable volumes of original Ashmolian documents, with historical introduction by C. H. Josten, ed., *Elias Ashmole (1617–1692).*
33. Pasi and Rabaté, *"Langue angélique, langue magique,"* 108. Ashmole's copies are preserved in the Ashmole collection of the Bodleian Library, Oxford, as MSS Ashmole 422, Ashmole 580, and Ashmole 1790. See Josten, ed., *Elias Ashmole (1617–1692),* vol. III, 1272, and vol. IV, 1335–36, 1843.
34. Where they comprise MS Sloane 3188 (the diary for December 22, 1581-May 23, 1583), MS Sloane 3189 (the "received book," *Liber Loagaeth*), and MS Sloane 3191 (including the four "received books," *48 Claves Angelica; Liber scientiae, auxilii, et victoriae Terrestris; De heptarchia mystica; Tabula bonorum angelorum*).
35. As Casaubon tells us in his preface.
36. This was first noted in Turner, *Elizabethan Magic,* 155.
37. See Table 1.2. Dee's version in Sloane 3188 f. 94b is originally in Latin characters, while the two others displayed Enochian letters. For ease of comparison I have translated all tables to their Latin equivalents.
38. It should be noted that Waite was quite convinced that Peter Smart was a forger. In Waite's opinion, Smart had forged MS Harley 6485, appearing to be a Rosicrucian text by John Dee. See Waite, *Brotherhood of the Rosy Cross,* 401. For a discussion of that manuscript, and of the Smart/Rudd connection, see the introduction to E. J. Langford Garstin, ed., *Rosie Crucian Secrets.* The latter also finds Thomas Rudd to be an unlikely candidate for the identity of "Dr. Rudd," while being more hesitant about dismissing that there was somebody behind Smart.
39. This argument is put in full in Asprem, "False, Lying Spirits."
40. See for instance McLean, ed., *Treatise,* 173–82.
41. McLean, ed., *Treatise,* 179–80.
42. Ibid., 175–76.
43. McLean, ed., *Treatise,* 33; emphasis mine.
44. Ibid., 36.
45. With the exception of Ebriah, who nevertheless may be connected to "Ebriel," the name of the ninth unholy sefirah according to Isaac ha-Cohen of Soria. See Gustav Davidson, *A Dictionary of Angels, Including the Fallen Angels,* 101.
46. See *The Goetia,* 31, 41.
47. See Skinner and Rankine, *Practical Angel Magic,* 38–43.
48. Ibid., 42.
49. Ibid., 41.
50. Ibid.
51. Saunders, "Rudd, Thomas (1583/4–1656)."
52. Rons, "Review: *The Practical Angel Magic of Dr. John Dee's Enochian Tables.*" This particular corruption is interesting, since it would have great impact later, notably on Aleister Crowley, through the central position Sloane 307 acquired

in the Golden Dawn. See also Rons's heavily detailed updated review, which does not come across any more positive than the original one. Rons, "*Practical Angel Magic:* An Updated Review."

53. I.e., as the official instruction *Book "H"*, prepared by W. W. Westcott.
54. We know that Crowley studied the document carefully. One major merit of Skinner and Rankine's otherwise problematic edition of Sloane 307 is the inclusion of Golden Dawn students' notes on the MS, including the notes of F. L. Gardner and Allan Bennett.

Chapter 3. Victorian Occultism and the Invention of Modern Enochiana

1. See Randall Styers, *Making Magic*, 3; cf. Hanegraaff, *Esotericism and the Academy*, chapter 3.
2. Granger, *A Supplement, Consisting of Corrections and Large Additions, to a Biographical History of England*, 94–95.
3. Burke, *The Annual Register*, "Characters" section, 51–52.
4. Cf. Hanegraaff, *Esotericism and the Academy*, chapter 3; idem, "Western Esotericism in Enlightenment Historiography."
5. Godwin, *Lives of the Necromancers*, 373–98; citation on 389.
6. Ibid., 390.
7. Ibid., 379.
8. The best way to form a picture of Hockley is by reading the material collected and commented in R. A. Gilbert and John Hamill, eds., *The Rosicrucian Seer*. See also Alex Sumner, "Angelic Invocations." Sumner compares Hockley's practices with those of other occult angelologies, including that of John Dee's conversations.
9. Ellic Howe, *Fringe Freemasonry*, 15.
10. See Francis King, "Introduction," 17; Barrett, *The Magus*. It is significant that *The Magus* contained no references to Enochian magic. This is a clear indication that Dee's magic was largely forgotten and/or neglected by practitioners in the eighteenth century.
11. This was his statement given to the London Dialectical Society, when speaking for their special Committee of Spiritualism on June 8, 1869. See Gilbert and Hamill, eds., *The Rosicrucian Seer*, 96.
12. Ibid., xxi.
13. See for instance Joscelyn Godwin, *The Theosophical Enlightenment*, ch. 9. I am also grateful to Daniel Kline, who let me read his unpublished paper on crystal gazing in early occultism.
14. Gilbert, "Secret Writing: The Magical Manuscripts of Frederick Hockley," 32.
15. See especially the excerpts from Hockley's "Crystal manuscripts," in Gilbert and Hamill, eds., *Rosicrucian Seer*, 109–28.
16. Godwin, *Theosophical Enlightenment*, 185.
17. King, "Introduction," 19.
18. For concise overviews of the history and significance of the Order, see Gilbert, "The Hermetic Order of the Golden Dawn"; cf. Asprem, "The Golden Dawn and the O.T.O."
19. See Joscelyn Godwin, *The Theosophical Enlightenment*, 333–79.
20. Former members of the original order were the first to speculate. Among these we find men such as the authors W. B. Yeats and Arthur Machen, and the occult

scholar A. E. Waite; all of whom touched upon the subject in their respective autobiographies. The standard scholarly discussion remains Howe, *Magicians of the Golden Dawn*, 1–25.

21. See Darcy Küntz, ed., *The Complete Golden Dawn Cipher Manuscript*. An online reproduction has also been made available. See: http://www.hermetic.com/gdlibrary/cipher/ (last accessed 09/06/2009).
22. See Gilbert, "Provenance Unknown"; idem, "Supplement to 'Provenance Unknown.'"
23. Talking about emic historiographies I refer to the uses of history and mythmaking in the process of constructing esoteric traditions, for example by delineating chains of transmission from mythical times through significant sages down to one's own group, presented as the current guardian of a "legitimate" esoteric "lineage." Cf. the detailed discussion in Hammer, *Claiming Knowledge*, 155–81.
24. The details of this episode are laid out in Howe, *Magicians of the Golden Dawn*, 1–25.
25. The most relevant evaluations of these issues are in Robert A. Gilbert, *The Golden Dawn;* idem, *The Golden Dawn Companion;* Ellic Howe, *The Magicians of the Golden Dawn;* R. A. Gilbert, "Provenance Unknown." I will mostly be following Gilbert, "Provenance Unknown," and Howe, *Magicians of the Golden Dawn* (especially pp. 1–25).
26. Several attempts to locate any traces of a German Rosicrucian Order at the indicated place and time, both by occultist and writer Gustav Meyrink, and by the scholar Ellic Howe, have proved unsuccessful. See Howe, *Magicians of the Golden Dawn*, 10. It is also well known that Westcott most probably forged a series of letters to make it appear as if the MS had come from this alleged German Order and their chief, "soror S.D.A." a.k.a. "Anna Sprengel." See ibid., 5–25.
27. See Lévi, *Transcendental Magic*, 99–103, 378–411; Howe, *Magicians of the Golden Dawn*, 2–3.
28. Howe, *Magicians of the Golden Dawn*, 2.
29. This position is convincingly argued for in Gilbert, "Provenance Unknown."
30. For a discussion and account of their meeting, see Christopher McIntosh, *Eliphas Lévi*, 117–23.
31. For my discussion of this form of creativity, its context and implication in the Golden Dawn and other occultist contexts, see Asprem, *"Kabbalah Recreata,"* esp. 133–37, 144–47.
32. On the place of "concordances" in Western esotericism generally, cf. Faivre, *Access to Western Esotericism*, 10–15.
33. See for example Anupassana [Suzan Wilson], "Introduction to the Elemental Grade Ceremonies," 135.
34. Asprem, *"Kabbalah Recreata,"* 144–47.
35. Cipher MS, f. 13.
36. Dee's final version of this being, as we have seen, in the *Tabula bonorum angelorum* of Sloane 3191.
37. Casaubon, ed., *True & Faithful Relation*, 173.
38. Ibid., 181.
39. Ibid.; cf. Sloane 3191, f. 52b-80b.
40. See Cipher MS f. 21 (Theoricus and "tablet of air"), f. 22, 26 (Practicus and "Great Western Quadrangle of water"), f. 34, 41 (Philosophus and "fire tablet").

41. This is relevant also because Mathers has often been blamed for the radical syncretism of the Order. See for instance King, "Introduction," 20.
42. See the reproduction of Westcott's letter to Mathers in Howe, *Magicians of the Golden Dawn,* 12.
43. See Howe, *Magicians of the Golden Dawn,* 75–90.
44. Cipher MS, folio 13.
45. See "Ceremony of the Zelator 1° = 10° Grade" in Regardie, ed., *The Golden Dawn,* 147–48.
46. See Regardie, ed., *The Golden Dawn,* 141, 156, 167–68, 182–83.
47. Darcy Küntz notes that it is part of a series of folios that were written and added later, probably forged by Westcott. See Küntz, ed., *The Complete Golden Dawn Cipher Manuscript,* 35. The folio itself is reproduced in ibid., 162–63.
48. See Casaubon, ed., *A True and Faithful Relation,* 179. The four tables are shown in a fourfold arrangement only in Casaubon, ed., "Actio Tertiæ," in *A True and Faithful Relation,* 15. However, here the Black Cross is not included. The arrangement of the tables shown on these pages (rearranged by Raphael in 1587) is nevertheless the one used in the Cipher MS and thus in the G.D. For manuscripts that show Dee's actual configuration of the Black Cross, see MS Sloane 3191, f. 52b-80b (*Tabula bonorum angelorum*).
49. The latter interpretation is not unreasonable, considering the novelty in the interpretation of the system generally. It would not be hard at all to find what the angels and Dee and Kelley thought about for instance the Great Table's use, as this is quite clearly stated even in Casaubon. In other words, it is not only possible but *likely* that the author knew, but did not care/had other plans.
50. See Casaubon, ed., *True and Faithful Relation,* 175–76, "Actio Tertia," in ibid., 15; Sloane 3191 f. 52b-558a; Cotton appendix XLVI f. 198b-201a.
51. See "The Book of the Concourse of the Forces," 630–58 in Regardie, ed., *The Golden Dawn,* 631–34. This document was circulated in the Inner Order of the Golden Dawn, and was probably written by Westcott. It is assumed, however, that the actual research was made by Mathers, who indeed is invoked and quoted several places in the document.
52. I have argued before that this syncretistic and progressive aspect of the Golden Dawn's frame of mind shows the Order as resonant with main aspects of Victorian Modernity. See Asprem, *"Kabbalah Recreata."*
53. "Ceremony of the Grade of Adeptus Minor," in Regardie, ed., *The Golden Dawn,* 231.
54. Ibid.
55. Ibid.
56. The five documents, or "books," are *Book "H": Clavicula Tabularum Enochi; Book "S": The Book of the Concourse of Forces; Book "T": The Book of the Angelical Calls; Book "X": The Keys of the Governance and Combinations of the Squares of the Tablets;* and *Book "Y": Rosicrucian Chess.* All but the first one were published by Regardie. See Regardie, ed., *Golden Dawn.* The significance of Regardie's exclusion will be thoroughly discussed in chapter 6.
57. See the whole list in, e.g., King, "Introduction," 28–29.
58. Regardie, "Introduction," 1–48 in idem, ed., *The Golden Dawn,* 43–44.
59. Regardie, *Golden Dawn,* 658.
60. Regardie's approach to questions of legitimacy and authenticity will be discussed more closely in chapter 6.
61. This manuscript, together with Sloane 3188, which was one of Elias Ashmole's documents on Enochian, was quite recently reproduced and published in

Rankine and Skinner, *The Practical Angel Magic of Dr. John Dee's Enochian Tablets: Tabularum Bonorum Angelorum Invocationes as Used by Wynn Westcott, Alan Bennett, Reverend Ayton*. However, as was discussed in chapter 2, there are several serious problems with the interpretative frame imposed on the material by the editors. Another edition of the *Book "H"* is available online at http://www.angelfire.com/ab6/imuhtuk/gdmans/rith.htm (retrieved 09/09/2007).

62. MS Sloane 3191, f. 52b-80b.
63. Casaubon, ed., *True and Faithful Relation,* 179.
64. As a matter of comparison, we may mention the notion of a purely "spiritual alchemy," which appeared in the middle of the nineteenth century with Mary Ann Atwood's *Suggestive Inquiry into the Hermetic Mystery* (1850). This book popularized a conception of medieval and early modern alchemists as talking entirely allegorically about the transmutation of metals, while in reality guarding a deep and very ancient spiritual insight. The conception, which has been remarkably resilient even in academic quarters, is now typically dismissed by serious scholars of alchemy as a nineteenth-century presentist projection. See, e.g., Lawrence Principe and William R. Newman, "Some Problems with the Historiography of Alchemy."
65. Most notably in another short piece by Westcott, "Further Rules for Practice," 669–70 in Regardie, ed., *The Golden Dawn*. Here he seems to keep the information of the different skills of the spirits, but blends it in with the elemental attributions to each table. More will be said about this short piece later.
66. Skinner and Rankine, *John Dee's Enochian Tables,* 49–50, 269–70.
67. "The Book of the Concourse of the Forces," 630–58 in Regardie, ed., *The Golden Dawn*.
68. Ibid., 638–42.
69. Ibid., 646–55.
70. Ibid., 655–56.
71. See "The Keys of the Governance and Combinations of the Squares of the Tablets," in Regardie, ed., *The Golden Dawn,* 659–62.
72. Ibid., 660.
73. Ibid., 661–62.
74. Casaubon, ed., *True and Faithful Relation,* 145.
75. This is elaborated in ibid., 153ff.
76. Sloane 3191.
77. "The Fourty-Eight Angelical Keys or Calls," in Regardie, ed., *The Golden Dawn,* 672–73.
78. One could add here that the former Golden Dawn magician Aleister Crowley went on to experiment with these "Aethyrs," first in 1901 and then again in 1909. See Crowley, Victor B. Neuburg, and Mary Desti, *The Vision & The Voice with Commentary*.
79. See the part "Enochian or Rosicrucian Chess," 683–96 in Regardie, ed., *The Golden Dawn*. This includes a lengthy commentary by Regardie, and original documents by Mathers.
80. For a history and introduction to the various Tarot games before it became an esoteric divinatory system, see Michael Dummet and Sylvia Mann, *The Game of Tarot*.
81. See for example Regardie, ed., *Golden Dawn,* 456–78.
82. The Adepts in question are Mrs. Helen Rand (Vigilate), Ms. Annie Horniman (Fortiter et Recte), Dr. H. Pullen-Berry (Anima Pura Sit), Dr. E. Berridge

(Resurgam), and Pamela Bullock (Shemeber). The Flying Roll is partially published two places. One half is in Regardie, ed., *The Golden Dawn*, 662–68, the other in King, ed., *Astral Projection, Magic, and Alchemy*, 81–87.

83. In King, ed., *Astral Projection*, 86–87.
84. Ibid, 87.
85. Moina Mathers, "Of Skrying and Travelling in the Spirit-Vision," reprinted in Regardie, *Golden Dawn*, 467–73.
86. Ibid, 470.
87. For a very rich and thoughtful elaboration on the role of scrying in Victorian occultism, see Alex Owen, *The Place of Enchantment*, especially chapter 5.
88. Regardie, *The Golden Dawn*, 683.
89. Howe, *Magicians of the Golden Dawn*, 228.
90. See Mary Greer, *Women of the Golden Dawn*, 141–42.
91. Ibid., 141.
92. Cited in ibid., 142.
93. Westcott, "Further Rules for Practice," 669–70 in Regardie, ed., *The Golden Dawn*.
94. Ibid., 668.
95. Ibid.
96. Ibid., 669.
97. Ibid., 699–70.
98. Ibid., 670.
99. Ibid.
100. See for instance the ritual written by Allan Bennett, performed with three other adepts, aimed at the evocation of the spirit Taphthartharath: Bennett, "Ritual for the Evocation unto Visible Appearance of the Great Spirit Taphthartharath."
101. Yeats cited in Greer, *Women of the Golden Dawn*, 141.
102. See Gnothi Seauton, Manuscript notebook, in the Gerald Yorke Collection, The Warburg Institute, "New Listing," 60, 66, 100. For a modern reproduction, see Küntz, ed., *The Enochian Experiments of the Golden Dawn*.
103. This group is an interesting chapter in the history of the Golden Dawn. For more on its workings, see, e.g., Greer, *Women of the Golden Dawn*, esp. chapters 21–24; Owen, *The Place of Enchantment*, 82, 129–30, 222.
104. This material is briefly discussed in Owen, *The Place of Enchantment*, 150, 291n.4.
105. See Küntz, ed., *The Enochian Experiments of the Golden Dawn*.
106. I am thinking here of the term as used by Olav Hammer, signifying the tendency in modern esoteric discourse to avoid citing originators of ideas, concepts, or themes. This can often be seen to give the presentation of the idea an aura of stability, sanctity, endurance, or even eternity. See Hammer, *Claiming Knowledge*, 180–81.

Chapter 4. The Authenticity Problem and the Legitimacy of Magic

1. For details, see Howe, *Magicians of the Golden Dawn*, 239–40.
2. Owen, *The Place of Enchantment*.
3. Luhrmann, *Persuasions of the Witch's Craft*.
4. Pasi, *La notion de magie*.
5. E.g., Wouter J. Hanegraaff, *New Age Religion and Western Culture;* Olav Hammer,

Claiming Knowledge; Christopher Partridge, *The Re-Enchantment of the West,* two volumes; Asprem and Granholm, eds., *Contemporary Esotericism.*

6. I.e., Hanegraaff, "How Magic Survived"; Asprem, "Thelema og ritualmagi." See also Hanegraaff's entry "Magic V" in the *Dictionary of Gnosis and Western Esotericism.*
7. There are indeed important magical currents that do not spring directly from the Golden Dawn synthesis, particularly those developed in continenteal Europe, particularly Germany, France, and Italy, at the *fin de siècle* and during the early decades of the twentieth century. Any list of important names and groups should include, e.g., Papus (Gerard Encausse), Giuliano Kremmerz (Ciro Formisano), Arturo Reghini, Julius Evola and the UR group, Gregor A. Gregorius (Eugen Grosche) and the Fraternitas Saturni, Maria de Naglowska, Franz Bardon, etc. For cursory overviews of some of these figures, see, e.g., Hans Thomas Hakl, "The Theory and Practice of Sexual Magic"; Massimo Introvigne, *Il Cappello del Mago;* Stephen Flowers, *Fire & Ice;* relevant entries in Hanegraaff et al., eds., *Dictionary of Gnosis and Western Esotericism.*
8. Webb, *The Flight from Reason.*
9. I.e., Hanegraaff, "The New Age Movement and the Esoteric Tradition"; idem, "How Magic Survived"; Owen, *Place of Enchantment;* Richard Noakes, "Spiritualism, Science and the Supernatural in mid-Victorian Britain."
10. For the former, see Godwin, Chanel, and Deveney, eds., *The Hermetic Brotherhood of Luxor.*
11. Regardie, ed., *The Golden Dawn.*
12. Such as Crowley, *Magick: Liber ABA.*
13. Colin Campbell, "The Secret Religion of the Educated Classes."
14. Peter Berger, ed., *The Desecularization of the World.*
15. Paul Heelas, *The New Age Movement;* Christopher Partridge, *The Re-Enchantment of the West,* two volumes.
16. Bruce, *God Is Dead,* 1–44.
17. E.g., Steve Bruce, "The New Age and Secularization"; Campbell, "The Cult, the Cultic Milieu, and Secularization."
18. Campbell, "The Secret Religion of the Educated Classes."
19. E.g., Hanegraaff, *New Age Religion and Western Culture.*
20. E.g., Luhrmann, *Persuasions,* 10–11.
21. See James R. Lewis, "New Religion Adherents: An Overview of Anglophone Census and Survey Data."
22. Hanegraaff, "How Magic Survived."
23. Ibid., 361–264.
24. Ibid., 366–267.
25. Ibid., 366ff. For a more detailed criticism of the "psychologization thesis", see Asprem, "'Magic Naturalized'?"
26. Ibid., 370.
27. Hanegraaff, "Magic V," 740.
28. Partridge, *The Re-Enchantment of the West,* Vol. 1, 40–41.
29. Ibid., 41; italics added. Quotes in text taken from Luhrmann, *Persuasions,* 164, 177–78.
30. I.e., Partridge, *Re-Enchantment of the West,* Vol. 1, 38–46.
31. Ibid., 84.
32. See especially Partridge, "Occulture Is Ordinary."
33. Ibid., 68, 70.

34. See for instance the articles in John Storey, ed., *Cultural Studies and the Study of Popular Culture.*
35. Cf. Asprem, "'Magic Naturalized'?"
36. LaVey, *The Satanic Bible,* 119.
37. LaVey, "Satanism," 440.
38. E.g., LaVey, "On Occultism of the Past."
39. Dyrendal, "Satan and the Beast"; LaVey, *The Compleat Witch.*
40. Asprem, "Thelema og ritualmagi," 122–24.
41. Ibid., 124.
42. Ibid., 124, 132–33.
43. See, e.g., Howe, *The Magicians of the Golden Dawn;* Gilbert, *The Golden Dawn;* Gilbert, *The Golden Dawn Companion.* For the aftermath and formation of new branches across the world, see Francis King, *Ritual Magic in England;* King, *Modern Ritual Magic.*
44. For instance, A. E. Waite, *Shadows of Life and Thought;* Arthur Machen, *Things Near and Far.*
45. Crowley, *Confessions,* 612–13.
46. Ibid.
47. Hammer, *Claiming Knowledge.*
48. E.g., ibid., 22–25, 42–46. The latter is not to be confused with the common philosophical meaning of "scientism."
49. For the polemical aspects of Scholem and other Kabbalah specialists, see esp. Huss, "Authorized Guardians." For the implications of Scholem's approach to the (neglect of) the study of modern occultism, see Asprem, *"Kabbalah Recreata,"* 132–33, 142–43.

Chapter 5. The Angels and the Beast

1. For a good survey of the literature, see Pasi, *Versuchung der Politik,* 23–32; cf. idem, "The Neverendingly Told Story."
2. See especially Lawrence Sutin, *Do What Thou Wilt*; Richard Kaczynski, *Perdurabo* for the most up-to-date biographical accounts.
3. Hugh Urban, "Unleashing the Beast;" idem, *Magia Sexualis.*
4. Pasi, *Aleister Crowley und die Versuchung der Politik.*
5. Alex Owen, "The Sorcerer and His Apprentice;" idem, *The Place of Enchantment,* 186–220.
6. E.g., Lon Milo DuQuette, *The Magick of Aleister Crowley;* Christopher Hyatt and DuQuette, *The Enochian World of Aleister Crowley;* Rodney Orpheus, *Abrahadabra.*
7. Some notable exceptions include Pasi, *La notion de magie;* Asprem, "Magic Naturalized?"; idem, *"Kabbalah Recreata";* Urban, *Magia Sexualis,* 109–39.
8. Owen, *The Place of Enchantment,* 186–220.
9. Ibid., 196.
10. For the details of this incident, see Howe, *Magicians of the Golden Dawn,* 219–32.
11. Sutin, *Do What Thou Wilt,* 80–117.
12. Ibid., 119.
13. On Allan Bennett, see John L. Crow, *The White Knight in the Yellow Robe.*
14. Ibid., 95. Cf. Pasi, "Lo yoga in Aleister Crowley."
15. For the relevance of this book to the interpretation and use of Kabbalah in

modern occultism, see Asprem, "*Kabbalah Recreata*." For Crowley's idea of these tabulations as a form of science, see Asprem, "Magic Naturalized?"

16. For these events, see Crowley, *Magick*, 405–43; idem, *Confessions*, 391–403; but cf. Sutin, *Do What Thou Wilt*, 115ff.
17. Sutin, *Do What Thou Wilt*, 120.
18. Ibid., 121.
19. Crowley's Thelemic revisions of these rituals are known respectably as "the Star Ruby" and "the Star Saphire" rituals. Both were published for the first time in Crowley's playful *Book of Lies*, as chapters 25 (5 x 5) and 36 (6 x 6). Among the main differences from the Golden Dawn rituals are that Hebrew god-names are exchanged for Thelemic ones, and that the new version of the hexagram ritual has been given more explicit sexual references.
20. For the most important commentaries on the Law of Thelema, see Crowley, *The Law is for*; idem, *Liber Aleph*.
21. E.g., Crowley, "Liber II."
22. McGregor Mathers had translated this ritual instruction from manuscripts in the Bibliothéque de l'Arsenal and published it in 1898. See Mathers, ed., *The Book of the Sacred Magic of Abramelin the Mage*.
23. Crowley, *Magick*, 494.
24. Ibid., 126.
25. Cf. Asprem, "Thelema og ritualmagi."
26. The Greek Αστρον Αργον has a double connotation, giving the English translation "the Still and Shiny Star." This is hinted at in Crowley's esoteric poem "One Star in Sight," where we read: "One star can summon them to wake / To self—star-souls serene that gleam / On life's calm lake."
27. Crowley, "Editorial," 2. For a thorough discussion of the meaning of science in the context of Crowley and the A∴A∴'s "Scientific Illuminism," see Asprem, "Magic Naturalized?"
28. For a concise overview of these events, see Asprem, "The Golden Dawn and the O.T.O."; cf. Pasi, "Ordo Templi Orientis."
29. The essence of Crowley's views on the Order in this respect was published already in 1919, in the so-called "Blue Equinox," being the first issue of the third volume of *The Equinox*.
30. The best studies of the O.T.O.'s institutional legacy—a largely underresearched field—are Martin P. Starr, *The Unknown God;* idem, "Chaos from Order."
31. Crowley, *Confessions*, 192; italics in original.
32. For Bennett's copy, see Rankine and Skinner, *John Dee's Enochian Tables*, 271–77. The editors note that Bennett must have made his copy between 1892 and 1894. Crowley's note to Bennett's copy is a technical suggestion for how to evoke Enochian spirits letter by letter, through the use of the "keys." See ibid., 277.
33. Ibid., 612–13; cf. Kaczynski, *Perdurabo*, 71.
34. For Crowley's claim that the event had been entirely unanticipated, see *Confessions*, 613.
35. Ibid.
36. Kaczynski, *Perdurabo*, 71.
37. Crowley, *Vision and the Voice*, 41–42.
38. Crowley, *Confessions*, 611.
39. See Crowley, ed., *The Goetia*, 95–124.
40. See Pasi and Rabaté, "Langue angélique, langue magique," 117, n82.
41. Crowley, *Confessions*, 611.
42. Cf. Kaczynski, *Perdurabo*, 151, 155.

43. Crowley and Neuburg, "Liber XXX Aerum" (1911); Crowley, "Liber LXXXIV vel Chanokh," parts I and II (1912).
44. Crowley would have access to Ashmole MS 422, Ashmole MS 580, and Ashmole MS 1790. See my overview of the transmission of Dee's manuscripts in chapter 2.
45. Ibid., 612–13.
46. See "Liber LXXXIV vel Chanokh," parts one and two.
47. Crowley, "Liber Chanokh," part one, 239.
48. Crowley, "Liber Chanokh," part two, 125.
49. Crowley, *Confessions*, 616. For a recent discussion of the event, see Owen, *Place of Enchantment*, 186–220.
50. Crowley and Neuburg, "Liber XXX Aereum."
51. Kaczynski, *Perdurabo*, 155.
52. Crowley, *Confessions*, 616.
53. Ibid.; Kaczynski, *Perdurabo*, 155.
54. Crowley et al., *The Vision and The Voice*, 86.
55. Ibid., 87n. For the role of this recreated kabbalistic hermeneutic, see Asprem, "*Kabbalah Recreata.*"
56. Crowley et al., *The Vision and the Voice*, 170.
57. Sutin, *Do What Thou Wilt*, 202–204.
58. See Sutin, *Do What Thou Wilt*, 204–205.
59. Crowley et al., *Vision and the Voice*, 156–57.
60. See Crowley, ed., *The Goetia*.
61. Kaczynski, *Perdurabo*, 159–60.
62. Ibid.
63. Ibid., 161–63.
64. Ibid., 162–63; Crowley et al., *The Vision and The Voice*, 168.
65. Crowley et al., *The Vision and The Voice*, 168–69.
66. Sutin, *Do What Thou Wilt*, 204.
67. Owen, *Place of Enchantment*, 211.
68. Crowley, *Confessions*, 628. See also Sutin, *Do What Thou Wilt*, 204–205.
69. Letter to J. F. C. Fuller, cited in Sutin, *Do What Thou Wilt*, 204.
70. This was written for the first time in 1911, but only published two years later, for the final issue of the first volume of *The Equinox*. Crowley, "A Syllabus of the Official Instructions of the A∴A∴." See also Richard Kaczynski, *Perdurabo*, 189.
71. Crowley, "A Syllabus of the Official Instructions," 46.
72. Ibid.
73. For instance, important god-like entities in Thelemic cosmology are not to be found in *Liber Legis*, but are introduced properly for the first time in these Enochian visions. This is notably the case with "Chaos" (mentioned in the visions pertaining to Aethyrs 14, 4, 3, and 2) and "Babalon" (speculations on this Thelemic goddess occupies much of the content of Aethyrs 12 through 2). See Crowley et al., *The Vision and the Voice*.
74. See, e.g., Kaczynski, *Perdurabo*, 210–11.
75. E.g., ibid., 211.
76. For the liturgy, see Crowley, "Liber XV, O.T.O. Ecclesiæ Gnosticæ Catholicæ Canon Missæ."
77. Chaos is described in the visions pertaining to Aethyrs 14, 4, 3, and 2, while the Thelemic goddess Babalon plays a central role in all the visions from Aethyrs 12 through 2. See Crowley et al., *The Vision and the Voice*.

78. Crowley et al., *The Vision and the Voice,* 206–11.
79. Crowley, "Liber XV, O.T.O. Ecclesiæ Gnosticæ Catholicæ Canon Missæ," 585. For solar-phallic religion and occultism, see Godwin, *The Theosophical Enlightenment,* 1–48. For a brief discussion of solar-phallicism in the O.T.O., see, e.g., Asprem, "The Golden Dawn and the O.T.O."
80. See especially Crowley et al., *Vision and the Voice,* 137–42.
81. Crowley, *Liber ABA,* 187.
82. Ibid.
83. Crowley et al., *The Vision and the Voice,* 116.
84. DuQuette, *The Magick of Aleister Crowley;* Orpheus, *Abrahadabra;* Gunther, *Initiation in the Aeon of the Child.*
85. See, e.g., Crowley et al., *The Vision and the Voice,* 36, 254–56.
86. E.g., DuQuette, *The Magick of Aleister Crowley,* 246, n2.
87. Detailed examples of how path-workings may function are described in the anthropological standard work on contemporary ritual magic: Luhrmann, *Persuasions of the Witch's Craft.*
88. Frater W.I.T., *Enochian Initiation.*

Chapter 6. Angels of Satan

1. See Anton Szandor LaVey, *The Satanic Bible,* 159–272. Compare with the version in Crowley, "Liber Chanokh," part two, 99–128. The spelling of the calls here are identical, while at the same time differing from those of the Golden Dawn papers published by Regardie, *Golden Dawn,* 673–82.
2. King, *Ritual Magic in England,* 110–11.
3. But see King, *Ritual Magic in England,* 94–191; cf. Howe, *The Magicians of the Golden Dawn,* 233–83.
4. Ibid., 95–96.
5. Regardie, ed., *Golden Dawn,* 683.
6. King, *Ritual Magic in England,* 107.
7. Zalewski, *Enochian Chess of the Golden Dawn.*
8. As is the opinion of Mary K. Greer: *Women of the Golden Dawn,* 251.
9. See, e.g., Greer, *Women of the Golden Dawn,* 348–58.
10. See Moina Mathers in Greer, *Women of the Golden Dawn,* 352.
11. Greer, *Women of the Golden Dawn,* 352–53.
12. Ibid., 353.
13. Perseverantia [P.F. Case], letter to Regardie, January 15, 1933; letter to Regardie, August 10, 1933.
14. Regardie, *The Garden of Pomegranates.* For the reception, cf. King, *Ritual Magic in England,* 153–54.
15. Case authored a book on the Tarot: see Case, *The Tarot.*
16. Case, letter to Regardie, January 1933.
17. Ibid.
18. "Ceremony of the Grade of Adeptus Minor" in Regardie, ed., *The Golden Dawn,* 231.
19. E.g., Asprem, *"Kabbalah Recreata."*
20. Case, letter to Regardie, August 10, 1933.
21. Cf. my discussion of Alex Owen's work on Crowley in chapter 5.
22. Ibid.
23. Case, letter to Regardie, January 15, 1933; emphasis added.

24. Ibid.; emphasis added.
25. See for instance their international Web site for more information: http://www.bota.org/.
26. Regardie, *The Golden Dawn*, 626. Unfortunately, Regardie does not reveal who these clairvoyants were, or when the experiments were conducted. It does not seem unreasonable, however, to suspect that it was in the Stella Matutina period.
27. Ibid.
28. It is nevertheless intriguing to note, as we did at the beginning of chapter 3, that the idea of Dee as an initiate of a Rosicrucian brotherhood was being spread in the Enlightenment historiography of the late eighteenth century.
29. Ibid.
30. Partially reproduced in Regardie, ed., *The Golden Dawn*, 627–28. Again, it is not stated when or where this was actually used. However, as the position has become influential also in a later period when defense against purists had become relevant, it is nevertheless an important document.
31. Ibid.
32. Ibid.
33. Ibid., 627–28.
34. Ibid., 628. The three names are Mor, Dial, Hctga.
35. Crowley, *Confessions*, 612.
36. Regardie, *The Golden Dawn*, 628–29.
37. Ibid.
38. Modern Satanism has started to receive more attention from scholars in later years, with the first international academic conference dedicated to the topic being held in Trondheim, Norway, in the fall of 2009. The same year saw the publication of the hitherto most complete anthology of modern religious Satanism, i.e., Jesper Aagaard Petersen, ed., *Contemporary Religious Satanism*. The first work to place it in the context of earlier religious and intellectual discourses on Satan and Satanism was Massimo Introvigne, *Enquête sur le satanisme*. It remains to this day the most complete treatment of the historical background, although Introvigne's discussion of modern Satanism has been rendered outdated by more recent research. Other works that touch upon the history of modern Satanism—some scholarly, some coming from emic perspectives—include Arthur Lyons, *The Second Coming;* Joachim Schmidt, *Satanismus;* Philip Stevens, "Satan and Satanism"; Jean LaFontaine, "Satanism and Satanic Mythology"; Gavin Baddeley, *Lucifer Rising;* James R. Lewis, *Satanism Today;* Jesper Aagaard Petersen, "Modern Satanism"; Petersen and Lewis, eds., *Encyclopedic Sourcebook of Satanism*.
39. See, e.g., Asbjørn Dyrendal, "Satan and the Beast." Introvigne also discusses the influence of earlier occult trends, especially the Californian Thelemic circle around Jack Parsons, on LaVey. See, e.g., Introvigne, *Enquête sur le satanisme*, 260ff. Cf. Pasi, "Dieu du désir, Dieu de la raison."
40. The now classic discussion of this process is Hanegraaff, *New Age Religion and Western Culture*.
41. Cf. the discussion in chapter 4.
42. E.g., Petersen, "Modern Satanism," 424–25; Partridge, *Re-Enchantment of the West*.
43. E.g., LaVey, "Satanism"; idem, "On Occultism of the Past."
44. Pasi, "Dieu du désir, Dieu de la raison" gives a discussion of the differences between LaVey and Aquino concerning the interpretation of the devil.

Although he does not explicitly use the dichotomy adopted here, it gives a good example of one of its main manifestations. See also the section on Aquino in this chapter.

45. Petersen, "Modern Satanism." One should however also note that applying the label "Satanism" to Aquino's position is not without its problems. For a discussion, see Kennet Granholm, "Embracing Others than Satan." Petersen's distinction is similar to an earlier fourfold typology made by Introvigne, which distinguished between "Rationalist Satanism" (Church of Satan), "Occultist Satanism" (Temple of Set), "Acid Satanism" (informal, youth oriented), and "Luciferian Satanism" (Gnostic). See Introvigne, *Auf den Spuren des Satanismus*. In the following I will be adhering to Petersen's dichotomy, which bases itself on Introvigne's "Rationalist"/"Occultist" distinction.
46. Petersen, "Modern Satanism," 444.
47. Ibid. Thus, it is "esoteric" in ways more similar to those movements, spokespersons, and texts defined and circumscribed by Antoine Faivre, e.g., *Access to Western Esotericism*. However, I do not here enter into the web of debate on the definition (or description) of "esotericism." See, however, Hanegraaff, *Esotericism and the Academy;* cf. von Stuckrad, *Was ist Esoterik?;* idem, "Western Esotericism."
48. It has been suggested, notably by Kennet Granholm, that referring to the Temple of Set as "Satanic" is misleading. The figure and symbolism of Satan is largely changed for other expressions (e.g., Set), and it would be more accurate to refer to the position by the more generic "Left-Hand Path." This also holds true for a range of later groups often denoted "Satanists" because of their heritage and links to LaVey and/or Aquino. See Granholm, "Embracing Others than Satan."
49. See Aquino, *The Church of Satan*, chapter 3.
50. Ibid, 52.
51. See LaVey, "Satanism," Appendix 1 to *The Church of Satan*, Aquino, 436–45.
52. Ibid, 444.
53. Lewis, "Diabolical Authority," 8.
54. Ibid; Aquino, *Church of Satan*, 65.
55. Crowley, "Liber LXXXIV vel Chanokh. A Brief Abstract Description of the Symbolic Representation of the Universe Derived by Doctor John Dee through the Skrying of Sir Edward Kelly," *The Equinox* I, nos VII and VIII (1912). Compare those in "A Brief Abstract...," *Equinox* VIII (1912): 99–128, with LaVey's in *The Satanic Bible*, 159–272. The spellings of the keys here are identical, while at the same time differing from those of the Golden Dawn published in Regardie, *Golden Dawn*, 673–82.
56. Aquino, *Church of Satan*, 65. See also Crowley, Victor B. Neuburg, and Mary Desti, *The Vision and The Voice*.
57. Aquino, *Church of Satan*, 52.
58. Although it should be made clear that it was not known at the time that Redbeard's tract was in fact the source of this part of the *Satanic Bible;* it was only named "The Book of Satan" and references to Redbeard were not included. Rather, the content was seen as compatible with the rest of the content of the satanic philosophy of life.
59. E.g., Campbell, "The Cult, the Cultic Milieu, and Secularization"; Olav Hammer, *Claiming Knowledge;* Partridge, *The Re-Enchantment of the West*, Vol. I.
60. Dyrendal's forthcoming "Satan and the Beast" gives a more thorough treatment

of this subject by comparing the notion of magic in Crowley, LaVey, and Aquino, their affinities and differences.

61. LaVey, *The Satanic Bible,* 111.
62. Dyrendal, "Satan and the Beast"; LaVey, *The Compleat Witch*. This book is really a sort of handbook for women in how to attract and manipulate men through various more or less mundane tricks.
63. LaVey, "Satanism," 439.
64. Ibid.
65. LaVey, *The Satanic Bible,* 110.
66. Ibid.
67. E.g., LaVey, "Enochian Pronunciation Guide"; idem, "Suggested Enochian Keys for Various Rituals and Ceremonies." Both reproduced on the CoS Web site: http://www.churchofsatan.com/Pages/EnochianGuide.html.
68. *The Satanic Bible,* 155.
69. Ibid. Also in LaVey, "Satanism," 442.
70. LaVey, "Enochian Pronunciation Guide."
71. Regardie cited in Aquino, *Church of Satan,* 65.
72. Ibid.
73. Ibid., 66. LaVey considered Regardie a personal friend, and it seems likely that his disappointment was due to this rather than any hope to be recognized by the established esoteric community.
74. Ibid. I have not succeeded in locating a copy of this article. However, Mr. Aquino has kindly told me that the article "was fairly brief, just making the point that Anton LaVey's modification of the Enochian Keys was only the latest in several successive modifications through the Golden Dawn and Crowley periods." Later on, however, Aquino would do more research into the original sources, acquiring a microfilm of the Dee material in the Ashmolean collection at the Bodleian Library. These studies were incorporated into his own position, which developed later. Aquino, e-mail to the author, February 20, 2008. More on Aquino's position follows below.
75. Aquino, *Church of Satan,* 66.
76. Aquino, e-mail to the author, February 20, 2008.
77. Lewis, "Diabolical Authority."
78. See Weber, *Wirtschaft und Gesellschaft,* Chapter III, §10.
79. Aquino, *Temple of Set,* 6–7.
80. See LaVey, "Phase IV message," appendix no. 116 in Aquino, *Church of Satan*.
81. Lewis, "Diabolical Authority," 5.
82. Aquino, *Temple of Set,* 7; emphasis added.
83. Aquino, *Temple of Set,* 9; emphases added.
84. Ibid., 7–8. This was Stephen Skinner's edition of Casaubon's *A True and Faithful Relation,* published as *John Dee's Action with Spirits*. It was a hardcover facsimile copy in a limited edition of 350 copies.
85. Aquino, *The Temple of Set,* 8. Aquino's engagement with U.S. military PSYOP, and the battalion's coterie of strange and unusual men is further outlined in his *Church of Satan,* 535–36.
86. Aquino, "The Book of Coming Forth By Night—Analysis and Commentary," 104–105.
87. Aquino, diary entry of March 9, 1974, cited in *The Temple of Set,* 8.
88. Aquino, *Temple of Set,* 9.
89. Aquino, "The Book of Coming Forth By Night—Analysis and Commentary," 105. For the full text of the result (which, amusingly, is in dialogue form

between the two mythological creatures mentioned in the title), see Aquino, "The Sphinx and the Chimera."

90. Ibid.
91. Aquino, *Temple of Set*, 9.
92. Aquino, "The Book of Coming Forth By Night—Analysis and Commentary," 105.
93. The current version of these translations is available as appendix 4 to Aquino's *Temple of Set*, 129–35.
94. Aquino, "The Book of Coming Forth By Night—Analysis and Commentary," 103; emphasis added.
95. LaVey, *The Satanic Rituals*, 173–202.
96. Aquino, "The Book of Coming Forth By Night—Analysis and Commentary," 104.
97. Ibid., 105.
98. The other seventeen were done much later, the whole composition being ready by 1981.
99. Aquino, *Word of Set*, 129.
100. Ibid.
101. Aquino, *Temple of Set*, 9.
102. Ibid.
103. For details, see Aquino, *The Book of Coming Forth by Night;* idem, "The Book of Coming Forth By Night—Analysis and Commentary."

Chapter 7. The Purist Turn

1. E.g., Dave Evans, *History of British Magic after Crowley*, 374–75.
2. Jean-François Lyotard, *The Postmodern Condition*.
3. Ibid., xxiv.
4. Ibid., xxv.
5. It may be interesting to compare this project with other attempts to preserve, save or even recreate "uniqueness." The theme has clear parallels to postcolonial discourse, the struggle against Western acculturation of natives, and the recovery of "subaltern" identities and voices. This of course impacted the Western religious landscape as well, notably perhaps with the flowering of neo-pagan currents, some of them at least attempting to reconstruct lost or repressed identities.
6. Pasi and Rabaté, "Langue angélique, langue magique," 120. It might be added that the perception that a "purist" tendency has gained ground over this period was recognized by Enochian magicians themselves, sometimes by that precise term (see, e.g., Gerald Schueler, "Re: Schueler's 'translations,'" Enochian-L, 13.10.1997; cf. the discussion in chapter 8). Incidentally then, I already developed a category of Enochian purism for my working hypothesis, before encountering it independently developed in Pasi and Rabaté's article.
7. *The Satanic Bible* is likely to have been one of the most popular occult books ever. In 1991 it had already sold more than 600,000 copies worldwide. In addition there have been illegal translations distributed in Spanish and Russian, and since the 1991 figures, other legal translations into Swedish, German, and French have been made. See Lewis, "Diabolical Authority," 9.
8. Skinner, ed., *John Dee's Action with Spirits*.
9. Aquino, e-mail to the author, February 20, 2008.

10. Vinci, *Gmicalzoma!*
11. See Pasi and Rabaté, "Langue angélique, langue magique," 119; Vinci, *Gmicalzoma!*, 12.
12. Laycock, *The Complete Enochian Dictionary*. Reprinted in 1994 by Weiser Books.
13. I.e., Laycock, "Angelic language or mortal folly?"
14. Skinner, "Preface to the Revised Edition," no page numbers.
15. It seems a promising vista for new research to chart out the extent to which something like the "purist turn" makes itself present more generally in the world of ritual magic from the 1970s and 1980s onward. Certainly, a considerable number of sourcebooks were published in this period. Some examples would include Skinner, ed., *The Fourth Book of occult Philosophy* (1978), the various editions by Adam McLean's Magnum Opus Hermetic Sourcework series, and editions of grimoires, such as Daniel Driscoll, *Sworn Book of Honorius* (1977).
16. King, *Ritual Magic in England,* 187.
17. Ibid.
18. Cited in King, *Ritual Magic in England,* 190.
19. For the reproduced self-initiation ritual, originally titled "The Magical Ladder of Frater L.Z.I., the 4 = 7 to 5 = 6 Workings," see King, *Ritual Magic in England,* 187–89. For Crowley's "Mass of the Phoenix," see Crowley, *The Book of Lies,* chapter 44.
20. Edwards, *Dare to Make Magic.*
21. Pasi and Rabaté do not treat this Order in their article, although Turner is mentioned in connection with the "*Necronomicon* scam," discussed below. See "Langue angélique, langue magique," 105–106.
22. Ashe, e-mail to the author, March 2, 2008. Steven Ashe was a member of the O.C.S. from 1979 to the early 1980s. Later he has acquired a name within contemporary occultism for his publications on occultist Kabbalah. See, e.g., his recent *Qabalah—The Complete Golden Dawn Initiate.*
23. Ashe, e-mail to the author, March 2, 2008.
24. Turner, ed., *The Heptarchia Mystica of John Dee*. First published in the Magnum Opus Hermetic Sourceworks series in 1983, reprinted with new introduction and additional material by Aquarian Press, 1986. Turner, *Elizabethan Magic.*
25. Turner, *The Heptarchia Mystica of John Dee,* xxii.
26. Ashe, e-mail to the author, March 2, 2008.
27. Ibid.
28. George Hay, ed., introduced by Colin Wilson, *The Necronomicon: Book of Dead Names.*
29. A full-length treatment of this phenomenon is available in Harms and Gonce, *Necronomicon Files.* For a scholarly analysis of Lovecraft's place in modern and contemporary esotericism, see Hanegraaff, "Fiction in the Desert of the Real."
30. H. P. Lovecraft, "A History of the *Necronomicon.*"
31. Ibid.
32. Ibid., 49.
33. In Sloane MS 3189.
34. For this account, see Harms, "The *Necronomicon* Made Flesh," 50.
35. Gonce, "A Plague of *Necronomicons,*" 129.
36. Ashe, e-mail to the author, March 2, 2008.
37. In Ashe's words, the success "went to Mr. Turner's head somewhat." Ibid.
38. See http://www.staffordtown.co.uk/tlodge.html (accessed Match 2, 2008).
39. Ashe, e-mail to the author, March 2, 2008. Forman's magical papers are in the

British Library, Add. MS 36674, ff. 47–56, f. 56. For more on Forman, see A. L. Rowse, *Simon Forman;* Barbara Traister, *The Notorious Astrological Physician of London;* Lauren Kassel, *Medicine and Magic in Elizabethan London.*

40. Turner, *The Heptarchia Mystica of John Dee,* 12.
41. This constructed tradition is set forth by Denning and Philips, *Robe and Ring,* xxx–xxxv.
42. Denning and Phillips, *The Magical Philosophy*, Book I, *Robe and Ring,* was published in 1974 by Llewellyn. Books II and III followed in 1975 (*The Appeal of High Magic* and *The Sword and the Serpent*), number IV in 1978 (*The Triumph of Light*), and number V in 1981 (*Mysteria Magica*). Hereafter I will refer to the volumes by their second titles.
43. According to a well-informed previous member, Al Billings, the few searches that have been done into the roots of the order have failed to find any trace of the turn of the century antiquarian society it claims to stem from, the Societas Rotae Fulgentis. The claimed lineage still seems to have wide currency among present members. Billings, e-mail to the author, March 10, 2008.
44. Dennings and Phillips, "The Heptarchical Doctrine." Although I have not been able to acquire a first edition of this book, there are strong indications that this material was not present when it was first published in 1974. *Vide infra.*
45. Ibid., 150.
46. Ibid., 149.
47. Ibid., 150–52.
48. Denning and Phillips, *The Apparel of High Magick.*
49. Idem, *The Sword and the Serpent,* esp. 139–41.
50. Idem, *The Triumph of Light.*
51. Idem, *Mysteria Magica,* 174–212, 213–54, 431–52.
52. Ibid., 184–208, 209–12.
53. Ibid., 232–44.
54. Ibid., 174–79.
55. James, *Enochian Evocation,* 194.
56. Ibid., 1–15.
57. Ibid., xxiv.
58. Ibid., xxii.
59. James, *The Enochian Magick of Dr. John Dee,* xii.
60. See, e.g., Hanegraaff, *New Age Culture,* 482–514.
61. Ibid., 179–91.
62. Pasi and Rabaté, "Langue angélique, langue magique," 120–21.
63. DuQuette and Hyatt, *Enochian World of Aleister Crowley,* 19–59 (exegesis/instructions), 61–102 *(Liber Chanokh).*
64. Ibid., 103–22.
65. DuQuette, "Instruction," in *Enochian World of Aleister Crowley,* 17; emphasis added.
66. Ibid.
67. For an intriguing personal account of DuQuette's magical biography, see his book *My Life with the Spirits*. Here, he also writes about his experiments with Enochian magic, which has been a long-term pursuit. DuQuette also mentions that he ran a study group called the Guild of Enochian Studies (G.O.E.S.). The group apparently met twice a week for three years, studying the available Crowley and Golden Dawn material on Enochian magic. Unfortunately, DuQuette does not provide us with an exact dating, but this seems to have taken place in the early 1980s. See *My Life With the Spirits,* 133–55.

68. Gerald Schueler has a background in the latter, being a member of the Association for Transpersonal Psychology (ATP). For his and Betty's *curriculum vitae,* see http://www.schuelers.com/bio.htm.
69. Especially "Liber Chanokh" and "The Vision and the Voice," published in Regardie, ed., *Gems from the Equinox,* 385–430, 431–591. Regardie's compilation was published for the first time in 1974.
70. Both these models are succinctly laid out on the Schuelers' Web site: see "Universe," http://www.schuelers.com/enochian/map.htm.
71. http://www.schuelers.com/enochian/index.htm.
72. See "Liber scientiae," "De Hep Mystica," and "Language" subsections at http://www.schuelers.com/enochian/index.htm. The Enochian language is also treated in G. and B. Schueler, *Enochian Magick,* predominantly from a G.D. and Crowley perspective.
73. G. Schueler, "Comments on the Heptarchia Mystica," linked to http://www.schuelers.com/enochian/index.htm.
74. Regardie, *The Golden Dawn,* 44.
75. "Schueler's Enochian Magic," javascript pop-up at http://www.schuelers.com/enochian/index.htm.
76. Ibid.
77. "Enochian healing," linked to http://www.schuelers.com/enochian/index.htm.
78. Ibid. This was first spelled out in G. and B. Scueler, *Advanced Guide to Enochian Magick*.
79. "Schueler's Enochian Magic," javascript pop-up at http://www.schuelers.com/enochian/index.htm.
80. G. and B. Schueler, *Angels' Message to Humanity,* acknowledgments page.
81. "Schueler's Enochian Magic," javascript pop-up at http://www.schuelers.com/enochian/index.htm.
82. This cosmology, which is succinctly explained on the Schueler Web site, borrows heavily from Blavatsky. The "higher" planes are, in order, the etheric, astral, lower and higher mental, and the divine plane. See also G. Schueler, *Enochian Physics*.
83. Cf. Hanegraaff's observation in "Magic V," 743.
84. Agrippa, *Three Books of Occult Philosophy.*
85. For a list and discription of his prolific production, see Tyson's Web site: http://www.donaldtyson.com/books.html.
86. It should nevertheless be noted that for Pasi and Rabaté the distinction between "purists" and "revisionists" is meant to indicate whether or not an author accepts the particular revisions done by the G.D. and Crowley (Pasi and Rabaté, "Langue angélique, langue magique," 119). In this sense, Tyson too is certainly a critic of the G.D. synthesis. With reference to the discursive strategies discussed in chapter 3, however, this is not the end of the story, since he also has a highly innovative side which is explored further here.
87. E.g., Tyson, *Enochian Magic for Beginners,* 35–47, 212, 220–25, 269, 271–74, 308, 309–51.
88. Ibid., 309–51.
89. E.g., ibid., 35–47, 225, 274–76.
90. Tyson, "The Enochian Apocalypse."
91. Tyson's other main innovation.
92. Ibid., 274. This seems to be the main criterion for Pasi and Rabaté. See note 26 above.

93. Ibid., 245ff, 283–308.
94. Tyson, "Foreword," xxiii–xxvi.
95. Tyson, *Power of the Word,* 170. Here he refers to the book as *Enochian Mandalas,* which seems to have been the working title of *Angels' Message.*

Chapter 8. Enochiana without Borders

1. The French context is briefly discussed by Pasi and Rabaté, "Langue angélique, langue magique," 121–23. Content-wise the Enochian material published in French is unremarkable, being mostly based on the G.D. material. See, e.g., Jean-Pascal Ruggiu, *La Magie Hénokéenne;* Étienne Morgant, *La magie enochienne.* The Norwegian context will be treated somewhat more in detail later, as it has had a greater influence on the recent development of Enochiana internationally as well.
2. The study of the Internet's impact on religion is rapidly developing. Some recent key studies include Douglas E. Cowan and Jeffrey K. Hadden, "Virtually Religious"; Lorne L. Dawson and D. E. Cowan, eds., *Religion Online;* Heidi Campbell, *Exploring Religious Community Online;* D. E. Cowan, *Cyberhenge;* Morten T. Højsgaard and Margrit Warburg, eds., *Religion and Cyberspace.* A good overview of the state of research is available in Doris R. Jakobsh, "Understanding Religion and Cyberspace."
3. Studies that focus more specifically on occult and related currents online include Dawson and Jenna Hennebry, "New Religions and the Internet"; Cowan and Hadden, "Virtually Religious"; and Cowan, *Cyberhenge.* For a thorough discussion on *how* and how *not* the Internet has affected modern religious groups (represented by pagan communities), see especially Cowan, *Cyberhenge,* 51–58. Cowan argues that there is nothing radically new about religion online (i.e., it does not become "virtual" per usage of "virtual reality"), but rather has given somewhat new patterns to old phenomena. For a discussion of methodological challenges related to studying online religion (and esotericism), see Petersen, "From Book to Bit."
4. Partridge, *Re-Enchantment of the West,* Vol. 1, 66.
5. Although it should be noted that researchers for a long time have pointed to a new global class divide along the lines of Internet access and information technology "haves and have-nots." See, e.g., Castells, *Internet Galaxy;* Lenhart, "The Ever-Shifting Internet Population."
6. K. G. Coffman and A. M. Odlyzko, "The Size and Growth Rate of the Internet," 13.
7. All the posts of this list are archived and accessible at http://www.hollyfeld.org/heaven/Email/Enochian-l/.
8. http://groups.yahoo.com/group/enochian/. Founded and moderated by "Frater Amoris" from Sidney. See his profile: http://profiles.yahoo.com/amoris313. Amoris also runs the group "Realmagick," a more general occult discussion forum which currently has more than 1,250 members. http://groups.yahoo.com/group/realmagick/.
9. http://hermetic.com/enochia/index.html.
10. http://hermetic.com/browe-archive/.
11. http://themagickalreview.org/.
12. http://www.enochian.org/new/enochiantools.shtml. The site has been

operative since 2006, and is run by a person writing under the name "Athena" in the Enochian Yahoo! group.

13. *Vide* the publications of Turner, Skinner, and Laycock in the bibliography.
14. E.g., DuQuette and Hyatt, *Enochian World of Aleister Crowley;* Crowley et al., *Vision and the Voice.*
15. "on line enochian resources?" Enochian-L, November 11, 1996. When citing posts from e-mail lists and online discussion forums, I will refer to the author, the subject title, name of list/forum, and date of posting. In the bibliography I give URLs to the archives of the forums and e-lists used (see the "Web sites and online sources" section), so that the reader can easily find the reference without it being necessary to litter the footnotes with URL addresses. The exact URL to online documents and essays can also be found in the bibliography.
16. Rowe, "Enochian Temples."
17. Rowe, "Enochian Magick Reference."
18. The first post in which he openly attacks the Schuelers' books on Enochian is "Re: Scheuler and context," Enochian-L, November 17, 1996.
19. Rowe, "Re: Tyson's system," Enochian-L, November 20, 1996.
20. E.g., Charla Williams, "Re: Tyson's system," Enochian-L, November 20, 1996.
21. Rowe, "Enochian Magick Reference," 52.
22. "Jerry" Schueler wrote his first post on October 12, 1997.
23. E.g., Rowe, "Schueler's \'translations'\," Enochian-L, October 9, 1997.
24. Rowe, "Re: Schueler's 'translations,'" Enochian-L, October 12, 1997. When quoting online posts I will generally leave the language and system of punctuation unedited. Since the language styles in discussion forums online tend to be rather liberal, the result is that several of the quotations will have odd punctuation and abundant spelling errors. For ease of reading I have chosen not to interfere with *sic!* in the most extreme cases, but rather let the texts stand as they are. As an exception, I have inserted italics where authors have indicated it through the use of underscores. For a discussion of styles and genres online, see Petersen, "From Book to Bit."
25. Schueler, "Re: Schueler's 'translations,'" Enochian-L, October 13, 1997.
26. Rowe, "'Enochian physics,' mostly," Enochian-L, October 14, 1997.
27. For Schueler's equation, see *Enochian Physics,* 156–57.
28. Rowe, "'Enochian physics,' mostly," Enochian-L, October 14, 1997.
29. Schueler, "Re: 'Enochian physics,' mostly," Enochian-L, October 14, 1997.
30. Schueler, "Re: Schueler's 'translations,'" Enochian-L, October 13, 1997.
31. Rowe, "'Enochian physics,' mostly," Enochian-L, October 14, 1997.
32. Ibid.
33. Ibid.
34. E.g., Hammer, *Claiming Knowledge,* 22–25, 44–45. See also my discussion in chapter 4.
35. Rowe, "Schueler's \'translations'\," Enochian-L, October 09, 1997.
36. See for instance the papers: Rowe, "The 91 Parts of the Earth"; idem, "The Lotus of the Enochian Temple: Sample Visions"; idem, "Experiments with the Second Enochian Key."
37. I.e., Rowe, "A Modified Hexagram Ritual for Enochian Workings"; idem, "A Ritual of the Heptagram." Rowe's most complete manifesto on Enochian magic is his "Godzilla meets E.T." (two parts).
38. Schueler, "Re: 'Enochian physics,' mostly," Enochian-L, October 14, 1997.
39. Ibid.

40. Frater_tommy, "enochian electrical field," Enochian Yahoo! group, August 26, 2005.
41. As is testified by for instance the fairly recent discussion on the Enochian Yahoo! group entitled "ritualistic enochian vs. spoken enochian," especially from the post by Dean Hildebrandt posted January 18, 2007, and onward.
42. Tim a.k.a. V. H., "Re: The Tablet of God," Enochian-L, November 14, 1996.
43. Rowe, "Are the Angels Real?" Enochian-L, November 15, 1996.
44. I.e., Asprem, "Thelema og ritualmagi."
45. Hanegraaff, "How Magic Survived"; Luhrmann, *Persuasions of the Witch's Craft*.
46. Rowe, "Are the Angels Real?" Enochian-L, November 15, 1996.
47. For a recent and thorough (philosophical) discussion, see Lipton, *Inference to the Best Explanation*. It should be noted that I found the same abductive line of argumentation in my study of ritual magicians in Norway. See Asprem, "Thelema og ritualmagi," 124.
48. In the following, I will normalize the spelling of his name, to read "Nigris" with a capital "N."
49. Nigris (333), "Re: Are the Angels Real?" Enochian-L, November 15, 1996.
50. Ibid.
51. Nigris (333), "Re: Are the Angels Real?" Enochian-L, November 23, 1996.
52. Nigris (333), "Re: Are the Angels Real?" Enochian-L, November 15, 1996.
53. Ibid.
54. Rowe, "Re: Are the Angels Real?" Enochian-L, November 16, 1996. The Aethyrs with geographical attributions, names, and sigils were given in Krakow, May 21–23, 1584, while the Great Table was revealed on June 25 the same year. Cf. Casaubon, *True and Faithful Relation,* 140ff, 172–81.
55. Rowe, "Re: Are the angels real?" Enochian-L, November 16, 1996.
56. Ibid.
57. Ibid.
58. E.g., Katz, ed., *Mysticism and Philosophical Analysis;* idem, ed., *Mysticism and Religious Traditions;* idem, ed., *Mysticism and Language;* Proudfoot, *Religious Experience.*
59. Rowe, "Re: Are the angels real?" Enochian-L, November 16, 1996.
60. Rowe, "Godzilla meets E.T."
61. Balt camp, and later oasis (from 1994), was founded in 1992, and was the third attempt to start an O.T.O. group in Oslo. The Balt group arose as a response to a conflict in the previous camp, Yggdrasil, which was run by Simen Berntsen. According to informed sources, the circle surrounding Karlsen's Balt group consisted of around twenty people, of which half were more or less stable and actively participating members. The group had a distinct emphasis on magical practice, including Enochian work. It was disbanded by its leader in 1997, due to what Karlsen experienced as homophobic discrimination embedded in the O.T.O. structure. This especially related to Karlsen's dissatisfaction with the Gnostic Mass, which he wanted to rewrite in order to incorporate two male priests instead of a priest and a priestess. During its period of existence, two other more or less competing O.T.O. camps were in existence in Oslo: Heimdall, and Aurora Borealis. While Balt focused extensively on ritual magic and Enochiana, Heimdall focused on the revival of Ásatrú (the group was run by Egil Stenseth, who played a pivotal role in establishing organized Ásatrú in Norway in the 1990s), while Aurora Borealis was preoccupied with Masonry. After the demise of Balt oasis, Heimdall largely took over as the main O.T.O.

body in Oslo. This continues to be the case, although with renewed leadership and somewhat weakened ties to the Ásatrú community. For references, see Karlsen, "A Recollection by Runar Karlsen"; for the O.T.O. in Norway, see O.T.O. Norway's official Web site, http://www.oto.no/; for reconstructionist Ásatrú in Norway and internal and external polemics, see Asprem, "Heathens Up North."

62. See Karlsen, "EM: The 9 Fire spirits," Enochian-L, January 4, 1998.
63. Karlsen, "Re: Intro & New Questions—Paraoan," Enochian-L, September 22, 1997.
64. Karlsen, "The Elements," Enochian-L, December 13, 1997.
65. Karlsen, "Re: Thoughts on the calls," Enochian-L, January 2, 1999.
66. Ibid.
67. To exemplify, the strophe in question reads "they are become 28 living dwellings, in whom the strength of man rejoices" (Enochian: "i noas *ni* paradial, casarmg ugear chirlan").
68. Karlsen, "EM: The nine Fire spirits," Enochian-L, January 4, 1998. One should note, however, that Karlsen, by his own statement, had already developed a great interest in Enochian, and especially the calls and its language.
69. Ibid.
70. This text, with Karlsen's translation, is found as an appendix to this book.
71. The translation he finally ended up with (by 1993) is claimed to be partially "received," but mostly his own. Looking closer at Karlsen's calls shows that some words are identical or very similar to those found, with translations, in the original calls (and later tabulated in the various Enochian dictionaries), while others do not resemble anything known.
72. See Karlsen, "About the I Ged Calls," http://home.no.net/karl24/aboutCalls.htm.
73. See the section of Karlsen's Web site where the *I Ged* is published, with all the squares and new calls: http://home.no.net/karl24/IgedIndx-rel.htm.
74. E.g., Hildebrandt, "Re: Thoughts on the calls," Enochian-L, January 2, 1999.
75. E.g., Hildebrandt, "Precession of the Equinoxes essay revisited," Enochian-L, April 23, 2001; W. P., "I GED Godname prayers," Enochian-L, May 27, 2001.
76. Zephyros93 [P. J. Rovelli], "New file uploaded to enochian," Enochian Yahoo! group, August 29, 2002. For the document, see Rovelli, "The DOzmt Index vel Dor OS zol ma thil: Commentary on the Runar Transmissions."
77. Hildebrandt, e-mail to the author, dated April 28, 2008.
78. http://home.no.net/karl24/. The Web site was taken down around 2009, but is expected to reappear at a new domain shortly: http://www.infinite-ways.net.
79. Shaffer, "Letter Essences of the Angelic Language," Enochian-L, June 4, 1998.
80. Ibid.
81. Ibid. Shaffer's theory has later been published online in a more condensed form. See http://members.aol.com/AJRoberti/enochale.htm.
82. Karlsen, "Re: Letter Essences of the Angelic Language," Enochian-L, June 5, 1998.
83. See http://home.no.net/karl24/audMindex.htm.
84. Ima Pseudonym, "Enochian and Gnosticism," Enochian Yahoo! Group, May 12, 2006.
85. I.e., Karlsen, "Re: Meta Re [enochian]: Re: Worldsoul of the Sun," Enochian Yahoo! group, June 7, 2004; Frater S.S.N.S., "A Modest Proposal," Enochian Yahoo! group, July 23, 2004.
86. Frater S.S.N.S., "A Modest Proposal," Enochian Yahoo! group, July 23, 2004.

Conclusion

1. See Hanegraaff, "Magic V," 743.
2. Regardie, *Golden Dawn,* 44.

Appendix

1. The introduction of this group of spirits is discussed in chapter 8 of the present book—E. A.
2. According to Karlsen, the awkward translation is an effect of a general lack of congruence between English and Enochian grammar. Karlsen's translations (those in the document given below included) follow a direct word-by-word approach, which tend to ignore aspects of grammar and syntax which remain unclear. The words added in brackets qualify merely as a best guess at the "correct" grammatical relation—E. A.
3. But see the discussions of Dee, Enochiana, and the construction of Rosicrucian lineage elsewhere in this book, particularly chapters 3 and 6. From the perspective of the academic historian, there is no evidence that Rosicrucianism existed before the early seventeenth century, i.e., after Dee's death—E. A.

BIBLIOGRAPHY

Primary Sources

Anupassana [Suzan Wilson]. "Introduction to the Elemental Grade Ceremonies." In *The Golden Dawn*, ed. Israel Regardie, 135–40. St. Paul: Llewellyn Publications, 1989.

Aquino, Michael. *The Book of Coming Forth by Night: Analysis and Commentary.* Appendix 3 to *The Temple of Set*, Draft 6, 2006. Available from Xeper.org: http://www.xeper.org/maquino/nm/TOSd6.pdf.

———. *The Church of Satan*. Fifth edition, 2002. Available from Xeper.org: http://www.xeper.org/maquino/nm/COS.pdf.

———. "The Sphinx and the Chimera." Appendix 1 to *The Temple of Set*, idem., Draft 6, 2006.

———. *The Temple of Set*, idem., Draft 6, 2006

———. *The Word of Set*. Appendix 4 to *The Temple of Set*, idem., Draft 6, 2006.

Ashe, Steven. *Qabalah—The Complete Golden Dawn Initiate.* Lulu Enterprises, U.K. Ltd., 2007.

Bennett, Allan. "Ritual for the Evocation unto Visible Appearance of the Great Spirit Taphthartharath." *The Equinox* 1, no. 3 (1910): 170–90.

Burke, Edmund. *The Annual Register, or a View of the History, Politics, and Literateure, For the Year 1774*. Second edition. London: J. Dosley, Pall-Mall, 1778.

Casaubon, Meric. *A True & Faithful Relation of What passed for many Yeers Between Dr. John Dee and some Spirits.* London, 1659.

Case, Paul Foster ["Perseverantia"]. Letter to Regardie, January 15, 1933. Made available by The Paul Foster Case Study Group at http://kcbventures.com/pfc., and the Fraternity of Inner Light at http://www.lvx.org/Archive/index.html.

———. Letter to Regardie, August 10, 1933. Made available by The Paul Foster Case Study Group at http://kcbventures.com/pfc/, and the Fraternity of Inner Light at http://www.lvx.org/Archive/index.html.

———. *The Tarot: A Key to the Wisdom of the Ages*. Richmond: Macoby, 1947.

Crowley, Aleister. *The Book of Lies: Which Is Also Falsely Called Breaks: The Wanderings or Falsifications of Frater Perdurabo Which Thought Is Itself Untrue.* San Francisco: Red Wheel/Weiser, 1981 (1st ed., 1913).

———. *The Confessions of Aleister Crowley*. London: Arcana Penguin Books, 1989.

———. "Editorial." *The Equinox: The Official Organ of the A∴A∴. Th e Review of Scientific Illuminism* 1, no. 1 (1909): 1–6.

———. *Gems from the Equinox: Instructions by Aleister Crowley for His Own Magickal Order.* Ed. Israel Regardie. Tempe: Falcon Press, 1986 (1974).

———. *The Law Is for All: The Authorized Popular Commentary of Liber AL vel Legis Sub Figura CCXX, The Book of the Law.* Ed. L. Marlow, W. Breeze, and L. U. Wilkinson. Tempe: New Falcon Publications, 1996.

———. "Liber II: The Message of the Master Therion." *The Equinox* 3, no. 1 (1919): 41–43.

———. "Liber XV, O.T.O. Ecclesiæ Gnosticæ Catholicæ Canon Missæ." In *Magick, Liber ABA*, idem, 584–97. San Francisco: Weiser Books, 1997.

———. "Liber LXXXIV vel Chanokh. A Brief Abstract Description of the Symbolic Representation of the Universe Derived by Doctor John Dee through the Skrying of Sir Edward Kelly." Part One. *The Equinox* 1, no. 7 (1912): 229–43.

———. "Liber LXXXIV vel Chanokh. A Brief Abstract Description of the Symbolic Representation of the Universe Derived by Doctor John Dee through the Skrying of Sir Edward Kelly." Part Two. *The Equinox* 1, no. 8 (1912): 99–128.

———. *Liber Aleph vel CXI: The Book of Wisdom or Folly.* York Beach: Red Wheel/ Weiser, 1991.

———. *Magick. Liber ABA. Book Four. Parts I–IV.* York Beach: Samuel Weiser, 1997.

———. "A Syllabus of the Official Instructions of the A∴A∴." *The Equinox* 1, no. 9 (1913): 41–56.

———, ed. *The Equinox Vol I.* Two volumes. York Beach: Red Wheel Weiser, 1999 (originally published 1909–1913).

———, ed. *The Goetia: The Lesser Key of Solomon the King. Clavicula Salomonis Regis.* Trans. Samuel Liddell Mathers. York Beach: Red Wheel/Weiser, 1995.

Crowley, Aleister, and Victor Neuburg. "Liber XXX Aereum, vel Saeculi sub Figura CCCCXVIII Being of the Angels of the 30 Aethyrs. The Vision and the Voice." Special supplement to *The Equinox* 1, no. 5 (1911).

Crowley, Aleister, Victor B. Neuburg, and Mary Desti. *The Vision and the Voice with Commentary, and Other Papers.* Ed. William Breeze. York Beach: Weiser Books, 1998.

Denning, Melita, and Osborne Phillips. "The Heptarchical Doctrine." In *The Magical Philosophy. Book I: Robe and Ring,* 135–55. St. Paul: Llewellyn, 1983 (1974).

———. *The Magical Philosophy. Book I: Robe and Ring.* St. Paul: Llewellyn, 1983 (1974).

———. *The Magical Philosophy. Book II: The Appeal of High Magick.* St. Paul: Llewellyn, 1975.

———. *The Magical Philosophy. Book III: The Sword and the Serpent.* St. Paul: Llewellyn, 1975.

———. *The Magical Philosophy. Book IV: The Triumph of Light.* St. Paul: Llewellyn, 1978.

———. *The Magical Philosophy. Book V: Mysteria Magica.* St. Paul: Llewellyn, 1981.

Driscoll, Daniel J. *Sworn Book of Honorius the Magician.* Gillette: Heptangle Books, 1977.

DuQuette, Lon Milo. *The Magick of Aleister Crowley: A Handbook of the Rituals of Thelema.* York Beach: Red Wheel/Weiser, 2003 (1st ed. 1994).

———. *My Life With the Spirits: The Adventures of a Modern Magician.* York Beach: Weiser Books, 1999.

Edwards, David. *Dare to Make Magic.* London: Rigel Press, 1971.

Gilbert, Robert A., and John Hamill, eds. *The Rosicrucian Seer: Magical Writings of Frederick Hockley.* Wellingborough: Aquarian Press, 1986.

Godwin, William. *Lives of the Necromancers: Or, an Account of the Most Eminent Persons in Successive Ages, Who Have Claimed for Themselves, or to Whom Has Been Imputed by Others, the Exercise of Magical Powers.* London: Frederick J. Mason, 1834.

Granger, James. *A Supplement, consisting of Corrections and large Additions, to A Biographical History of England.* London, 1774.

Gunther, J. Daniel. *Initiation in the Aeon of the Child: The Inward Journey.* Lake Worth, FL: Ibis Press, 2009.

Hay, George, ed. *The Necronomicon: The Book of Dead Names.* Introduced by Colin Wilson. St. Helier, Jersey Channel Islands: Neville Spearman, 1978.

Hedegård, Gösta, ed. *Liber Iuratus Honorii: A Critical Edition of the Latin Version of the Sworn Book of Honorius.* Stockholm: Almqvist og Wicksell International, 2002.

Hildebrandt, Dean. "Essay on Enochian." First posted at the enochian e-maillist, January 7, 2001. http://home.no.net/karl24/DeanOnEnochiana.htm. (Accessed April 23, 2008).

Hyatt, Christopher S., and Lon Milo DuQuette. *The Enochian World of Aleister Crowley: Enochian Sex Magic.* Tempe, AZ: New Falcon Publications, 1991.

James, Geoffrey. *Enochian Evocation of Dr. John Dee.* Gillette: Heptangle Books, 1984.

———. *The Enochian Magick of Dr. John Dee: The Most Powerful System of Magick in Its Original Unexpurgated Form.* St. Paul: Llewellyn, 1998.

Josten, C. H., ed. Elias Ashmole (1617–1692). *His Autobiographical and Historical Notes, his Correspondence, and Other Contemporary Sources Relating to his Life and Work.* Volumes I, III and IV. Oxford: Clarendon Press, 1966.

Karlsen, Runar. "About the I Ged Calls." 2001. http://home.no.net/karl24/aboutCalls.htm (Accessed April 23, 2008).

———. *Dor OZ zol ma thil.* 1991 (later commentaries not dated). http://home.no.net/karl24/boeindex.htm. (Accessed April 23, 2008).

———. *The I Ged Index.* 1992 (later commentaries not dated). http://home.no.net/karl24/IgedIndx-rel.htm. (Accessed April 23, 2008).

———. "A Recollection by Runar Karlsen." In *The O.T.O. Phenomenon*, ed. Peter Koenig. Online at: http://user.cyberlink.ch/~koenig/sunrise/runar.htm. (Accessed April 23, 2008).

Küntz, Darcy, ed. *The Complete Golden Dawn Cipher Manuscript.* London: Holmes, 1995.

———, ed. *The Enochian Experiments of the Golden Dawn: The Enochian Alphabet Clairvoyantly Examined.* Sequim: Holmes Publishing Group LLC, 1996.

Kupperman, J. S. ,trans. and ed. *The Cipher Manuscript.* http://www.hermetic.com/gdlibrary/cipher/. (Last accessed September 24, 2007). Undated.

Langford Garstein, E.J., ed. *The Rosie Crucian Secrets: Their Excellent Method of Making Medicines from Metals, Also Their Lawes and Mysteries.* Wellingborough: Atlantis, 1985.

LaVey, Anton Szandor. *The Compleat Witch.* New York: Lancer Books, 1970.

———. "Enochian Pronunciation Guide." In *The Cloven Hoof*, May issue (1970). Online reprint by Church of Satan: http://www.churchofsatan.com/Pages/EnochianGuide.html.

———. "On Occultism of the Past." *The Cloven Hoof*, September (1971). http://www.churchofsatan.com/Pages/LaVeyPastOccultism.html.

———. "Phase IV message." Appendix no. 116 in Aquino, *The Church of Satan.* Fifth ed., 2002.

———. *The Satanic Bible.* New York: Avon Books, 1969.

———. *The Satanic Rituals.* New York: Avon Books, 1972.

———. "Satanism." Appendix no. 1 in Aquino, *The Church of Satan*, 436–45. Fifth ed., 2002.

———. "Suggested Enochian Keys for Various Rituals and Ceremonies." In *The Cloven Hoof*, June issue (1970). http://www.churchofsatan.com/Pages/EnochianGuide.html.

Laycock, Donald. *The Complete Enochian Dictionary: A Dictionary of the Angelic Language as Revealed to Dr. John Dee and Edward Kelley.* London: Askin, 1978.

———. "Enochian: Angelic Language or Mortal Folly?" In *The Complete Enochian Dictionary*, ed. Donald Laycock and Stephen Skinner, 19–64. Boston: Weiser Books, 1994.

———, and Stephen Skinner, eds. *The Complete Enochian Dictionary: A Dictionary of the Angelic Language as Revealed to Dr. John Dee and Edward Kelley.* York Beach: Weiser Books, 1994.

Lévi, Eliphas. *Transcendental Magic: Its Doctrine and Ritual.* Trans. A. E. Waite. York Beach: Weiser Books, 2001.

Lovecraft, H. P. "A History of the *Necronomicon*." In *Necronomicon Files: The Truth Behind Lovecraft's Legend*, ed. Daniel Harms and John Wisdom Gonce III, 303–305. York Beach: Red Wheel/Weiser, 2003 (1998).

Machen, Arthur. *Things Near and Far*. London: Martin Secker, 1923.

Mathers, S. L. MacGregor et al. *Astral Projection, Ritual Magic, and Alchemy*. Ed. Francis King. London: Neville Spearman, 1971.

Mathers, S. L. MacGregor, ed. *The Book of the Sacred Magic of Abramelin the Mage.* Mineola, NY: Dover, 1975 (Facsimile of 1900 second ed.).

McLean, Adam, ed. *A Treatise on Angel Magic*. York Beach: Weiser Books, 2006 (1989).

Morgant, Étienne. *La magie enochienne*. Paris: Guy Trédaniel Éditeur, 1995.

Orpheus, Rodney. *Abrahadabra: Understanding Aleister Crowley's Thelemic Magick.* Stockholm: Looking Glass Press, 1995.

Peterson, Joseph, ed. *John Dee's Five Books of Mystery. Original Sourcebook of Enochian Magic*. York Beach: Red Wheel/Weiser, 2003 (First edition by Magnum Opus Hermetic Sourcework series, 1985).

Rankine, David, and Stephen Skinner, eds. *The Practical Angel Magic of Dr. John Dee's Enochian Tables.* Singapore: Golden Hoard, 2004.

Regardie, Israel. *The Garden of Pomegranates: Skrying on the Tree of Life*. St. Paul: Llewellyn, 1995 (First ed. 1932).

———, ed. *Gems from the Equinox: Instructions by Aleister Crowley for His Own Magical Order.* St. Paul: Llewellyn, 1974.

———, ed. *The Golden Dawn. The Original Account of the Teachings, Rites and Ceremonies of the Hermetic Order of the Golden Dawn.* St. Paul: Llewellyn, 1989 (First ed. 1937–1940).

———. "Introduction." In: *The Golden Dawn*, ed. Israel Regardie, 1–48. St. Paul: Llewellyn, 1989.

Rovelli, Paul Joseph [a.k.a. Zephyros93]. "The Dozmt Index vel Dor OS zol ma thil: Commentary on the Runar Transmissions." Available from Enochian Yahoo! group, at: http://f1.grp.yahoofs.com/v1/EJIVSL9b4EP_wa0RaVzGxHDzU2VKr3hTPeCGi6-CD9B0v83-Xw_buSWOGu0C7Sj7RkpzD9NZ6PKylKwCl0B1yjKu050/Essays%20%26%20Writings%20from%20Members/Runar%27s%20Transmission%20Commented.doc. (Accessed April 28, 2008).

Rowe, Benjamin. "The 91 Parts of the Earth." http://www.hermetic.com/browe/91intro.html. Independently published, 1994. (Accessed April 23, 2008).

———. "Enochian Magick Reference." Independently published, 1997. http://hermetic.com/browe-archive/enochian.htm. (Accessed April 23, 2008).

———. "Enochian Temples: Chapbook." http://hermetic.com/browe/etemple.html. Independently published, 1992. (Accessed April 23, 2008).

———. "Experiments with the Second Enochian Key." http://hermetic.com/browe/keytwo.html. Independently published, 1987, 1992. (Accessed April 23, 2008).

———. "Godzilla meets E.T." http://www.hermetic.com/browe/godzill1.html (part one); http://www.hermetic.com/browe/godzill2.html (part two). Independently published, 1994. (Accessed April 23, 2008).

———. "The Lotus of the Enochian Temple: Sample Visions." http://hermetic.com/browe/lot-vis.html. Independently published, 1993. (Accessed April 23, 2008).

———. "A Modified Hexagram Ritual for Enochian Workings." http://www.hermetic.com/browe/hexrit.html. Independently published, 1988, 1992. (Accessed 23.04.2008).

———. "A Ritual of the Heptagram." http://www.hermetic.com/browe/heptagrm.html. Independently published, 1990, 1992. (Accessed April 23, 2008).

Ruggiu, Jean-Pascal. *La Magie Hénokéenne de l'Ordre Hermétique de la Golden Dawn: Le Livre de la Convergence des Forces.* Paris: Éditions Télètes, 1994.

Schueler, Gerald. *Enochian Physics: The Structure of the Magical Universe.* St. Paul: Llewellyn, 1988.

Schueler, Gerald, and Betty. *Advanced Guide to Enochian Magick: A Complete Manual of Enochian Magick.* St. Paul: Llewellyn, 1995.

———. *Angels' Message To Humanity: Ascension to Divine Union. Powerful Enochian Magick.* St. Paul: Llewellyn, 1996. (2002 edition with a foreword by Donald Tyson).

———. *Enochian Magick: A Practical Manual: The Enochian Language Revealed.* St. Paul: Llewellyn, 1996 (first edition 1985).

———. *The Enochian Tarot.* St. Paul: Llewellyn, 1989.

———. *Enochian Tarot: A New System of Divination for a New Age.* St. Paul: Llewellyn, 2002.

———. *Enochian Yoga: Uniting Humanity and Divinity.* St. Paul: Llewellyn, 1995.

Shaffer, Patricia. "Angelic Letter Essences." Not dated. http://members.aol.com/AJRoberti/enochale.htm. (Accessed April 23, 2008).

Skinner, Stephen. "Preface to the Revised Edition." In *The Complete Enochian Dictionary,* ed. Donald Laycock and Stephen Skinner, unpaged. Boston: Weiser Books, 1994.

———, ed. *The Fourth Book of Occult Philosophy.* Berwick, ME: Ibis Press, 2005 (First ed., 1978).

———, ed. *John Dee's Action with Spirits.* London: Askin, 1974.

———, and David Rankine. *The Goetia of Dr. Rudd: The Angels & Demons of Liber Malorum Spirituum Seu Goetia Lemegeton Clavicula Salomanis with a Study of the Techniques of Evocation.* Singapore: Golden Hoard Press, 2007.

———. *The Practical Angel Magic of Dr. John Dee's Enochian Tables.* Singapore: Golden Hoard, 2004.

Torrens, R.G. *The Secret Rituals of the Golden Dawn.* Wellingborough: Aquarian Press, 1973.

Turner, Robert. *Elizabethan Magic: The Art and the Magus.* Shaftesbury: Element, 1989.

———. *The Heptarchia Mystica of John Dee.* Wellingborough, Northamptonshire: Aquarian Press, 1986.

———, ed. *The Heptarchia Mystica of John Dee.* Edinburgh: Magnum Opus Hermetic Sourceworks 17, 1983.

Tyson, Donald. "The Enochian Apocalypse." *Gnosis: A Journal of the Western Inner Traditions* 40 (1996).

———. *Enochian Magic for Beginners: The Original System of Angel Magic.* St. Paul: Llewellyn, 1997.

———. "Foreword." In Betty and Gerald Schueler, *Angels' Message to Humanity,* ix–xxvi. St. Paul: Llewellyn, 1996.

———. *Power of the Word: The Secret Code of Creation.* St. Paul: Llewellyn, 2004. [Second edition of *Tetragrammaton*].

———. *Tetragrammaton: The Secret of Evoking Angelic Powers and the Key to the Apocalypse.* St. Paul: Llewellyn, 1995.

Vinci, Leo. *Gmicalzoma! An Enochian Dictionary.* London, New York: Regency Press, 1976.

Waite, A. E.. *Shadows of Life and Thought: A Retrospective Review in the Form of Memoirs.* London: Selwyn and Blount, 1938.

Weekly News. "Secrets of the Rosicrucians." March 22, 1910. Reproduced online by lashtal.com: http://www.lashtal.com/nuke/module-subjects-viewpage-pageid-2.phtml.

Westcott, William Wynn. *Book "H": Clavicula Tabularum Enochi.* Online edition by Frater Alastor, not dated, at: http://www.angelfire.com/ab6/imuhtuk/gdmans/rith.htm.

———. "Further Rules for Practice." In *The Golden Dawn*, ed. Israel Regardie, 669–70.

Whitby, Christopher, ed. *John Dee's Actions with Spirits.* Two volumes. New York: Garland, 1988.

W.I.T., Frater (Scott Brush). *Enochian Initiation: A Thelemite's Journey into the Ultimate Transcendence.* Parker: Outskirts Press, 2006.

Zalewski, Chris. *Enochian Chess of the Golden Dawn: A Four-Handed Chess Game.* St. Paul: Llewellyn, 1994.

Manuscript Sources

British Library, London:

Cotton Appendix XLVI. (Dee's diary from May 28, 1583, to May 23, 1587, plus March 20 to September 7, 1607. Later reproduced by Casaubon as *T&FR*.)

Harley 6482. ("Dr. Rudd's" *Treatise*.)

Harley MS 6483. ("Dr. Rudd's" Goetia.)

Sloane MS 307. ("Invocation of Angels", with copy of Dee's Great Table.)

Sloane MS 3188. (Dee's diary for December 22, 1581-May 23, 1583.)

Sloane MS 3189. (Dee's *Liber Loagaeth*.)

Sloane MS 3191. (Dee's *48 Claves Angelica; Liber scientiae, auxilii, et victoriae Terrestris; De heptarchia mystica; Tabula bonorum angelorum*.)

Sloane MSS 3624–3628. (Diaries of magical operations between the years 1671–1688.)

Sloane MS 3821. ("Tractatus Magici et Astrologici"; copy of Great Table, as in Sloane 307.)

Web sites and online archival sources

Donald Tyson's Supernatural World. http://www.donaldtyson.com/. (Accessed April 27, 2008).

Enochian-L Archives. 1996–2001. http://www.hollyfeld.org/heaven/Email/Enochian-l/ (Accessed April 27, 2008).

Enochian Yahoo! group. 2002-present. http://groups.yahoo.com/group/enochian/. (Accessed April 27, 2008).

Enochian Linguistics. http://members.aol.com/AJRoberti/enochlng.htm. (Accessed April 27, 2008).

Enochian Tools and Supplies. http://www.enochian.org. (Accessed April 27, 2008).

The Equinox Vol. I Online. http://www.the-equinox.org/vol1/index.html (Accessed April 27, 2008).

The Hermetic Library. http://hermetic.com/. (Accessed April 27, 2008).

Ored Dhagia: The Infinite Ways. Ed. Runar Karlsen and Dean Hildebrandt. http://home.no.net/karl24/. (Accessed April 27, 2008). New Web site to appear at http://www.infinite-ways.net/.

Realmagick Yahoo! group. http://groups.yahoo.com/group/realmagick/. (Accessed April 27, 2008).

Schueler's Online. Edited by Gerald and Betty Schueler. http://www.schuelers.com/. (Accessed April 27, 2008).

References and Secondary Literature

Appleby, John H. "Woodall, John (1570–1643)." In *Oxford Dictionary of National Biography*. Oxford: Oxford University Press, 2004. Online: http://www.oxforddnb.com/view/article/29902.

Ashworth, William B. "Natural History and the Emblematic Worldview." In *Reappraisals of the Scientific Revolution*, ed. Robert S. Westman and David C. Lindberg, 303–32. Cambridge: Cambridge University Press, 1990.

Asprem, Egil. "'Enochian' Language: A Proof of the Existence of Angels?" *Skepsis*, December 13, 2006. Online: http://www.skepsis.no/marginalia/enochian_language_a_proof_of_t.html.

———. "False, Lying Spirits and Angels of Light: Ambiguous Mediation in Dr Rudd's 17th Century *Treatise on Angel Magic*." *Magic, Ritual, and Witchcraft* 3, no. 1 (2008): 54–80.

———. "The Golden Dawn and the O.T.O." In *Cambridge Handbook of Mysticism and Western Esotericism*, ed. Glenn Magee. New York: Cambridge University Press, forthcoming 2012.

———. "Heathens Up North: Politics, Polemics, and Contemporary Norse Paganism in Norway." *The Pomegranate* 10, no.1 (2008): 42–69.

———. "Kabbalah Recreata: Reception and Adaptation of Kabbalah in Modern Occultism." *The Pomegranate: The International Journal of Paganism Studies* 9, no. 2 (2007): 132–53.

———. "Magic Naturalized? Negotiating science and occult experience in Aleister Crowley's Scientific Illuminism." *Aries* 8, no. 2 (2008): 139–65.

———. "Thelema og ritualmagi: med magi som livsholdning i moderne vestlig esoterisme." *Chaos* 46 (2006): 113–37.

———, and Kennet Granholm, eds. *Contemporary Esotericism*. London: Equinox, forthcoming 2012.

Baddeley, Gavin. *Lucifer Rising: Sin, Devil Worship and Rock 'n' Roll*. London: Plexus, 2003.

Bäcklund, Jan. "In the Footsteps of Edward Kelley." In *John Dee: Interdisciplinary Studies*, ed. Stephen Clucas, 295–330. Dordrecht: Springer, 2006.

Bassnett, Susan. "Absent Presences: Edward Kelley's Family in the Writings of John Dee." In *John Dee: Interdisciplinary Studies*, ed. Stephen Clucas, 285–94. Dordrecht: Springer, 2006.

Berger, Peter, ed. *The Desecularization of the World: Resurgent Religion and World Politics*. Grand Rapids: Eerdmans, 1999.
Bruce, Steve. *God is Dead: Secularization in the West*. Malden / Oxford / Carlton: Blackwell Publishing, 2002.
———. "The New Age and Secularisation." In *Beyond New Age. Exploring Alternative Spirituality*, ed. Steven Sutcliffe and Marion Bowman, 220–36. Edinburgh: Edinburgh University Press, 2000.
Campbell, Colin. "The Cult, the Cultic Milieu, and Secularization." *A Sociological Yearbook of Religion in Britain* 5 (1972): 119–36.
———. "The secret religion of the educated classes." *Sociological Analysis* 39, no. 2 (1978): 146–56.
Campbell, Heidi. *Exploring Religious Community Online: We Are One in the Network*. New York: Peter Lang, 2005.
Castells, Manuel. *The Internet Galaxy: Reflections on the Internet, Business, and Society.* New York: Oxford University Press, 2001.
Clark, Stuart. *Thinking with Demons: The Idea of Witchcraft in Early Modern Europe.* Oxford: Oxford University Press, 1997.
Clulee, Nicholas. "At the Crossroads of Magic and Science: John Dee's Archmastrie." In *Occult and Scientific Mentalities in the Renaissance*, ed. Brian Vickers, 57–71. New York: Cambridge University Press, 1984.
———. "Dee's Natural Philosophy Revisited." In *John Dee: Interdisciplinary Studies in English Renaissance Thought*, ed. Stephen Clucas, 23–37. Dordrecht: Springer, 2006.
———. *John Dee's Natural Philosophy: Between Science and Religion*. London: Routledge, 1988.
Clucas, Stephen. "John Dee's Angelic Conversations and the Ars Notoria." In *John Dee: Interdisciplinary Studies*, ed. Stephen Clucas, 231–73. Dordrecht: Springer, 2006.
———. "'Non est legendum sed inspiciendum solum': Inspectival Knowledge and the Visual Logic of John Dee's Liber Mysteriorum." In *Emblems and Alchemy*, ed. Alison Adams and Stanton J. Linden, 109–132. Glasgow Emblem Studies, 1998.
———, ed. *John Dee: Interdisciplinary Studies in English Renaissance Thought.* Dordrecht: Springer, 2006.
Cohn, Norman. *Europe's Inner Demons: The Demonization of Christians in Medieval Christendom,* rev. ed. Chicago: University of Chicago Press, 1993.
Coffman, K. G., and A. M. Odlyzko. "The size and growth rate of the Internet." *AT&T Labs Research*. Online: http://www.dtc.umn.edu/~odlyzko/doc/internet.size.pdf, 1998.
Copenhaver, Brian P. "Natural Magic, Hermeticism, and Occultism in Early Modern Science." In *Reappraisals of the Scientific Revolution,* ed. David C. Lindberg and Robert S. Westman, 261–302. Cambridge: Cambridge University Press, 1990.
Cowan, Douglas E. *Cyberhenge: Modern Pagans on the Internet*. London: Routledge, 2005.
———, and Jeffrey K. Hadden. "Virtually Religious: New Religious Movements and the World Wide Web." In *The Oxford Handbook of New Religious Movements,* ed. James R. Lewis, 119–36. Oxford: Oxford University Press, 2004.
Crow, John L. *The White Knight in the Yellow Robe: Allan Bennett's Search for Truth*. Research MA thesis, History of Hermetic Philosophy and Related Currents, University of Amsterdam, privately published by author, 2009.
Davies, Owen. "Angels in Elite and Popular Magic, 1650–1790." In *Angels in the*

Early Modern World, ed. Peter Marshall and Alexandra Walsham. Cambridge: Cambridge University Press, 2006.

Dawson, Lorne L., and Jenna Hennebry. "New Religions and the Internet: Recruiting in a New Public Space." In *Cults and New Religious Movements: A Reader*, ed. Lorne L. Dawson, 271–91. Malden: Blackwell, 2003.

Dawson, Lorne L., and D. E. Cowan, eds. *Religion Online: Finding Faith on the Internet*. New York: Routledge, 2004.

Delatte, Armand. *La Catoptromancie Grecque et ses derives*. Paris: Droz, 1932.

Dummet, Michael, and Sylvia Mann. *The Game of Tarot: From Ferrara to Salt Lake City*. London: Gerald Duckworth, 1980.

Dyrendal, Asbjørn. "Satan and the Beast. The Influence of Aleister Crowley on Modern Satanism." In *Aleister Crowley and Western Esotericism*, ed. Henrik Bogdan and Martin P. Starr. Forthcoming.

Eco, Umberto. *The Search for the Perfect Language*. Trans. James Fentress. Oxford: Oxford University Press, 1995.

Elert, Claes-Christian. "Andreas Kempe (1622–1689) and the Language Spoken in Paradise." *Historiographica Linguistica* 5 (1975).

Evans, Dave. *The History of British Magic after Crowley: Kenneth Grant, Amado Crowley, Chaos Magic, Satanism, Lovecraft, The Left Hand Path, Blasphemy and Magical Morality*. N.p.: Hidden Publishing, 2007.

Faivre, Antoine. *Access to Western Esotericism*. Albany: State University of New York Press, 1994.

———, and Wouter J. Hanegraaff, eds. *Western Esotericism and the Science of Religion: Selected Papers presented at the 17th Congress of the International Association for the History of Religions, Mexico City 1995*. Leuven: Gnostica (2), 1998.

Fanger, Claire. "Virgin Territory: Purity and Divine Knowledge in Late Medieval Catoptromantic Texts." *Aries* 5, no. 2 (2005): 200–24.

Flowers, Stephen E. *Fire and Ice: The History, Structure, and Rituals of Germany's Most Influential Modern Magical Order: The Brotherhood of Saturn*. St. Paul: Llewellyn, 1994.

Forshaw, Peter. "The Early Alchemical Reception of John Dee's Monas Hieroglyphica." *Ambix* 52, no. 3 (2005): 247–69.

Foucault, Michel. *The Order of Things: An Archaeology of the Human Sciences*. London: Routledge, 1989 (1966).

French, Peter. *John Dee: The World of an Elizabethan Magus*. Dorset Press, 1971.

Gilbert, Robert A. *The Golden Dawn: Twilight of the Magicians*. Wellingborough: Aquarian Press, 1983.

———. *The Golden Dawn companion. A guide to the history, structure, and workings of the Hermetic Order of the Golden Dawn*. York Beach: Weiser Books, 1986.

———. "Hermetic Order of the Golden Dawn." In *Dictionary of Gnosis and Western Esotericism*, ed. Hanegraaff, in collaboration with Antoine Faivre, Roelof van den Broek, and Jean-Pierre Brach, 544–50. Leiden: Koninkleijke Brill, 2005.

———. "Provenance Unknown: A Tentative Solution to the Riddle of the Cipher Manuscript of the Golden Dawn." In *Wege und Abwege: Beiträge zur europäischen Geistesgeschichte der Neuzeit*, ed. Albrecht Götz von Olenhausen, 79–89. Freiburg: Hochschul Verlag, 1990.

———. "Secret Writing: The Magical Manuscripts of Frederick Hockley." In *Rosicrucian Seer: Magical Writings of Frederick Hockley*, ed. R. A. Gilbert and J. Hamill, 26–33. Wellingborough: Aquarian Press, 1986.

———. "Supplement to 'Provenance Unknown': The Origins of the Golden

Dawn." In *The Complete Golden Dawn Cipher Manuscript*, ed. Darcy Küntz, 11–13. Edmonds, WA: Holmes, 1996.

Godwin, Joscelyn. *The Theosophical Enlightenment*. Albany: State University of New York Press, 1994.

———, Christian Chanel, and John Patrick Deveney, eds. *The Hermetic Brotherhood of Luxor: Initiatic and Historical Documents of an Order of Practical Occultism*. York Beach: Samuel Weiser, 1995.

Gonce, John Wisdom. "A Plague of *Necronomicons*." In *Necronomicon Files: The Truth Behind Lovecraft's Legend*, ed. Daniel Harms and John Wisdom Gonce III. York Beach: Red Wheel/Weiser, 2003 [1998].

Granholm, Kennet. "Embracing Others than Satan: The Multiple Princes of Darkness in the Left-Hand Path Milieu." In *Contemporary Religious Satanism. A Critical Anthology*, ed. Jesper Aagaard Petersen, 85–101. Farnham: Ashgate, 2009.

Greer, Mary. *Women of the Golden Dawn: Rebels and Priestesses*. Rochester, VT: Park Street Press, 1995.

Håkansson, Håkan. *Seeing the Word: John Dee and Renaissance Occultism*. Lund: Lunds Universitets Forlag, 2001.

Hakl, Hans Thomas. "The Theory and Practice of Sexual Magic, Exemplified by Four Magical Groups in the Early Twentieth Century." In *Hidden Intercourse: Eros and Sexuality in the History of Western Esotericism*, ed. Wouter J. Hanegraaff and Jeffrey J. Kripal, 446–78. Leiden: Brill, 2008.

Hammer, Olav. *Claiming Knowledge: Strategies of Epistemology from Theosophy to the New Age*. Leiden: Brill, 2001.

———, and Kocku von Stuckrad, eds. *Polemical Encounters: Esoteric Discourse and its Others*. Leiden and Boston: Brill, 2007.

Hanegraaff, Wouter J. *Esotericism and the Academy: Rejected Knowledge in Western Culture*. Cambridge: Cambridge University Press, forthcoming 2012.

———. "Fiction in the Desert of the Real: Lovecraft's Cthulhu Mythos." *Aries* 7, no. 1 (2007): 85–109.

———. "Forbidden Knowledge: Anti-Esoteric Polemics and Academic Research." *Aries* 5, no. 2 (2005): 225–54.

———. "How Magic Survived the Disenchantment of the World." *Religion* 33 (2003): 357–88.

———. "Magic V: 18th-20th Century." In *Dictionary of Gnosis and Western Esotericism*, ed. Hanegraaff, in collaboration with Antoine Faivre, Roelof van den Broek, and Jean-Pierre Brach, 738–44. Leiden: Koninkleijke Brill, 2006.

———. "The New Age Movement and the Esoteric Tradition." In *Gnosticism and Hermeticism from Antiquity to Modern Times*, ed. Roelof van Den Broek and Wouter J. Hanegraaff, 359–82. Albany: State University of New York Press, 1998.

———. *New Age Religion and Western Culture: Esotericism in the Mirror of Secular Thought*. Albany: State University of New York Press, 1998.

———. "Western Esotericism in Enlightenment Historiography: The Case of Jakob Brucker." In *Constructing Tradition: Means and Myths of Transmission in Western Esotericism*, ed. Andreas Kilcher. Leiden: Brill, 2009.

Harkness, Deborah. *John Dee's Conversations with Angels: Cabala, Alchemy, and the End of Nature*. Cambridge: Cambridge University Press, 1999.

———. "Shews in the Shewstone: John Dee's Angelic Conversations." *Renaissance Quarterly* 49 (1996): 707–37.

Harms, Daniel. "The *Necronomicon* Made Flesh." In *Necronomicon Files: The Truth Behind Lovecraft's Legend*, ed. Daniel Harms and J.W. Gonce. York Beach: Red Wheel/Weiser, 2003 [1998].

———, and John Wisdom Gonce III. *Necronomicon Files: The Truth Behind Lovecraft's Legend*. York Beach: Red Wheel/Weiser, 2003 [1998].

Heelas, Paul. *The New Age Movement: The Celebration of the Self and the Sacralization of Modernity.* Oxford: Blackwell Publishing, 1996.

Howe, Ellic. *Fringe Freemasonry*. Sequim: Holmes, 2006.

———. *The Magicians of the Golden Dawn: A Documentary History of a Magical Order 1887–1923*. York Beach: Samuel Weiser, 1978.

Hunter, Michael, ed. *Elias Ashmole 1617–1692: The Founder of the Ashmolean Museum and His World.* Oxford: Ashmolean Museum, 1983.

Huss, Boaz. "'Authorized Guardians': Polemics of Academic Scholars of Jewish Mysticism against Kabbalah Practicioners." In *Polemical Encounters: Esoteric Discourse and Its Others,* ed. Kocku von Stuckrad and Olav Hammer, 81–105. Leiden: Brill, 2007.

Højsgaard, Morten T., and Margrit Warburg, eds. *Religion and Cyberspace*. London: Routledge, 2005.

Idel, Moshe. "Prisca Theologia in Marsilio Ficino and in Some Jewish Treatments." In *Marsilio Ficino: His Theology, His Philosophy, His Legacy,* ed. Michael J. B. Allen and Valery Rees, with Martin Davies, 137–58. Leiden: Brill, 2002.

Introvigne, Massimo. *Auf den Spuren des Satanismus*. Vienna: Mödling, 1991.

———. *Il Cappello del Mago: I nuovi movimenti magici, dallo spiritismo al satanismo.* Milan: SugarCo, 1990.

———. *Enquête sur le satanisme: satanistes et antisatanistes du XVIIe siecle à nos jours.* Trans. Philippe Baillet. Paris: Dervy, 1997.

Jakobsh, Doris R. "Understanding Religion and Cyberspace: What Have We Learned, What Lies Ahead?" *Religious Studies Review* 32, no. 4 (2006): 237–42.

Josten, C. H. "A Translation of John Dee's 'Monas Hieroglyphica' (Antwerp, 1564), With an Introduction and Annotations." *Ambix* 12 (1964): 112–221.

Kaczynski, Richard. *Perdurabo, The Life of Aleister Crowley.* Tempe: New Falcon Publications, 2002.

Kassel, Lauren. *Medicine and Magic in Elizabethan London: Simon Foreman.* Oxford: Clarendon Press, 2005.

Katz, Steven T., ed. *Mysticism and Language*. New York: Oxford University Press, 1992.

———, ed. *Mysticism and Philosophical Analysis*. London: Sheldon Press, 1978.

———, ed. *Mysticism and Religious Traditions*. Oxford: Oxford University Press, 1983.

Kieckhefer, Richard. *Magic in the Middle Ages*. Cambridge: Cambridge University Press, 1990.

King, Francis."Introduction." In S. L. MacGregor Mathers et al., *Astral Projection, Ritual Magic, and Alchemy,* ed. King, 7–29. London: Neville Spearman, 1971.

———. *Modern Ritual Magic: The Rise of Western Occultism.* Garden City Park, NY: Avery Publishing Group, 1989.

———. *Ritual Magic in England: 1887 to the Present Day.* Jersey: Spearman, 1970.

Klaassen, Frank. "Medieval Ritual Magic in the Renaissance." *Aries* 3, no. 2 (2003): 166–200.

Kuntz, Marion Leathers. *Guillaume Postel, Prophet of the Restitution of All things: His Life and Thought.* The Hague: Martinus Nijhoff Publishers, 1981.

La Fontaine, Jean. "Satanism and Satanic Mythology." In *Witchcraft and Magic in Europe, (Vol 6): The Twentieth Century,* ed. Bengt Ankerloo and Stuart Clark, 81–140. London: Athlone Press, 1999.

Lang, Benedek. "Angels around the Crystal: The Prayer Book of King Wladislas and the Treasure Hunts of Henry the Czech." *Aries* 5, no. 1 (2005): 200–24.

Lenhart, Amanda. "The Ever-Shifting Internet Population: A New Look at Internet

Access and the Digital Divide." *Pew Internet and American Life Project*. Online at http://www.pewinternet.org/pdfs/PIP_Shifting_Net_Pop_Report.pdf. (Accessed April 21, 2008). Published April 16, 2003.

Lewis, James R. "Diabolical Authority. Anton LaVey, *The Satanic Bible*, and 'Tradition.'" *Marburg Journal of Religion* 7, no. 1 (2002).

———. "New Religion Adherents: An Overview of Anglophone Census and Survey Data." *Marburg Journal of Religion*, 9, no. 1 (2004). Online: http://web.uni-marburg.de/religionswissenschaft/journal/mjr/art_lewis_2004.html (accessed January 15, 2008)].

———. *Satanism Today: An Encyclopedia of Religion, Folklore, and Popular Culture.* Santa Barbara: Abc-Clio Ltd., 2001.

———, and Jesper Aagaard Petersen, eds. *The Encyclopedic Sourcebook of Satanism*. Buffalo: Prometheus Books, 2008.

Lipton, Peter. *Inference to the Best Explanation. Second Edition.* London: Routledge, 2004 [First ed. 1991].

Luhrmann, Tanya. *Persuasions of the Witch's Craft*. Cambridge, MA: Harvard University Press, 1989.

Lyons, Arthur. *The Second Coming: Satanism in America*. New York: Mysterious Press, 1970.

Lyotard, Jean-François. *The Postmodern Condition: A Report on Knowledge*. Manchester: Manchester University Press, 1979.

McIntosh, Christopher. *Eliphas Lévi and the French Occult Revival*. New York: Samuel Weiser, 1974.

McLean, Adam. "Dr. Rudd's Treatise—Some New Insights into the Enochian System." *The Hermetic Journal* 16 (1982).

———. "Introduction." In "Dr. Rudd," *A Treatise of Angel Magic,* ed. McLean, 9–20. York Beach: Weiser Books, 2006 [1989].

Murphy, Tim. "Discourse." In *Guide to the Study of Religion,* ed. Willi Braun and Russell T. McCutcheon, 396–408. London and New York: Cassell, 2000.

Noakes, Richard. "Spiritualism, Science, and the Supernatural in mid-Victorian Britain." In *The Victorian Supernatural*, ed. Nicola Brown et al., 23–43. Cambridge: Cambridge University Press, 2004.

Owen, Alex. *The Place of Enchantment: British Occultism and the Culture of the Modern.* Chicago, London: University of Chicago Press, 2004.

———. "The Sorcerer and His Apprentice: Aleister Crowley and the Magical Exploration of Edwardian Subjectivity." *Journal of British Studies* 36 (1997): 99–133.

Partridge, Christopher. "Occulture is Ordinary." In *Contemporary Esotericism*, ed. Egil Asprem and Kennet Granholm. London: Equinox, forthcoming 2012.

———. *The Re-Enchantment of the West: Alternative Spiritualities, Sacralization, Popular Culture and Occulture.* 2 vols. London: T and T Clark International, 2004/2005.

Pasi, Marco. *Aleister Crowley und die Versuchung der Politik*. Graz: Ares Verlag, 2006.

———. "Dieu du désir, Dieu de la raison (Le Diable en Californie dans le années soixante)." In: *Le Diable*, 87–98. Paris: Dervy, 1998.

———. "The Neverendingly Told Story: Recent Biographies of Aleister Crowley." *Aries* 2, no. 3 (2003): 224–45.

———. *La notion de magie dans le courant occultiste en Angleterre (1875–1947)*. Unpublished PhD dissertation. Paris: Ecole Pratique des Hautes Etudes, 2004.

———. "Lo Yoga in Aleister Crowley." In *The Ordo Templi Orientis Phenomenon*, ed. Peter Koenig. 2000. Online at: http://user.cyberlink.ch/~koenig/sunrise/pasi/pasi.htm.

———, and Philippe Rabaté. "Langue angélique, langue magique, l'énochien." *Politica Hermetica* 13 (1999): 94–123.

Petersen, Jesper Aagaard. "From Book to Bit: Enacting Satanism Online." In *Contemporary Esotericism,* ed. Egil Asprem and Kennet Granholm. London: Equinox, forthcoming 2012.

———. "Modern Satanism: Dark Doctrines and Black Flames." In *Controversial New Religions,* ed. James R. Lewis and Jesper Aagaard Petersen. Oxford: Oxford University Press, 2005.

———, ed. *Contemporary Religious Satanism: A Critical Anthology*. Farnham and Burlington: Ashgate Publishing, 2009.

Principe, Lawrence, and William R. Newman. "Some Problems with the Historiography of Alchemy." In *Secrets of Nature: Astrology and Alchemy in Early Modern Europe,* ed. W. R. Newman and Anthony Grafton. Cambridge: MIT Press, 2001.

Proudfoot, Wayne. *Religious Experience*. Berkeley: University of California Press, 1985.

Reeds, John. "John Dee and the Magic Tables in the *Book of Soyga*." In *John Dee: Interdisciplinary Studies in English Renaissance Thought,* ed. Stephen Clucas, 177–204. Dordrecht: Springer, 2006.

Rons, Ian. "*Practical Angel Magic*: An Updated Review." *The Magical Review* (2009). Online: http://www.themagickalreview.org/reviews/practical-angel-magic-update/Practical-Angel-Magic-Updated-Review.pdf. (Accessed January 12, 2010).

———. "Review: *The Practical Angel Magic of Dr. John Dee's Enochian Tables,* by Stephen Skinner and David Rankine." *The Magickal Review* (2005). Online: http://www.themagickalreview.org/reviews/Enochian-tables.php. (Accessed June 28, 2009).

Rowse, A. L. *Simon Forman: Sex and Society in Shakespeare's Age*. London: Weidenfeld and Nicolson, 1974.

Rummel, Erika. *The Humanist-Scholastic Debate in the Renaissance and Reformation*. Cambridge: Harvard University Press, 1995.

Saunders, Andrew. "Rudd, Thomas (1583/4–1656)." In *Oxford Dictionary of National Biography*. Oxford: Oxford University Press, 2004. Online: http://www.oxforddnb.com/view/article/24247?_fromAuth=1. (Accessed April 28, 2008).

Schmidt, Joachim. *Satanismus: Mythos und Wirklichkeit*. Marburg: Diagonal Verlag, 1992.

Secret, Francois. *Les Kabbalistes chrétiens de la Renaissance.* Paris: Dunod, 1964.

Serjeantsen, R. W. "Casaubon, (Florence Estienne) Meric (1599–1671)." *Oxford Dictionary of National Biography*. Oxford: Oxford University Press, 2004. Online: http://www.oxforddnb.com/view/article/4852.

Sledge, James Justin. "Between 'Loagaeth' and 'Cosening': Towards an Etiology of John Dee's Spirit Diaries." *Aries* 10, no. 1 (2010): 1–36.

Spanos, Nicholas P. *Multiple Personalities and False Memories: A Sociocognitive Perspective*. Washington, DC: American Psychological Association, 1996.

Starr, Martin P. "Chaos from Order: Cohesion and Conflict in the Post-Crowley Occult Continuum." *The Pomegranate* 8, no. 1 (2006): 84–117.

———. *The Unknown God: W.T. Smith and the Thelemites.* Bollingbrook: Teitan Press, 2003.

Stevens, Philip. "Satan and Satanism." In *The Encyclopedia of the Paranormal,* ed. Gordon Stein, 657–70. Buffalo: Prometheus Books, 1996.

Storey, John, ed. *Cultural Studies and the Study of Popular Culture: A Reader*. 2nd rev. ed. Edinburgh: Edinburgh University Press, 2003.

Styers, Randall. *Making Magic: Religion, Magic, and Science in the Modern World.* Oxford: Oxford University Press, 2003.

Szőnyi, György E. *John Dee's Occultism: Magical Exaltation through Powerful Signs.* Albany: State University of New York Press, 2004.

———. "Paracelsus, Scrying and the *Lingua Adamica*." In *John Dee: Interdisciplinary Studies in English Renaissance Thought*, ed. Stephen Clucas. Dordrecht: Springer, 2006.

von Stuckrad, Kocku. "Discursive Study of Religion: From States of the Mind to Communication and Action." *Method & Theory in the Study of Religion* 15 (2003): 255–71.

———. *Was ist Esoterik? Kleine Geschicte des Geheimen Wissens*. Munich: Beck, 2004.

———. "Western Esotericism: Towards an Intgegrative Model of Interpretation." *Religion* 34 (2005): 78–97.

Sumner, Alex. "Angelic Invocations." *Journal of the Western Mystery Tradition* 10, no. 1 (2006). Online: http://www.jwmt.org/v1n10/angelic.html (retrieved August 30, 2007).

Sutin, Lawrence. *Do What Thou Wilt, A Life of Aleister Crowley*. New York: St. Martin's Press, 2000.

Traister, Barbara. *The Notorious Astrological Physician of London: Works and Days of Simon Forman*. Chicago: University of Chicago, 2001.

Urban, Hugh. *Magia Sexualis. Sex, Magic, and Liberation in Modern Western Esotericism*. Berkeley: University of California Press, 2006.

———. "Unleashing the Beast: Aleister Crowley, Tantra and Sex Magic in Late Victorian England." *Esoterica* 5 (2003).

Waite, A. E. *Brotherhood of the Rosy Cross: Being Records of the House of the Spirit in Its Inward and Outward History*. London: Rider, 1961 [1924].

Webb, James. *The Flight from Reason*. London: Macdonald, 1971.

Weber, Max. *Wirtchaft und Gesellschaft: Grundriss der Ferstehenden Soziologie*. 1922. Online edition: http://www.textlog.de/weber_wirtschaft.html.

Whitby, Christopher. "John Dee and Renaissance Scrying." *Bulletin of the Society for Renaissance Studies* 3, no. 2 (1985): 25–37.

Wilding, Michael. "A Biography of Edward Kelly, the English Alchemist and Associate of Dr. John Dee." In *Mystical Metal of Gold*, ed. Stanton Linden, 25–92. New York: AMS Press, 2007.

Yates, Frances. *Giordano Bruno and the Hermetic Tradition*. London: Routledge and Kegan Paul, 1964.

———. *The Occult in the Elizabethan Age*. London: Routledge and Kegan Paul, 1979.

———. *The Rosicrucian Enlightenment*. London: Routledge and Kegan Paul, 1972.

INDEX

Made in the USA
San Bernardino, CA
30 July 2015